Virginians Will Dance or Die!

Virginians Will Dance or Die!

The Importance of Music in Pre-Revolutionary Williamsburg

Joshua R. LeHuray

McFarland & Company, Inc., Publishers
Jefferson, North Carolina

LIBRARY OF CONGRESS CATALOGUING-IN-PUBLICATION DATA

Names: LeHuray, Joshua R.
Title: Virginians will dance or die! : the importance of music in
    pre-revolutionary Williamsburg / Joshua R. LeHuray.
Description: Jefferson, North Carolina : McFarland & Company,
    2016 | Includes bibliographical references and index.
Identifiers: LCCN 2016022315 | ISBN 9781476662848 (softcover :
    acid free paper) ∞
Subjects: LCSH: Music—Social aspects—Virginia—Williamsburg—
    History—18th century. | Williamsburg (Va.)—Social life and
    customs—18th century.
Classification: LCC ML3917.U6 L44 2016 |
    DDC 780.9755/425209033—dc23
LC record available at https://lccn.loc.gov/2016022315

BRITISH LIBRARY CATALOGUING DATA ARE AVAILABLE

ISBN (print) 978-1-4766-6284-8
ISBN (ebook) 978-1-4766-2409-9

© 2016 Joshua R. LeHuray. All rights reserved

No part of this book may be reproduced or transmitted in any form
or by any means, electronic or mechanical, including photocopying
or recording, or by any information storage and retrieval system,
without permission in writing from the publisher.

Front cover image of "The Victory Ball, 1781," painted in 1929 by
Jean-Leon Gerome Ferris (Virginia Historical Society)

Printed in the United States of America

McFarland & Company, Inc., Publishers
  Box 611, Jefferson, North Carolina 28640
  www.mcfarlandpub.com

Acknowledgments

I would like to thank my wife Dawn for her encouragement during this entire process, for contributing crucial ideas and suggestions, as well as for being a sounding board for my thoughts and concerns; also for putting up with the huge mess of papers and books that covered our computer room floor for a year. I would also like to thank Dr. Carolyn Eastman for assisting me with the process of writing sections of this book and her invaluable feedback. Thank you also to my parents, and all of my friends and family who encouraged me during this entire process. Finally, I would like to thank all members of the Janesville Fife and Drum Corps, past, present, and future, for helping me discover my love of the 18th century and its music, and for always being like a second family.

Table of Contents

Acknowledgments	v
Preface	1
Introduction	4
1. The Progression of Williamsburg's Musical Marketplace	7
2. Virginians Will Dance or Die!	40
3. Casual Music and Common Folk	71
4. The Vibrant Stage of Williamsburg's Colonial Theaters	99
Epilogue	130
Appendix I: Music Master Cuthbert Ogle's Musical Estate	133
Appendix II: Concerts and Dances of Williamsburg	135
Appendix III: Slaves and Servants Valued for Their Music or Dancing Skills	144
Appendix IV: Plays and Performances at the Williamsburg Theatres	154
Appendix V: The Articles of Association, October 20, 1774	165
Chapter Notes	169
Bibliography	177
Index	183

Preface

This book explores the pre–Revolutionary War music of Williamsburg, Virginia, the colonial capital and sole major city in the colony, as well as the importance of music to the citizens of this town and its surrounding areas. Due to Virginia being a plantation economy, many individuals were only in the capital during court sessions and experienced music in other cities near Williamsburg or in their homes during the rest of the year. The first chapter of the book analyzes the importance of music to those in the upper levels of society in colonial-era Williamsburg in order to highlight the complex, diverse musical economy that developed during the eighteenth century, in part due to the cultural necessity which dictated the interests of Virginia's elites. The importance of music to Williamsburg's elite citizens and the expansion of a musical marketplace were intrinsically linked as the genteel needed to spend increasing amounts of money to maintain their social status. By adopting the music and musical entertainment found in Europe, Virginia's gentility helped create and define a cultural identity they considered to be increasingly similar to that of the British elite. In addition, the first and second chapters explore how this musical marketplace changed over the course of approximately sixty years and some of the various musical services available to these well-to-do Virginians. For clarification, the term "marketplace" is intended to encompass a diverse economy of music instructors, instrument and sheet music makers/sellers, and various forms of musical entertainment—in other words, not one organization or monolithic business, but a growing universe of businesspeople who sought to capitalize on colonists' increasing interest in various types of music. In the third chapter the book goes on to explore the music of "common folk," those without the disposable income to necessarily influence the musical marketplace, but who nevertheless embraced popular music and integrated it into many aspects of their daily lives. Finally, the fourth chapter examines the Williamsburg theater and its role in the lives of all Williamsburg citizens, both rich and poor alike.

Though heavily focused on the eighteenth century, the scope of the book begins around 1619 when the first enslaved Africans arrived in the American colonies and a fiddler named John Utie arrived in Jamestown. Just shy of one hundred years later in 1716, William Levingston, a Virginia merchant, proposed to build the Williamsburg theater—the first theater anywhere in the American colonies. Shortly afterward, concerts, operas, and other forms of music began to appear in large, wealthy cities along the eastern seaboard, including Williamsburg. The scope of the book ends in 1775, for much has been written about music during and after the American Revolution. Finally, many scholars have already dedicated serious research to the study of religious music, discovering that this type of music was much more influential in the New England area than in America's middle and southern colonies. As such this book focuses primarily on secular music, though it does touch upon Bruton Parish Church's importance to Williamsburg, the use of psalm books, and the establishment of psalmody singing schools in Williamsburg.

Few historians have specifically studied the subject of music in colonial-era Virginia, and even fewer have studied music in the city of Williamsburg; additionally, a large percentage of these works were written well over fifty years ago. One of the most detailed scholarships of music in Williamsburg surrounds the discovery of Cuthbert Ogle's estate inventory, mentioned below. A transcript of the estate originally appeared in the *William and Mary Quarterly*, while Maurer Maurer wrote a more in-depth article years later further exploring his life. Despite the attention given to Ogle, his story is only one small piece of the puzzle of how music wove its way through the lives of colonial Virginians. Another highly specific example of scholarship is John Molnar's *Songs from the Williamsburg Theatre*, which similarly provides deep insight into the theater's role in the Williamsburg music scene. Other historians have specifically explored the music of Virginia and Williamsburg but within the context of general social histories. Philip Bruce, for example, incorporated certain musical elements into his *Social Life of Virginia in the Seventeenth Century*. I have drawn on these scholars, but my analysis covers a much broader chronology and subject base.

Despite the importance of music to the lives of elite Virginians, few scholars have explored the rise of the music industry and the ways it shaped cultural life and identity in colonial Virginia. In developing my analysis of the Williamsburg marketplace, I especially drew on the work of two scholars. In his book *The Refinement of America*, Richard Bushman explores the increasing importation of material goods to the colonies, as well as the increasing size and complexity of elite domestic residences and their use in genteel entertainments. T.H. Breen's *Marketplace of Revolution* delves further into the American marketplace and how colonists' consumption of imported goods led to massive debts, feeding into the growing schism with Britain which resulted in the American Revolution. Though neither scholar focuses on the music industry specifically, both prove fundamental for understanding the growing complexity of the colonial marketplace, as well as the importance of credit and debt to citizens who spent increasing amounts of money to stay on par with the European genteel.

A large percentage of research done specifically regarding colonial music in the American colonies focuses on New England, and the Puritans specifically. These studies explore the origins of Puritan church music and how it was taught, read, modified, and understood. Other studies focus specifically on Boston or other New England towns, or on Quaker and German music in Pennsylvania. Charleston, South Carolina, is also frequently explored in various books. These works have been integral to my work because while it briefly touches on religious music, I have sought to emphasize secular and often fashionable music as it circulated in Virginia, and music which was important in Williamsburg frequently had ties to music which was fashionable in other colonies.

More broadly, my analysis benefits from an array of recent studies that examine the subject of music in early America from a variety of perspectives. Historians such as Kate Keller and Joy Cleef have published books and articles examining different types of dancing and its accompanying music, while Mary Stanard and Louis Wright look at culture in the colonies and the various ways in which colonists entertained themselves. Other works explore colonial concert life and theaters, taverns and drinking, and the music of African Americans. One popular historical genre explores a broad history of music, from early colonial times to modern music we hear today, including works by Gilbert Chase, Charles Hamm, and Richard Crawford. These and other studies have provided valuable insight into the various roles music played in colonists' lives during the eighteenth century. Perhaps most importantly, the Colonial Williamsburg Foundation has published numerous research reports online documenting their findings regarding many of the buildings which stood in Williamsburg during the pre–Revolutionary period. These reports have proved invaluable when researching the history of Williamsburg's theaters and other important buildings. The Foundation has also made the *Virginia Gazette* available through their website, a resource which again proved invaluable during the research portion of this book.

Introduction

When a Williamsburg music teacher named Cuthbert Ogle died in 1755, the executors of his estate had his belongings listed in the *Virginia Gazette*, as was common practice at the time. What made Ogle's estate listing unique was that it included a detailed list of the instruments and sheet music he owned, including a concerto by Charles Avison (valued at one shilling, four pence) and George Handel's "Apollos Feast" (valued at five shillings) with an overall total value of the music-related items greater than thirty-five pounds, equivalent to the considerable amount of approximately three thousand pounds, or just shy of five thousand dollars, in today's money. More frequently in such estate inventories administrators simply listed music as a "lot" or "bundle" and gave one overarching value to the whole. This detailed list of Ogle's musical library provides an unusual view of at least one individual's access to music during the eighteenth century, and perhaps also a broader glimpse of Virginians' musical tastes. Just as important, Ogle's music collection offers a way for historians to scrutinize one aspect of the growing desire for music that emerged in the city of Williamsburg, Virginia's metropolitan hub during the pre–Revolutionary period, an era during which colonists increasingly spent more time and money on music, as well as placing a greater emphasis on music's social value. Over the course of these decades, inhabitants gained access to music via concerts, plays, or music lessons in the home, and became aware of an even broader musical world by seeing advertisements for dances, theater performances, and music lessons in the paper or advertised by peddlers. This work examines that growing musical world in order to better understand the significance of music for colonial Virginians.

Many of Williamsburg's citizens experienced music in one form or another during the eighteenth century. Any person walking into a tavern in town would have heard a fiddler or other instrumentalist playing the most popular tunes of the time for the customers' entertainment. Yet despite the ubiquity of music in Virginia, the highly diversified commercial industry that developed surrounding it was not directed towards the common citizen, but rather to the upper class gentility of the colony. These elite Virginians were quite aware of their British heritage and desired to emulate the fashions, habits, and pastimes of their overseas brethren. They believed by adopting the lifestyle of London's upper classes they might evade the European stereotype of Americans as backwoods country farmers compared to British citizens of equal status.

To do so, over the course of the eighteenth century, Williamsburg's wealthiest citizens increasingly spent more of their disposable income on musical instruments, lessons, and entertainment to elevate their cultural status. Acquisition of instruments and printed music was mandatory for the genteel, and hiring music or dancing masters from Europe helped teach proper techniques to adults and children alike. Gentlemen amateurs regularly held concerts for their peers, though it was considered taboo for them to accept any form of payment as it would have lowered their social status to that of a tradesman for hire. Williamsburg's governors integrated music into their social lives and often held concerts and dances at the governor's mansion or the Virginia capitol, and treated dignitaries to the sorts of entertainment they could expect in Europe, often with slaves playing the accompanying music. Virginia's citizens were quite well aware of how music was utilized in elite British society, as the *Virginia Gazette* regularly published accounts of the balls, concerts, and theatrical performances held by and for European royalty. These articles gave Williamsburg's upper crust up-to-date knowledge of the most fashionable European music and performers, allowing them to experience this music for themselves.

Elite citizens held balls and dances regularly, with tickets sold at prices only the well-off could generally afford, generating previously unavailable revenue for the organizers. With dancing as highly prized as instrumental proficiency, elites also hired dancing masters to teach the intricate steps for complex dances such as the minuet, as well as some of the associated niceties of European etiquette and physical bearing that would likewise distinguish the genteel from country hicks. These teachers educated Virginians on how to act the part of a European-style upper class, not only when dancing but in all public situations.

As this musical economy flourished and grew in Williamsburg, lower status citizens, or "common folk," also integrated more and more music into their daily lives. Many attended frequent events such as harvest feasts, birthdays, and funerals where music played an important role in the festivities.

The dances most popular to Virginia's less-elite citizens, commonly known as "country dances," grew in popularity during the century and were used by both rich and poor alike for a variety of events. Bawdy and lowbrow folk songs, the popular music of the day and frequently heard in taverns and parties, became more prevalent in Williamsburg, even appearing on the theatrical stage due to popular demand. Slaves also encouraged the growth of music in Virginia, as many blacks gained musical talent and brought instruments and African-style music with them across the Atlantic following their enslavement. White Virginians often adopted this music and its associated dancing at their own parties, and utilized talented slave musicians at formal balls and dances, increasing the value of these particular slaves and further growing the musical economy.

Both elites and common folk alike also patronized multiple theaters that arrived in Williamsburg in the eighteenth century. Though slow to take off, by 1752 the theaters featured theatrical companies and operas that had appeared in London and other parts of Europe and the colonies, allowing Virginians to feel equal in cultural literacy to their British peers. By spending increasing amounts of money on these musical activities, Williamsburg's elite citizens helped themselves to grow closer in culture and manners to the English gentry, while at the same time establishing a complex musical economy in colonial Virginia. Most importantly, however, all Virginians, regardless of social status, gained access to musical entertainment through the theaters.

My sources for this book come from a wide variety of genres, most especially the *Virginia Gazette* and records from the Williamsburg theater. I have also explored numerous other areas, ultimately utilizing transcribed letters, diaries, and manuscripts of Williamsburg residents and visitors. Additionally, George Washington and Thomas Jefferson's account ledgers provided valuable financial information regarding their expenditures for theater tickets, and meeting notes from the College of William and Mary shed light on the school's involvement with dancing instruction. All quotations retain original punctuation and spelling including errors, but frequent capitalization has been reduced to ease reading.

1

The Progression of Williamsburg's Musical Marketplace

> "Ben is in a wonderful fluster lest he shall have no company to-morrow at the dance—But blow high, blow low, he need not be afraid; Virginians are of genuine blood—They will dance or die!"
> —Philip Fithian, August 25, 1774

In October 1767 an account appeared in the *Virginia Gazette* taken from an English paper. The writer, only identified by the pseudonym Socratissa, had observed a conversation while dining at the home of a Lady Ramble. Ramble's sister had decided to question her niece, a young eleven-year-old girl known as Miss, about her duty in life as a woman. Standing before the group, Miss was asked among other questions what was the business of a fine lady, to which she replied, "To play at cards, go to routs, balls, plays, operas, &c. and carry on intrigues." Having heard this response, Ramble's sister declared, "I vow my niece is very perfect in her education, and will make a fine accomplished woman." As the girl had so eloquently described the duties of an eighteenth-century woman, Socratissa decided to have Miss's answer published as "it may be of service to other young Ladies of Quality."[1] Besides providing an interesting glimpse into the mindset of an eighteenth-century pre-teenager, this amusing anecdote captured the extent to which a "fine lady" must dedicate her time to musical activities as a part of her daily business, and an important element of how the citizens of England and the American colonies used music to define who they were and their role in society.

It comes as no surprise that the editors of the *Virginia Gazette* decided to run this particular piece of social commentary, for Virginia in 1767 was in the middle of a musical renaissance, with Williamsburg at its epicenter. Plantation owner Landon Carter noted in his diary while walking through the town, "I hear from every house a constant tuting may be listened to, from one instrument or another."[2] Virginians increasingly integrated music into their daily lives during the course of the eighteenth century, allowing it to grow intertwined with their business and political dealings. Those living in or near the city were constantly exposed to activities and events associated with music, and part of their social duties included attending the balls, plays, and operas frequently held in the area. An anonymous writer in the *Virginia Gazette* identified only as Old Sterling noted, in a critical fashion, the people of Virginia had become constant "resorters to plays, balls, operas, masquerades, [and] concerts."[3]

This desire for musical entertainment helped Virginians, and especially those in the upper classes, to associate themselves with and emulate the genteel lifestyle of British citizens. This meant in order to perceive themselves as equals, early Americans needed to copy the habits and entertainments of their European counterparts, including their clothing and fashions, hobbies, the way they acted and presented themselves in public, as well as acquiring the physical goods that separated the social elites from those beneath them. Part of this emulation took the form of acquiring instruments and books consisting of musical compositions by famous European composers, so as to better integrate music into home life and raise one's social status. Newspaper ads and an increase in a North American consumer culture helped propel these sales, further expanding the influence of music in the daily lives of the citizens of Williamsburg.

In 1699, following a fire which destroyed the statehouse in Jamestown, the Virginia legislature voted to move the state capital to the city of Williamsburg. Though located a decent distance away from the water, the city was conveniently located between the James and York rivers, with Queen Mary's port and Princess Anne's port offering access only a few miles away to allow the easy transportation of goods and people into the town. The city at the time was already the home of William and Mary, the second oldest college in the colonies, which further underscored its importance to wealthy citizens of the state. Soon after, important buildings began to appear in the town: by 1701 a capitol building was under construction, followed shortly by the building of the governor's mansion, started in 1706. These were followed by Bruton Parish Church, a jail, taverns, a hospital, and other typical colonial buildings.[4] By the middle of the 1700s Williamsburg had grown from a few buildings into the largest city in Virginia. Despite being the largest town, Williamsburg was quite small compared to the prominent towns in its sister colonies, such as Charles Town, Boston, New York, and Philadelphia, where populations ranged from 12,000 to 40,000 citizens.[5] In comparison, Williamsburg's permanent eighteenth-century population probably never exceeded fifteen hundred persons, though according to one estimate the population tripled or quadrupled during the June court session.[6] During those times thousands of Virginians from plantations and farms flooded the city, riding on carriages, wagons, and horses, filling the streets with raucous noise, laughter, and various entertainments designed to capture as much money as possible from these temporary visitors.

The city was described by the traveler Reverend Andrew Burnaby, who toured through the colonies on a trip from England in 1759. He noted that Williamsburg contained about two hundred houses and approximately one thousand residents. He commented upon the "handsome square in the center, through which runs the principal street, one of the most spacious in North America, three quarters of a mile in length, and above a hundred feet wide."[7] The principal street Burnaby referenced in his journal is the current Duke of Gloucester Street, the main thoroughfare still today in Colonial Williamsburg. Burnaby also described the college and capitol buildings, noting their locations at either end of the street and shingle-covered wooden houses that lined it: "The whole makes a handsome appearance." He also believed that "the governor's palace is tolerably good, one of the best upon the continent." He observed ten or twelve gentlemen's families resided in the town, in addition to merchants and tradesmen. Though the population did not match the size and density of other colonial cities like Boston or Philadelphia, the minister remarked that during the time of the Virginia assemblies and general courts, Williamsburg "is crowded with the gentry of the country." According to him, when these wealthy merchants and plantation owners gathered in the city for these events, inevitably wealthy Williamsburg families or the governor would host "balls and other amusements."[8]

Burnaby was right that the governors in Williamsburg frequently made music and dances part of their annual Virginia court sessions. These activities represented the refinement and elite status of the participants, and were similar to those that would have been experienced in European governmental sessions. The Reverend Hugh Jones, mathematics professor at William and Mary, commented in his 1724 book *The Present State of Virginia*, that "at the capitol, at publick times, may be seen a great number of handsom, well-dress'd, compleat gentlemen. And at the governor's house upon birth-nights, and at balls and assemblies, I have seen as fine

The Bodleian Plate, engraved around 1740 by an unknown artist. This copper plate was discovered in 1929 at the Bodleian Library at Oxford University. It contains the only known eighteenth-century architectural drawings of the College of William and Mary (top), the capitol building (middle left) and the governor's palace (middle right), along with flora and fauna of Virginia. This engraving proved vital to the restoration of Williamsburg in the early twentieth century. It is currently housed in the collections of the Colonial Williamsburg Foundation.

an appearance, as good diversion, and as splendid entertainments in Governor Spotswood's time, as I have seen any where else."[9] The *Virginia Gazette* announced in 1746 that balls and assemblies would be held every other night during that year's court session, "for the entertainment of gentlemen and ladies."[10] During the session of 1768 the governor threw frequent "stately receptions to which flocked ladies and gentlemen in court apparel; there was no end of music, dancing, and private entertaining, and there was a two months' theatrical season."[11] These entertainments showed that Virginia's governors and their guests might be as civilized as Britain's governmental leaders.

Virginia's governors also used musical entertainment to honor and impress those of different cultures considered to be of a high social status. According to the *Virginia Gazette*, on September 5, 1755, "Two great warriors of the Cherokee nation, with their attendants, are come to town, in order to give a proof of their love and friendship for their brethren the English; and we hear are much pleased with their entertainment at the governor's, and the cloaths and presents he has made them."[12] On another occasion in November 1752 Governor Robert Dinwiddie received the "Emperor of the Cherokee nation with his Empress and their son, the young Prince, attended by several of his warriors and great men and their ladies." That night the honored guests were taken to see a performance of *Othello* with musical accompaniment at the second Williamsburg playhouse. The *Gazette* subsequently reported that during the play the actors fought with "naked swords on the stage," causing the Cherokee Empress, who apparently did not understand the concept of play-acting, to order her warriors to stop the on-stage fighting and "prevent their killing one another."[13] By observing a European-style performance the Cherokee experienced one of the ways in which Virginia's governors utilized musical theater to integrate British culture into their governmental proceedings, and the misunderstandings about the on-stage fighting, whether true or not, allowed readers to witness a sharp contrast between the sophisticated whites of Williamsburg and the perceived cultural ignorance of neighboring tribes of Native Americans.

Governors also held frequent private concerts for privileged and important members of the town. Governor Francis Fauquier became acquainted with a young Thomas Jefferson through George Wythe, Jefferson's mentor in Williamsburg. Fauquier, who was also a musician, invited Jefferson to play violin at his weekly concerts along with future Virginia Governors John Tyler and Patrick Henry.[14] Though these private concerts were held in the drawing room of the governor's palace, professional chamber concerts were also frequently performed in the palace's ballroom for larger crowds.[15] In fact, according to historian Daniel Mendoza de Arce, seemingly the first organized concert in the American colonies was held at the governor's mansion in Williamsburg in 1720.[16] Though Mendoza de Arce does not elaborate on this particular concert, he is probably referring to an incident in April 1720 when Governor Alexander Spotswood was involved in a disagreement with William Byrd II, the wealthy owner of Westover Plantation located between Richmond and Williamsburg. Byrd had recently returned to Virginia after a long absence in London, and King George I appointed him to the Council of Virginia, overruling any objections the governor or lieutenant governor may have had with this appointment.[17] The tension between Spotswood and Byrd, as well as the remaining council members, lasted for five days after Byrd received his official appointment letter from the king. Finally on April 29 the governor appeared to have a change of heart, inviting all of the council members to dinner and, according to Byrd, "entertained us very hospitably and the guns were fired and there was illumination all the town over and everybody expressed great joy." This celebration concluded with "a concert of music at the governor's" with all participants drinking until 11 o'clock.[18]

Virginia's governors hardly needed governmental meetings, visiting dignitaries, dispute settlements, or organized concert performances to justify throwing elaborate parties. Election days, holidays, muster days, and the commencement of William and Mary were sufficient reasons to obtain the services of musicians and hold a ball, an event frequently accompanied by city-wide illuminations and other festivities.[19] Street lighting for the most part had not appeared in Williamsburg in the early eighteenth century, and the array of events listed above gave regular citizens an opportunity to participate in the frivolities by illuminating the windows of their houses throughout the city. Homeowners placed rows of candles on their window sills, one for every pane of glass in the house. Large bonfires would be built, frequently in Market Square along Duke of

This portrait of William Byrd II was painted by Sir Godfrey Kneller, the official painter of London's royal court, around 1700–1704. Byrd owned the Westover Plantation between Williamsburg and Richmond, and frequently participated in dances and other entertainments while visiting the capital. Byrd hung this painting in his house at Westover. It is currently housed in the collections of the Colonial Williamsburg Foundation.

Gloucester Street. Combined with the lights shining in the cupolas of the governor's mansion and capitol building, Williamsburg lit up during these special events, creating a joyous atmosphere for all the residents. In addition to the illumination of the city, cannon fire from the governor's home combined with an often elaborate display of fireworks added to the excitement experienced by all citizens and visitors.[20] Governor William Gooch celebrated King George II's birthday in October of 1736 with a "firing of guns, illuminations, and other demonstrations of loyalty" and to cap off these festivities, "at night there was a handsome appearance of gentlemen and ladies, at His Honour the Governor's, where was a ball, and an elegant entertainment for them."[21] In 1755 in honor of George, Prince of Wales's birthday, Governor Dinwiddie gave "a ball and entertainment at the palace, where was a splendid appearance of gentlemen and ladies, and the evening was concluded with the greatest demonstration of mirth and loyalty."[22] George, Prince of Wales, who would of course become King George III in 1760, was famously known for his role in the American Revolution. Later in 1755 to once again celebrate a royal birthday, this time for King George II, the governor threw yet another ball at the palace, as well as illuminating the entire city to underscore the grandness of the occasion.[23]

Scheduling musical festivities was important to Williamsburg's leaders as the dates they were held often corresponded with momentous events or celebrations in Britain. As such, governors needed to choose which of these events deserved special attention and which could be overlooked. In 1766, eleven years after Governor Dinwiddie's 1755 celebrations, Governor Fauquier and other "principal gentlemen of this city" decided that it would be a mistake to throw a ball or find other means of honoring King George III's birthday. Rather, they believed, it would make more sense to postpone it and celebrate in conjunction with the king's ascendancy date in October as Williamsburg had "a great deal of company generally being in town at that season of the year."[24] It is a possibility this decision was made in protest of the Stamp Act, a much-despised bill creating a tax on most printed materials in the colonies, which had passed the previous year in March 1765 and taken effect eight months later on November 1. The leaders of Virginia certainly did not hesitate to throw an elaborate celebration when Colonel George Mercer, the King's Stamp Act Commissioner and appointed enforcer of the law in the colony, arrived in Williamsburg on October 30, 1765. Uncertain if Mercer would begin collecting the hated fees at the beginning of November, the governor and other important gentlemen immediately began pestering him to see if he planned to enforce the law or not. Given a short amount of time to consider, Mercer made a public statement to Williamsburg's citizens indicating, "I will not, directly or indirectly, by myself or deputies, proceed in the execution of the act until I receive further orders from England, and not then without the assent of the General Assembly of this colony."[25] To celebrate this victory over the reviled tax collections, Virginia's elite organized an illumination and musical festivities:

> [Mercer] was immediately born out of the capitol gate, amidst the repeated acclamations of all present. Then he was conducted to a public house, and an elegant entertainment ordered to be provided, where he spends the evening with a number of gentlemen. He had no sooner arrived there than the acclamations of the company were redoubled, drums, French-horns, &c. sounding all the while. As soon as night set in the whole town was illuminated, the bells set a ringing, and every mark of joy shown, at this gentleman's declining, in such a genteel manner, to act in an office so odious to his country. In short, we have never had so much, and so general rejoicing upon any occasion, in so short a time; and to crown the whole, there will be tomorrow night a splendid ball.[26]

By the time Virginia's leaders decided to postpone the king's birthday celebration in early June 1766, eight months after Colonel Mercer's festivities, the Stamp Act had been repealed for over two months, but the official news of the act's repeal did not appear in the *Virginia Gazette* until the week after the party was postponed. Once the good news formally arrived, the genteel citizens of Williamsburg, in conjunction with Governor Fauquier and other members of the local government, did not hesitate to throw a ball at the capitol building in June 1766 "upon the joyful occasion of the repeal of the Stamp Act."[27] Other Virginia cities joined in the celebration, including the town of Portsmouth where its citizens gathered together to celebrate "with the greatest harmony, friendship, and joy, on the happy accommodation of all differences between Great Britain and her colonies. After dining in the common hall ... toasts were drunk, under a discharge of many cannon, display of colours, sound of trumpets, French-horns, and drums, with bonefires [sic] and illuminations. The whole was conducted with the utmost order and decorum."[28] In Norfolk the town's leaders greeted the news with the ringing of bells and a day of celebrations, concluded by "a very elegant ball and entertainment, given at the house of Mr. Stephen Tanchard, at which was present a very numerous company of ladies and gentlemen, who made a brilliant appearance ... the whole was conducted with the utmost regularity, dignity, and decorum."[29] Virginia's political leaders were quite adept at integrating dancing and music into their political celebrations, while making a point to emphasize all music-related activities maintained a certain level of propriety and dignity as befit their rank and title in the colony.

1. Williamsburg's Musical Marketplace

At the opposite end of Duke of Gloucester Street from the capitol building, William and Mary College also encouraged the growth of the musical arts as most of its students came from the upper levels of society. In 1716 William Levingston, a merchant in nearby New Kent County, decided to open a dancing school in Williamsburg and approached the William and Mary Board of Visitors for permission to use one of the college buildings to hold his classes. On March 26, 1716, not only did the Board allow him "use of the lower room at the south end of the colledge [sic]," but encouraged Levingston to teach the scholars and students of the college to dance.[30] The Reverend Hugh Jones, writing as a former mathematics professor at the school, felt it necessary to offer suggestions on how best to run the college in his *The Present State of Virginia*. Though Levingston had opened his dancing school in a William and Mary classroom eight years earlier, this was a temporary situation until a proper school could be built elsewhere in Williamsburg. As the city lacked such a school, it appeared to Jones that the college needed to at least occasionally teach the musical arts, and felt the need to recommend to school leaders that "as for the accomplishments of musick, dancing, and fencing, they may be taught by such as the President and Masters shall appoint at certain times, as they shall fix for those purposes."[31] Aware of the importance of dancing and music to upper class students, those in charge of the college made sure to teach dances like the minuet and country-style dances and reels, offering these classes "well before its academic faculty was complete."[32]

Aside from formal dancing classes, Virginia's early governors utilized the College of William and Mary for casual music and dancing as the main college hall was also the governor's home until the new mansion on the north side of the Palace Green was habitable in 1716, though it was not fully completed until 1722. As it doubled as a residence, the school became a place of relaxation as well as study for those on the campus grounds. In 1705 Thomas Story visited the college, noting, "The Governor ordered the president of the college for the time being, to shew [sic] us the buildings of it; and he being of a pleasant natural temper, he told us, when he came into their chapel, that that was the most useful place in all the college; for, said he, 'Here we sometimes preach and pray, and sometimes we fiddle and dance; the one to edify, and the other to divert us.'"[33] It would seem then that not only the governor but the head of the school believed William and Mary's role in Williamsburg was not just education, but also entertainment for those living and working at the college.

Of course, music was not used at the school for only happy occasions, but sad ones as well. Upon news of King William III's death in 1702, a visitor named Francis Louis Michel observed a memorial service for the king at the college in what he called "Willemsburg." Not all were in mourning, however, as this event was combined with "the proclamation of and rejoicing over the new queen," Queen Anne. At this service three grandstands were built in front of the school buildings to set off fireworks, and approximately two thousand soldiers appeared, including cavalry on horseback. According to Michel's description, the college had three balconies at the time and "on the uppermost were the buglers from the warships, on the second, oboes and on the lowest violinists, so that when the ones stopped the others began. Sometimes they all played together. When the proclamation of the king's death was to be made they played very movingly and mournfully." Following this the musicians played as they marched with the clergy and the governor to a tent "where a touching oration was delivered, which caused many people to shed tears." Finally at noon the festivities transitioned from mourning into a celebration of their new queen when "the musicians began to play a lively tune" accompanied by three salutes from the cannons and small arms, plus rum and brandy drinks for the crowd.[34] This grand event, designed to remember one former ruler and celebrate the rise of another, shows just one way Williamsburg's leaders and the College of William and Mary used music and musicians to elevate the importance of their official functions early in the 1700s, a custom which only grew over the following decades.

As these passages indicate, music increasingly became associated with refinement during the eighteenth century in Williamsburg. By participating in events like balls and concerts, and using music as a part of official festivities and celebrations, many of the city's elite citizens integrated music, instruments, and musical activities into their daily lives in an effort to attain a level of gentility. During the eighteenth century the term "genteel" had come to loosely mean polite, polished, refined, tasteful, and other terms that represented the concept of being well-bred and upper class. As Richard Bushman has shown, later in the century use of "genteel" spread to encompass "a host of objects, situations, persons, and habits ... genteel persons with genteel educations practiced genteel professions." Clothing, food, furnishings, towns, and schools were all referred to as *genteel* in an effort to gentrify certain aspects of life.[35] The concept of gentility created a "cultural and social gulf" between elites and those of the lower social ranks in Virginia. Those of a lower sort deferred to those above them, a rule that held true also among the elite themselves. Eventually everything about the genteel, from the clothing, food, houses, and entertainment, differentiated them from the lower social ranks.[36]

1. Williamsburg's Musical Marketplace 17

Those who considered themselves to be genteel in Williamsburg had a social obligation to be refined in manners and the ways in which they presented themselves, including their participation in musical activities. One contributor to the *Virginia Gazette*, writing under the pseudonym Hector, offered his advice on one fashionable activity the genteel should pursue: "You must often go to the playhouses, and there always distinguish yourself as highly as possible."[37] Though Hector took a sarcastic tone in his letter as he felt the youths of the time had a tendency to get out of control, advice such as this still instructed Virginians how to properly act the part of the British-style gentry in the types of activities they should pursue.

Hector's tongue-in-cheek advice reflected a growing genre of writing during the eighteenth century when Virginians imported a wide array of courtesy manuals and other guides for manners designed to educate those aspiring towards gentility, including instructions for proper dancing techniques, signaling the "arrival of the genteel code."[38] These books instructed the reader on the ways to be a gentleman, including conversational skills, proper physical placement of hands, feet, and arms, and how to manage human body functions such as belching or spitting. Probably the most famous example of an eighteenth-century courtesy manual was George Washington's *Rules of Civility & Decent Behaviour in Company and Conversation*. This book consisted of 110 rules Washington copied at the age of fourteen from a French book of manners, and many of these became an integral part of how he conveyed himself for the rest of his life. Examples of the strict demands on the body while in public include "If you cough, sneeze, sigh, or yawn, do it not loud but privately; and speak not in your yawning, but put your handkerchief or hand before your face and turn aside" and "Shake not the head, feet, or legs; roll not the eyes; lift not one eyebrow higher than the other; wry not the mouth; and bedew no man's face with your spittle by approaching too near him when you speak."[39] Based on these examples, being a gentleman in the eighteenth century was a full time job, requiring constant monitoring of all physical gestures and actions in public, even when monitoring how high one eyebrow was raised compared to the other. Despite these stringent rules, many Williamsburg elites strove to attain this level of physical discipline in order to be considered genteel in Virginia society.

Part of the instructional requirements for the genteel also included learning the "'polite' arts, dancing, and other forms of sociability as the principal amenities of such a privileged mode of existence."[40] Contemporary letters and diaries reveal how important Virginians considered those lessons. For example, Philip Vickers Fithian, who worked as a tutor at Nomini Hall plantation for Robert Carter III from 1773 to 1774, kept a diary and recorded many of his experiences with the elite family employing him, including his observations on the activities of the genteel. While writing to another tutor to advise him on obtaining a teaching job in Virginia, he noted, "Any young gentleman travelling through the colony, as I said before, is presum'd to be acquainted with dancing, boxing, [and] playing the fiddle."[41]

Dancing was an integral part of what made a person genteel, as "an indispensable symbol of high breeding was the southern gentleman and lady's ability to dance."[42] In his diary Fithian noted the gentlemen around him regularly solicited him to join them in their dances, though he always declined, and lamented on multiple occasions that he never learned to dance and wished "that it had been a part of my education to learn what I think is an innocent and an ornamental, and most certainly, in this province is a necessary qualification for a person to appear decent in company!"[43] Ladies gained from their ability to dance as it gave each one an "opportunity to demonstrate her dignity and skill at moving gracefully." Gentlemen were also required to be good dancers, though not necessarily excellent ones, as "being too proficient in executing fancy steps, his masculinity might be called into question," as historian Ronald Davis puts it.[44]

While many of the older generations involved themselves with gossip and merrymaking, young men and women took these dancing opportunities to partake in the "intrigues" mentioned previously by the young "Miss" at the opening of this chapter. Dances brought elite citizens together, allowing the young to showcase their dancing prowess. Dancing in Virginia, "especially the jig, with its vigorous alternating pursuit and retreat—was a stylized representation of bold, active courtship on the part of both sexes."[45] In July 1766 Landon Carter commented that nothing could stop his daughter Judy from attending a dance at her uncle's, though it was an extremely hot night and he was worried she would become ill. This prediction subsequently proved to be the case when she came down with a stomach flu the next day. Carter noted in his diary that attending these dances in the heat with their late hours and rich food was making Judy "bear ungovernable the whole summer through, eating extravagantly and late at night of cucumbers and all sorts of bilious trash."[46]

Attending dances held such social significance and importance to Virginians it was certainly not uncommon for them to ignore their illnesses so they could make an appearance. On one occasion William Byrd II had made plans to attend a ball held at the governor's mansion in Williamsburg,

1. Williamsburg's Musical Marketplace   19

a gathering any genteel individual was required to attend to keep up their mandatory social appearances. The night before, however, Byrd developed a cold that "grew exceedingly bad so that I thought I should be sick." Trying to recover before the dance, he drank some sage tea provided by his sister that did nothing but "made me mad all night so that I could not sleep but was much disordered by it." The following day, after rising around 9 o'clock, Byrd "was so bad I thought I should not have been in condition to go to Williamsburg." Considering how poorly he felt, his wife volunteered to stay home with him, but rather than forcing her to miss out on an essential social interaction, and missing it himself, he "resolved to go if possible," and sure enough Byrd pressed on, having a fine time at the dance though his cold persisted for the next several days.[47]

As demonstrated by William Byrd's insistence on attending the governor's ball even while ill, these dances and other entertainments were considered almost mandatory by the Virginia gentry as they were part of polite society. Despite lacking dancing skills, Philip Fithian found it almost impossible to avoid these types of genteel social gatherings. He noted following church service several different gentlemen inevitably invited him to various dinners, feasts, and balls.[48] While living in Virginia, almost every week Fithian noted he was "strongly invited" to a "luxurious entertainment" filled with "charming music."[49] Apparently one Williamsburg citizen felt the need to comment, in a somewhat sarcastic manner, on the importance of these musical activities to upper class Virginia citizens. A March 1752 *Virginia Gazette* news item indicated that, due to the death of the Queen of Denmark, the Danish king had issued an edict banning all plays, balls, operas, and concertos for a year. Following this piece of news, *Gazette* editor William Hunter wryly commented, "Heaven preserve us from such mourning which would send at least half of our gay polite gentry to the grave."[50] Apparently this news contributor felt if Williamsburg's citizens were forced to live without their musical entertainments in honor of the deceased, it would in fact end up killing half of the gentility during the mourning period, perhaps from boredom. Luckily for Virginians they apparently felt no need to honor the Danish king's request.

In Virginia, genteel social events like balls and concerts helped define a person's place in society. While information about weather and trade filled the diaries of farmers, elites kept note almost religiously of the various formal entertainments they had attended, including balls, concerts, tea parties, or other assemblies. As gentility expanded in the eighteenth century from the wealthiest to some of middling status, these types of activities spread along geographical lines from cities and towns to more rural areas with high concentrations of planters. To be clear, these events were not generally found in the countryside among common farmers, but rather existed in elite plantation society or in cities. Balls took days to plan, and provided the participants with days' worth of gossip to tide them over until the next event.[51]

Even Virginia's publically accessible spaces established a degree of social demarcation. Those elite citizens living in cities established their own areas where the wealthier were permitted to go, while average citizens were generally shunned, though in many cases they were not explicitly forbidden from entering these places; genteel society simply established unofficial locations where social peers could gather together to be among their own. Certain streets and fenced parks, generally located near government buildings or luxury shops catering to the upper class, were utilized predominantly by the well-to-do, where they could expect to encounter people of their own social level and conveniently bypass those of a lower station.[52] In Williamsburg these areas most likely would have included the Palace Green just to the south of the governor's mansion, certain parts of Duke of Gloucester Street, and near the capitol building on the east side of the city. Again, though these areas were predominantly utilized by the higher status citizens living and working near them, certainly there would have been a bit of mixing with the merchant class, considered respectable but still beneath the Virginia elites, and even those on the bottom of the social ladder still had to go about their business through the town. This would have been especially true during the times when the courts were in session and a myriad of merchants, farmers, politicians, and other characters flooded the city for weeks on end, breaking down the social barriers that had been established in day-to-day Williamsburg.

The established rules of social interaction applied not just to outside spaces, but to interior ones as well. Conversation, games, dancing, and music were regular activities in which genteel citizens participated in Williamsburg's taverns. While cities fostered many such establishments, some would be available to common citizens, while others were reserved solely for the use of polite society. Frequently these taverns were located close to the places of power in a city, like the capitol building or governor's mansion in Williamsburg, allowing convenient access to musical entertainment for the city's upper class. Not only did dancing and musical performances take place in these businesses, but admittance "to the public activities of polite society" was "the ultimate test of one's position and culture." The conversation, games, dancing and music experienced by elites in public spaces might be no different than that experienced by the lower sorts, yet experiencing it surrounded by the genteel elevated the activity to a higher social level.[53] Tavern keepers frequently kept their own instruments available for customers' use, perhaps as much to keep those patrons spending money in the establishment as to keep them entertained.[54] In addition to hosting balls and other festivities, these taverns also served meals for political figures and sometimes housed government meetings. The Raleigh Tavern in Williamsburg hosted the Virginia legislature for a time in 1774 when Governor Dunmore suddenly dissolved the assembly after he learned they had formed a committee to address their growing antagonism towards taxes levied by the crown.[55] By utilizing taverns, members of the elite were able to extend a genteel environment away from their estate houses and plantations, as well as giving them a place in Williamsburg to feel comfortable while surrounded by people of their own social status. Incorporating music and music-related activities like dancing and singing into their public social gatherings enhanced the sensation of participating in proper elite activities, while at the same time livening up the mood and festive atmosphere at their favorite taverns.

Although public spaces became more prominently utilized by the gentry during the eighteenth century, large plantation houses remained the primary locations of balls, concerts, and other socializations. These grand houses first appeared in cities up and down the East Coast, and eventually merchants and politicians began building a few miles outside of town. Beginning about 1725, planters in Virginia began to build large mansion-style houses on their plantations. Elite citizens built these grand houses due to an economic boom that took place during the eighteenth century, when per capita wealth increased fifty to one hundred percent between 1760 and 1770.[56] Whereas most Virginia houses during this period consisted of hewn logs covered in clapboards and comprised one room and an attic, these new mansions had two stories with an attic with multiple rooms dedicated to single purposes like bedrooms and parlors, while also being made of brick, which created a stark contrast with the small, unpainted wooden structures of their neighbors.[57]

The interiors of these houses were also designed to promote a genteel lifestyle and contribute to the social interactions necessary in the lives of upper tier citizens. The new Georgian-style house incorporated a central hall upon entry with rooms to either side. This isolated visitors from the private activities of the house, and seemed to imply that guests must wait for permission to enter certain areas designated for the evening's entertainment.[58] Spaces for entertainment were an important concern when choosing to either build or purchase a house in the eighteenth century. A

1770 *Virginia Gazette* advertisement for a large mansion and grounds for sale indicated the house was "very commodious" as it had a large room which was forty feet by twenty feet that, "would make a good ball room," a necessity for the kind of individual likely to purchase the dwelling. The seller, a B. Grymes, also listed a different large building he believed "would make a good theatre, which might be very beneficial to the town in general, and country adjacent," though not just anyone should be allowed to perform in this theater since only "proper persons, and of good demeanor" could contribute to the well-being of the city and surrounding area.[59]

Colonial Virginians' obsession with gentility partially arose from a desire to emulate their European brethren. This emulation required them to act as the British, French, and other enlightened countries did in regards to social etiquette, as well as copy their forms of entertainment as "they were determined they should not revert to barbarism in the wilderness. At no time did they allow themselves to forget that they were inheritors of British civilization," according to historian Hunter Farish. This meant the Virginia elite needed to fashion their manners and activities around those found in the lives of British gentlemen and ladies.[60] It appears, to some observers at least, that Virginians successfully adopted the European lifestyles they craved. Hugh Jones noted as early as 1724 that "the habits, life, customs, computations, etc., of the Virginians are much the same as about London, which they esteem as their home ... they live in the same manner, dress after the same fashion, and behave themselves exactly as the gentry in London."[61] In the third quarter of the eighteenth century, music in British society was one of those activities extremely popular among the genteel, with the *Virginia Gazette* noting in 1769:

> It is very justly observed, by many hundreds of the fair sex, as also by the gentlemen of the several musical societies dispersed over England, that musick was never so much in vogue as at this time, which is in no great measure attributed to that great and amiable patroness, our most gracious Queen, who in a very masterly manner plays on the organ, harpsichord, and piano forte; which seems to have stirred up the youth of both sexes, nay even grown persons, to attain this great and most agreeable of all accomplishments.[62]

To mimic the actions of the elite British citizenry, Virginians first needed to learn how, specifically, their overseas counterparts integrated music into their lives.

The theater became one such focus. In March 1751 the *Virginia Gazette* commented upon the passing of Maurice de Saxe, a Marshal General of France, noting that he had built a theater in his castle at Chambord. It was not enough, however, to simply state that the theater had been built, but it was also necessary to elaborate this particular theater featured decorations which cost more than 60,000 French livres (over $600,000 today) and that "his company of players was composed of excellent actors and actresses."[63] By highlighting the enormous expense Saxe had invested in his theater, as well as the skill of his performers, Virginians emphasized the importance of theatrical and musical extravagance in an elite culture. This news item also potentially encouraged American citizens to integrate theatrical entertainments into their own dwellings; perhaps B. Grymes's advertisement pronouncing that a room in his home would make an excellent theater reflected that message. Surely any individual prestigious enough to own their own theater would stand out among their peers as a truly elite citizen.

Accounts reflecting the importance of the theater to the genteel also appeared from England. In August 1751 the *Virginia Gazette* dedicated almost the entire first page to a *London Daily Advertiser* review of a performance of William Shakespeare's *Othello* at the Drury Lane theatre in London. This appraisal notes the play was performed by "persons of distinction," and the gentlemen who put on the play had been "long celebrated for their taste and spirit in gallantry." As noted by the author, these types of entertainments were designed for the genteel by the genteel: "Theatrical performances have lately been often exhibited by persons of the first fashion." As such, those putting on the play made sure the genteel in attendance were kept separate from "all improper people among them." The author lavished additional attention on the royal family in attendance, the elaborate stage decorations and embroidery work on the sets, "magnificent" and "well fancied" dresses worn by the women, and, perhaps the most important aspect of any stage show, "The band of musick, was a very fine one."[64] This *Virginia Gazette* account highlights most of the criteria of what made a person genteel: The activities they attended, their distance from those of a lower status, and the spectacle of the items in which they surrounded themselves. Reprinting stories like these from London conveyed important information about proper genteel behavior in regards to musical and theatrical entertainment to Virginia colonists.

Descriptions of British entertainments appeared regularly in the Williamsburg paper, highlighting how Virginians gained a sense of this form of musical cultural consumption and presentation. Editors of the *Virginia Gazette* also made it a point to include brief descriptions of grand balls, concerts, and theater performances that took place in England, briefly highlighting how many people were involved and their ranks, the specific types of entertainment, and the clothing styles worn by the attendees. In 1752 a ball held in London and attended by the Prince of Wales, Princess Augusta, the Duke of Cumberland, and Prince Edward was described as "the most splendid that has been known for many years," with the royals dancing minuets.[65] When George II took a summer vacation to Hanover, Germany, the paper noted the king "ordered French plays to be acted three times a week, and alloted [sic] the other days for assemblies, balls and concerts." Keeping up on the king's summer vacation, it noted George "take[s] three times a week the diversion of seeing a play," and during one of his afternoon meals "there was a fine concert."[66] The newspaper described a ball in 1766 at St. James's in London as "the most brilliant and numerous that has been for many years." The Duke of York and Princess Louisa Anne danced minuets, and after they withdrew country dances were initiated by the nobles, lasting until 2 a.m.[67] This focus on how royalty and nobles listened to concerts, attended plays, and danced at elaborate balls informed the Virginia elite about an entire world of entertainment, manners, and gentility required to be considered on par with their European counterparts.

Reading these *Virginia Gazette* accounts gave Virginians an overarching view of how European lords, ladies, and other elites integrated music into their lives and social activities. However, the best clues came from the intricate details published in the paper, allowing Americans to implement specific dances, music, and entertainments into their own frivolities. For example, in the June 30, 1768, *Virginia Gazette* a story from London appeared detailing a dinner and its subsequent post-meal dance. Not content with generalities, the story listed minute details of the particular dances and interactions between the participants, noting the ball started when "45 ladies entered the room; then the dances immediately began, and each lady was saluted at the end of every dance, which were nine minuets, nine rigadoons, nine cotillions, and eighteen country dances, being in the whole 45. After the ladies had been kissed around 45 times, and 45 couple of jellies were eaten, the company retired with great mirth and festivity at 45 minutes past 3 o'clock."[68] This fascination with the step-by-step details was multipurpose. For one, it was simply entertaining and a good story for the paper's readers. It also provided the subscribers, as mentioned above, a glimpse of what was fashionable and popular in London, the city they most wished to emulate. Thirdly, and perhaps most importantly, it told the readers of Williamsburg how specifically to copy their peers overseas. Not content to simply throw a ball, they now knew how many dances were acceptable, some of the interactions to expect between the guests, how long the dance should last, and even one of the food items which was served. Using this information they could then copy London's genteel as closely as possible, bringing the Americans one step closer to the Europeans.

The desire of the Virginia gentry to emulate the British was not solely limited to public events such as concerts, plays, and balls, but also extended to owning the same consumer goods as the European elite. The middle third of the eighteenth century witnessed a dramatic consumer revolution selling British goods to the colonies. Before this time, exporters in Europe were slow to realize the potential markets that existed for their goods in America. Just as important, even if these businesses had been willing and able to ship their items overseas, before the 1740s many elite Americans could not have afforded to buy the items they desired.[69] As a result of easy credit and a growing consumer mentality, however, by 1773 American colonists were buying almost twenty-six percent of all goods produced in England, compared to a mere six percent at the beginning of the century.[70] The total value of goods Britain imported into America during the mid–1740s amounted to just shy of £900,000, of which Maryland and Virginia alone purchased forty-three percent of that total. By 1771 imports had increased to an astonishing £4,500,000 (approximately $450 million in today's money) of imported merchandise for the colonists to purchase, of which the two Chesapeake colonies still purchased approximately thirty percent.[71] This massive increase in purchasing imported goods was not just limited to the upper classes of Virginia. By approximately the 1740s "manufactured goods inundated the households of people of all classes" in the Chesapeake, leading some scholars to refer to the rise in consumer spending as "rapid and unprecedented."[72] Desiring to emulate their social betters, as that group in turn wanted to be like the British elite, middle and lower rank Virginians demanded luxury goods like instruments and music books in order to more closely copy the lifestyles of those above them.

Part of the reason for this explosion in consumer purchases by the colonials was that their population had vastly increased during the century. Between 1700 and 1770 the colonial population, both black and white, had increased from approximately 250,000 to over two million citizens. During the period following 1740 alone the population grew an astounding one hundred thirty-seven percent.[73] Unsurprisingly, this is also the period when American consumer spending also increased at a dramatic pace. As more people came to live in the colonies they required more British goods to sustain the lives they desired. Another reason consumer purchases increased in the latter half of the eighteenth century is that social and economic conditions improved during this time, giving the gentility more leisure time to spend on entertainment activities.[74]

One of those activities was the purchasing and playing of a wide variety of musical instruments. Having the skills to play an instrument, Virginians believed, increased an individual's social image by having them partake in an activity associated not only with the upper crust, but with the European culture Americans craved in the 1700s. Men and women often played different types of instruments, with men focusing on the flute and violin and women primarily playing keyboard instruments like the harpsichord, virginal, spinet, clavichord and fortepiano, all predecessors to modern pianos and similar in that they used a series of keys to propel hammers against tightened strings, creating various musical notes. The flute and violin were generally not played by genteel women as "it was considered unladylike for girls to learn to play them," according to historian Ronald Davis. Many likewise frowned upon gentlemen learning to play most wind instruments as the wind variety had a tendency to "puff out the face in vulgar fashion," as one of Davis's sources indicated.[75] Washington addressed this social faux pas in his 16th "Rule of Civility" noting, "Do not puff up the cheeks; loll not out the tongue, rub the hands, or board, thrust out the lips, or bite them, or keep the lips too open or close."[76]

Some instruments like the guitar were played by both sexes, and there was, of course, some degree of crossover between the instruments played by men and women. When playing concerts in the home or the drawing room, the preferred choices among males were generally the violin and flute, despite the great variety of instruments available to the colonists.[77] John Blair, Sr., onetime president of William and Mary and future Acting Governor of Virginia, noted in his diary in January 1751 that he had two acquaintances visit him, and as part of their visiting a "Mr. J.R. play'd on his violin & Dr. Hackerston on his G flute."[78] Philip Fithian and Ben Carter, one of his students, frequently played the flute together at the behest of Robert Carter, owner of Nomini Hall. Fithian also encouraged Ben to play the flute for him when he retired for the evening, being paid "half a bit a week" for this duty.[79]

The violin, often referred to as the fiddle in colonial writings, was one of the most prominent instruments in the eighteenth century. The instrument's popularity represented a radical change in attitude from the 1600s, when "most Virginians regarded professional fiddlers as rogues and rascals almost by definition and perfectly capable of theft or most any other unscrupulous act" according to historian Ronald Davis.[80] Indeed, a fiddler named John Utie migrated to Jamestown from England in August 1620 and shortly thereafter was elected to the Virginia House of Burgesses, a quite prestigious position. While serving in this government role, Utie occasionally played the fiddle for the amusement of himself and his friends. This musical fun was quickly seized upon and used as a partisan attack by William Tyler, a neighbor and political enemy, who sought to unseat Utie from his government position. In one personal disagreement involving stolen tobacco that ended up in Jamestown's General Court, Utie accused Tyler of growing "very high and loftie," to which Tyler sarcastically replied, "I wil be as high as a fidler," then mocking Utie for being a professional fiddler in England. This statement was apparently so provocative Utie "flung a stick at" Tyler, despite the fact it was true. Later in front of the court, witnesses proclaimed Tyler also publicly disparaged Utie's character, labeling him as a "Fidlinge Rogue and Rascall."[81] Apparently though Utie enjoyed playing the violin for an audience, as well as personal pleasure, his character was besmirched in the eyes of the public simply by playing the instrument. By the beginning of the 1700s, however, the fiddle's association with rascals dissipated and violins appeared frequently at balls, dances, and various other forms of public entertainment. In one public celebration twenty fiddlers played in a contest of musical skill, with the best player winning a new violin. Of course, it was required the contestants own their own instruments, as no one had "the liberty of playing, unless he brings a fiddle with him." Following the contest the participants all played a variety of tunes together in celebration of the event.[82]

As previously noted, one of Thomas Jefferson's favorite instruments was the violin and he often played it with other influential Williamsburg figures at the governor's mansion, rising at 5 a.m. at times to practice.[83] According to nineteenth-century biographer Henry Randall, while living in Williamsburg Jefferson purchased a small violin he called a "kit," used chiefly by dancing masters, along with a small case that fit on his saddle. He took this violin with him everywhere in town as it afforded him a "capital way of whiling away the time before the people were up where he was staying." Due to its quiet tone, he could practice wherever he pleased without disturbing anyone nearby, including indoors, at least if the walls were thick.[84] Eager to acquire a new violin, Jefferson wrote to John Page in 1763 about his desire to purchase "a good fiddle" in Italy.[85] In 1768 he subsequently purchased one in Williamsburg from Dr. William Pasteur, an apothecary and seller of a variety of items, instruments included.[86] Fiddles were so popular in Williamsburg one anonymous individual in town was apparently infatuated enough with his own instrument he wrote a poem and sent it to the *Virginia Gazette* for publication, titling it "A Gentleman's Address to his Violin":

> Pretty little charming thing,
> Raptures flow from ev'ry string;
> Mindful of thy lively strains,
> Charmer both of nymphs and swains.
> Drousy in my lonesome cot,
> Welcome, ev'ry sprightly note!
> Kindling soft and easy joys,
> Mirthful, ev'ry damp destroys.
> Partner of my peaceful hours,
> Gladdens more than mild amours;
> Fleeting though thy pleasures be,
> Guiltness they-no stings from thee.
> Thou canst sooth each vain desire,
> Thou canst virtuous thoughts inspire,
> Thou canst make me not repine;
> Sure, sweet creature! thou'rt divine.[87]

In addition to the violin, members of the Virginia elite purchased many other instruments to showcase their genteel credentials. At Nomini Hall, plantation owner Robert Carter owned and played a vast array of instruments, including a harpsichord, fortepiano, guitar, violin, and German flutes. It was not unusual for Philip Fithian to spend "most of the day at the great house hearing the various instruments of music." It is striking that a plantation owner like Robert Carter dedicated a large amount of time to playing music. The Nomini Hall plantation consisted of over 70,000 acres of land, and though plantation owners generally would not have participated in the physical work on the grounds, many like George Washington and William Byrd spent hours every day touring their lands to supervise the day-to-day operations. By devoting a good amount of time to playing music, enough that Fithian felt the urge to mention it in his diary, Carter showed that this activity was equally as important as his other duties as the owner of a huge Virginia plantation. For the gentility in the eighteenth century it was not enough to simply be successful and wealthy; one also needed to be skilled at playing a variety of musical instruments. Carter even converted one unused end of Fithian's classroom into a concert room which could hold the great variety of instruments he owned and to provide "a place for practice, as well as entertainment."[88] Also in Carter's possession was an exceptional organ that had been built specifically for him in London to his own specifications. Thomas Jefferson so appreciated this instrument that he offered to purchase it from him, though Carter declined as it was eventually going to be used to teach his daughters how to play.[89]

Robert Carter not only owned and played a variety of instruments, but had additional skills to maintain and adjust the complicated implements. Carter invented a tool for tuning his harpsichord and forte-piano consisting of a number of whistles of various sizes "so as to sound all the notes in one octave."[90] Robert Carter then was similar to Thomas Jefferson in that both were wealthy Virginia planters who used some of their spare time to invent gadgets designed to improve their lives and property, including their musical instruments. In 1786 Jefferson wrote to his friend Francis Hopkinson, also an individual who enjoyed tinkering with instruments, and described a metronome, a modified musical piece on which he had been working. Metronomes are small mechanical devices used to indicate a tempo or beat by using clicks or other sounds to assist musicians in maintaining a consistent speed while playing music. However, modern metronomes similar to those available today did not appear until the early nineteenth century. In Jefferson's time the company Renaudin of Paris made two versions of the predecessor of the metronome, and after he purchased one of these models he decided

This portrait of Robert Carter III of Nomini Hall, painted around 1753 by London artist Thomas Hudson, shows the music-loving plantation owner at the age of 25, twenty years before Philip Fithian wrote of his experiences at Nomini Hall. Note Carter's proper, genteel posture and elegant clothes. His clothing suggests Carter wore this outfit to a masquerade ball, where music no doubt played a role, as he is holding a mask in his left hand. This painting was located in Robert Carter's townhouse in Williamsburg and eventually moved to Nomini Hall until his death in 1804. The original painting is located at the Virginia Historical Society.

it would be possible to improve on the design. Though the model from Paris had multiple settings for different tempos, or speeds at which the music should be played, there was no indicator on the device to tell the musician how many beats per minute there were in each tempo, an important piece of information when it came to accurately reading the music. Jefferson discovered by making a simple pendulum on the wall using a string and the metronome, through counting the vibrations of the string he could accurately track the number of beats for each tempo.[91] Their dedication to maintaining and tweaking their instruments, and subsequently sharing these discoveries with their fellow elites, indicates music was more than a hobby or necessity to gentlemen like Jefferson and Carter. Instead, as the last quarter of the eighteenth century approached music had become an integral part of life for Virginians, especially those with the free time and money to dedicate themselves fully to its enjoyment.

Many of the Founding Fathers appreciated music in multiple forms, including acquiring a variety of musical instruments. Some, like Benjamin Franklin, even invented their own instruments when those in the marketplace did not live up to their expectations. In 1761 Benjamin Franklin was in London when he saw a concert of musical glasses performed by E.H. Delaval. This performance consisted of glasses placed on a table filled with different amounts of water. The musician then could produce varying musical notes by wetting their fingers and rubbing them around the rims of the glasses. After seeing this concert, Franklin wrote to his friend Father Beccaria in Italy, describing the music as being adapted to "soft and plaintive" music. Franklin described being "charmed with the sweetness of its tones," though he believed the musical glasses could be reconstructed in a more convenient fashion to play them. Rather than placing the glasses on a table, Franklin instead affixed them in a row to a horizontal wooden rod or spindle which spun by using the feet to depress a pedal. The musician would then dip his fingers in water, and hold them against the glasses as they spun to produce the pleasing sound.[92] Initially this instrument was known as a "glassy-chord," while Franklin preferred giving it the Italian-sounding name of an "armonica," though most colonists generally referred to the instrument as a glass harmonica.[93]

The glass harmonica quickly became a popular instrument in Virginia. Thomas Jefferson was "fascinated" with them and considered purchasing one. However, being the musical connoisseur he was, Jefferson wanted a six-octave model, but was informed by his friend John Trumbull that the glass harmonica only came in a three-octave version which could be purchased in London from the store of Longman and Broderip;

Jefferson never did purchase the instrument, however.[94] Robert Carter, on the other hand, did purchase a glass harmonica and added it to his musical collection at Nomini Hall. One evening he played the musical glasses for Philip Fithian, who was listening to them for the first time. He described the music as "charming," and noted, "The notes are clear and inexpressibly soft, they swell, and are inexpressibly grand; & either it is because the sounds are new, and therefore please me, or it is the most captivating instrument I have ever heard. The sounds very much resemble the human voice, and in my opinion they far exceed even the swelling organ."[95]

Aside from those mentioned above, a vast array of other instruments flooded the Virginia marketplace in the latter half of the eighteenth century. Jefferson expressed interest in purchasing pianos and clavichords for Monticello, and admired a small instrument Benjamin Franklin carried with him called a sticcado, which "resembled a small dulcimer with glass bars and keys and had a three-octave compass."[96] In August 1757 a professional musician named Charles Love fled along a road in Westmoreland County north of Williamsburg holding in his saddlebags a violin, a German flute, an oboe, and a prized bassoon stolen from Philipp Ludwell Lee of Stratford Hall. The latter instrument was valuable enough that Lee took out a newspaper advertisement asking the public to be on the lookout for Love.[97] In orchestras performing in Williamsburg it was possible to find "members of the string family, flutes, oboes, horns, and bassoons," occasionally cymbals, and clarinets after the mid-eighteenth century.[98] As the century progressed the variety of instruments grew, with the string bass, cello, and viola appearing in concerts. As the variety grew so too did the number played overall at one time, oftentimes with multiple musicians playing the same instruments in harmony.[99] Though less common than violins or keyed instruments, bagpipes, guitars, Jews harps, bugles, fifes, hunting horns, hautboys (similar to an oboe), drums, and banjos were also heard in the colonies, with the latter being a favorite instrument of slaves.[100] According to Jefferson, who referred to this instrument as the "banjar," the banjo was brought to America by African slaves and was "the original of the guitar."[101]

As a multitude of instruments flooded the nascent American musical marketplace, customers needed a way to acquire these goods for their personal use. Most Virginians likely purchased their instruments directly from a seller or manufacturer in Europe, though some individuals such as Benjamin Bucktrout of Williamsburg had his own spinets and harpsichords for sale.[102] Due to the limited existing purchase records, it is impossible to know exactly how many instruments were shipped to the colonies, but examples like Bucktrout were unusual compared to the number purchased from Europe.[103] By ordering instruments directly from the source, purchasers bypassed the usual method of items being shipped to stores or merchants in Virginia, and expedited the time it would take to receive their goods. Colonists had enough consumer savvy to know that specific English instrument makers created objects of great value. Instruments like spinets and harpsichords would sometimes be made by regular manufacturers, but at other times master craftsmen such as Roger Plenius or Jacob Kirkman would personally work on the items. Kirkman was the instrument maker to the queen, so any musical device he made would have been of exceedingly high quality and highly sought after by consumers, no matter the cost.[104] As early as 1730 superior violins from the Cremona region of Italy, home of the renowned instrument maker Stradivari, were available in the colonies, sometimes offered as prizes in fiddling contests. Jacob Stainer, a predecessor of Stradivari in the Cremona region, also had exceptional quality string instruments for sale in the colonies. If a genteel person could not afford instruments made by these master craftsmen, high quality copies were available for purchase.[105]

By the time packing charges, freight, and commissions were added to the cost of the merchandise, it represented a considerable expense for colonists to purchase and import an instrument. Soon after their invention, Benjamin Franklin's glass harmonicas were being commercially built in London and were a well-known and very popular instrument. These harmonicas were sold at the store of Longman and Broderip, an instrument manufacturer and book publisher in London, for £21, which in today's money would be equal to just shy of £1600 or $2500. It should be noted this was simply the sale price, and did not include the extra expenses mentioned above.[106] The Williamsburg Post Office's May 1771 advertisement in the *Gazette* noted they had for sale "Tip-top violins, with elegant screw bows, at five pounds a piece."[107] Even these smaller and far more common instruments, as compared to the glass harmonica, cost approximately £320, or $500 in today's money, a substantial sum and well outside the budgets of many in Williamsburg. Despite these financial outlays, many would have viewed such costs as necessary expenses. Genteel citizens gladly paid high prices as the musical instruments were considered essential to elevate a person's status above that of a common citizen.

Not all transactions were necessarily conducted in money, however, especially in a plantation economy like the one found in Virginia where trade goods were their own form of currency. In 1766 Mary Savage of

Northampton, Virginia, wrote to John Norton, a merchant in London, thanking him for the fiddle he shipped to her on the *Rachel & Mary*. In this letter Savage apologizes that she did not send Norton as much tobacco for payment as she would have liked due to a small crop that year. She did, however, promise to send Norton more tobacco the following year, and even requested another shipment of items, seeming to imply some London merchants were flexible in their financial dealings.[108] High prices and extraneous fees would have been a necessary expense for the Virginia elite, regardless of the form of currency used, as these instruments would add to the perception that the purchaser was in a high social circle and thus were considered a mandatory purchase in Williamsburg and the surrounding areas.

By the time Hugh Jones wrote his notes on the colony of Virginia, Williamsburg had already grown into what he described as a "market town." The capital by that point was "well stock'd with rich stores, of all sorts of goods, and well furnished with the best provisions and liquors."[109] Specialty stores did not exist in Williamsburg at this point, so most sellers would advertise and sell a great variety of goods, from foodstuffs and practical household items to medicine and instruments. Other items were simply sold from the post office or at the *Virginia Gazette*'s office. Among the various instruments sold by the stores in Williamsburg were spinets, harpsichords, bells, Jews harps, flutes, harps, pipes, hand organs, hunting horns, and various others. Included in this impressive list of instruments were some notable items, such as a 1767 "complete harpsichord, with three stops, just imported from London, made by Kirkman, the Queen's instrument maker, and supposed by good judges to be the best in the colony."[110] A year later this item was relisted as for sale for unknown reasons, but this time the harpsichord was "to be disposed of under prime cost," a steal for those desiring to be genteel but on a limited budget.[111]

Also for sale in 1767, recently imported from London, was "a very neat hand organ, in a mohogany [sic] case, with a gilt front, which plays sixteen tunes on two barrels; it has four stops, and every thing is in the best order." Hand organs worked on the same principle as larger pipe organs, though they were much smaller and rather than keys used a hand crank to turn a series of gears which played a variety of songs through small pipes. Though this hand organ was originally sold for sixteen pounds, "the lady being dead it came in for, any person inclining to purchase it may have it on very reasonable terms."[112] In case a purchaser was unsure of how a particular instrument would affect their social standing, advertisers reassured them that their new item was "very genteel," sure to increase their prestige in Williamsburg, as one barrel organ merchant promised in the *Gazette*.[113] Sellers increasingly advertised not only the instruments but the many "genteel" musical accessories required to accompany them. For example, the *Gazette* explained in an advertisement that John Prentis's store featured "an exceeding elegant spinnet, in a genteel mahogany case, with a music desk, spare wires, quills, &c.," which taught newspaper readers that an instrument was simply one part of a well-appointed music room.[114]

As noted in Prentis's advertisement, it was not just the musical instruments themselves sold by Williamsburg's merchants. Included with these goods were those supplies necessary for the maintenance and accessorizing of the harpsichords, violins, and other instruments. Violins alone needed replacement strings, bridges, pegs, and bows, and merchants like John Greenhow in Williamsburg gladly sold these items. Thomas Jefferson frequently had to purchase replacement violin strings for his instruments as they had a tendency to break.[115] Greenhow also sold catgut strings for drums, harps and guitars, spinet wire, and hammers for the hammer dulcimer, a percussion instrument where the musician uses two small hammers to strike strings stretched over a trapezoid-shaped board.[116]

Merchants did not just focus on instruments and musical accessories, however, but also the printed instructions and music books necessary to utilize those instruments, as well as the dancing manuals to accompany the music. As observed in Cuthbert Ogle's will inventory from 1755, Virginians developed a taste for purchasing musical compositions to accompany their instruments in the latter half of the eighteenth century. After they had acquired the physical instruments themselves, citizens still needed the ability to effectively play music to establish their genteel credentials. Not only would such talents show they were upstanding citizens, but acquiring the newest English music brought a sense of proximity to European culture: the music being played in a Virginia tavern might be the same played at the king's birthday celebration in London. Most of this imported music was originally published approximately between 1710 and 1752, with a majority of it coming after 1745. London music houses or printers issued all of the music, though it often consisted of German and Italian composers, and the books slowly made their way across the Atlantic and into the possessions of those in Virginia.[117] The mid- to late-eighteenth century experienced a type of musical renaissance, with famous composers such as Antonio Vivaldi, Jean-Philippe Rameau, Johann Sebastian Bach, George Frideric Handel, Franz Joseph Haydn, and Wolfgang Amadeus Mozart almost simultaneously writing and performing music in Europe, providing an almost unprecedented wealth of material for amateur musicians to perform at concerts and in their homes.

Of course, the citizens of Williamsburg needed some way to purchase these imported music books. Purdie and Dixon, owners of one version of the *Virginia Gazette*, advertised in 1771 that, in addition to new instruments they had acquired, they also offered "musick, namely instructions for the harpsichord, violin, and German flute." Included in this list of instructions was music for famous eighteenth-century compositions such as *The Padlock, Love in a Village, Maid of the Mill, Cunning Man*, as well as Italian sonatas and numerous "eminent composers" like Vivaldi.[118] The post office in Williamsburg advertised "instructions for the violin and flute" were for sale, as well as the music for famous plays like "The Beggars Opera, Love in a Village, and The Padlock, set to musick, a great variety of other musick by the best masters, and blank musick books," for those desiring to compose on their own.[119] Robert Carter purchased a book of vocal music in Williamsburg which he showed to Philip Fithian and which he described as "a collection of psalm-tunes, hymns, & anthems set in four parts for the voice; he seems much taken with it & says we must learn & perform some of them in the several parts with our voices & with instruments."[120] This musical book and the others listed here represent only a small portion of the variety of printed music which was available in Williamsburg in the latter half of the eighteenth century.

Not all music came from overseas, however. As the eighteenth century progressed and Williamsburg became wealthier and more cosmopolitan, Virginians took it upon themselves to stake their own claim in the music scene. Edward Cumins published the first book of theater songs in Williamsburg's printing office in 1772.[121] *The Storer, or American Syren: Being a Collection of the Newest and Most Approved Songs* was named for a young actress named Maria Storer. In 1771 Maria performed in Williamsburg as Lucinda in the play *Love in a Village* as part of the American Company, and the book was named after her in honor of her musical talents.[122] No longer were Virginians content to purchase music from London and play what was already old to the British elite. Now they began publishing their own music books, establishing a unique musical culture and elevating themselves to contemporaries of London's musical scene rather than its followers. By the beginning of the nineteenth century American publishers had produced over five hundred different pocket-sized collections of songs called "songsters," and an amazing fifteen thousand individual songs via sheet music, rivaling many European publishers.[123]

The ability to profit from musical composition was not necessarily

AN ESSAY

For the further

IMPROVEMENT OF

DANCING;

Being a COLLECTION of

Figure Dances,

Of several Numbers,

Compos'd by the most Eminent Masters; Describ'd in CHARACTERS after The newest Manner of Monsieur *Feuillet*.

By E. PEMBERTON.

To which is Added,
Three Single DANCES, *viz.*
A Chacone by Mr. Isaac,
A Passacaille by Mr. L'Abbe,
And a Jig by Mr. Pecour, *Master of the Opera at* Paris.

London Printed, and Sold by *J. Walsh* at the *Harp* and *Hautboy* in *Catherine-street* near *Somerset-House* in the *Strand, J. Hare* at the *Viol* and *Flute* in *Cornhill* near the *Royal-Exchange*, and at the Author's next the *Fire-Office* in St. *Martin's-Lane*, 1711.

Price Half a Guinea.

An Essay for the Further Improvement of Dancing, written by E. Pemberton in 1711. Dancing manuals and other music-related books like this one became more and more popular as the eighteenth century progressed and were frequently sold in Williamsburg's stores. Image courtesy of the Library of Congress.

limited to publishing music books, however. Others who learned this valuable skill could sell their talents to anyone desiring unique, one of a kind music for any special occasion. In August of 1774, according to the *Virginia Gazette,* an "odd accident" happened to a Doctor Arne, who had been "engaged to hire a band, and write music to an ode to be performed that day for the benefit of a public charity." After finishing his musical arrangement, "he accordingly packed up his composition, along with some instruments, in a hackney coach, and set out for the appointed place. Stopping at a coffeehouse just by, to enquire for a gentleman at the bar, he desired the coachman to take care of his papers, and he would be out immediately. The coachman, from this caution, we suppose, imagining them of more value, took a French leave, and has not been heard of since, to the great disappointment of the doctor, who forgot to take the number of his coach, as well as the audience." Seeing fit to wrap up this amusing anecdote with a musical pun, the editors wryly commented, "that it is rather surprising so excellent a judge in music as Doctor Arne could be so easily hummed."[124] Despite most likely losing his pay in addition to his work, Doctor Arne's story indicates one additional way music composition could be profitable in Williamsburg, though of course written musical work of this sort could never match the extensive audience of printed music books.

Newspapers played a critical role in reaching those audiences and increasing music book and instrument sales in Virginia. As the eighteenth century began newspapers became a necessity for any city or colony desiring to appear at the same social level as Europe. When they first appeared these publications typically consisted of four pages, about half of which was a collection of various anonymously-written stories from overseas or neighboring colonies, letters to the editor, or perhaps general interest stories such as political or celebratory matters; stories about individuals were rare as they were considered personal. The other half of the four-page paper consisted of advertisements for various goods and services, supplying the publisher with the majority of their income.[125] In one of the earliest known examples of publishers soliciting these purchases, on October 8, 1736, William Parks, editor of the *Virginia Gazette,* inserted in his paper an "Advertisement, concerning Advertisements" requesting, "All persons who have occasion to buy or sell houses, lands, goods or cattle; or have servants or slaves runaway; or have lost horses, cattle &c. or want to give any publick notice; may have it advertis'd in all these Gazettes printed in one week, for three shillings, and for two shillings per week for as many weeks afterwards as they shall order." Parks sweetened the sales pitch to his potential customers by noting, "As these papers will circulate (as speedily as possible) not only all over this, but also the neighbouring colonies, and will probably be read by some thousands of people, it is very likely they may have the desir'd effect; and it is certainly the cheapest and most effectual method that can be taken, for publishing any thing of this nature."[126]

Despite William Parks's 1736 sales pitch, it should be noted that advertisements selling instruments in the *Virginia Gazette* did not appear until 1751, marking this as a later development in the musical commerce of Williamsburg.[127] Psalm books showed up in advertisements as early as 1739 in Virginia, though books containing secular music first appeared in 1751, around the same time as instruments for sale.[128] However, as noted previously, since many individuals purchased their merchandise directly from Europe it seems likely the beginning of advertising for instrument and book sales coincided with an increase in general colonial mercantilism rather than a newly-formed desire for musical goods, and these earlier overseas purchases would never have appeared in newspaper advertisements. Also, many colonial advertisers did not list specific items they had for sale, instead choosing to use bundling terms like "a large assortment," "goods of all sort," or simply using "etc etc etc" to indicate more items were available, so it is difficult to ascertain for certain the amount of musical merchandise which may have been on sale at any given time in Williamsburg's stores.[129]

As instruments and books of music began to appear for sale in the latter half of the eighteenth century, the style of advertisements changed at this time as well. Before the 1750s advertisements in papers "were generally small, one-column texts, but after mid-century it was not uncommon to encounter two-column spreads, announcing newly arrived consumer goods." Advertisers began to pay more attention to "layout, ornamental borders, and creative variations in type size." These design features helped differentiate different merchants from their competitors as the number of sellers increased in proportion to the amount of goods sold in the colonies. Following 1760 the total space dedicated to advertisements generally equaled or exceeded the amount of space to publish the news of the day. By 1775 it was not uncommon for some papers to have advertisements filling an entire page, which represented a new era in colonial commerce.[130]

This increase in advertising space paralleled the growth of the musical marketplace during the 1700s as it grew from a sometimes frowned-upon pastime to a societal obligation necessary to establish one's place in Virginia. As the eighteenth century progressed, the genteel of Williamsburg developed a fascination with how the British aristocracy and upper crust lived their lives. In an effort to reduce their image as backwoods, ignorant planters, Virginians strove to adopt the culture of their overseas counterparts, including their fascination with music. They integrated musical activities into a vast array of their social and governmental functions including balls and dances held during court sessions, and instrumentalists played at establishments frequented by the genteel. On an individual basis, gentility required that one must purchase the same instruments popular in Britain at the time, as well as the music books containing the most popular songs so they could hear the same operas and concertos that appealed to the British gentry. As the century progressed it was not good enough to own just one of these instruments or music books, and soon Virginia's well-to-do citizens acquired sufficient quantities of musical accessories to consider themselves on par with Britons. Now that the ability to create music was flooding Virginia, the citizens of Williamsburg needed to further expand on those venues which allowed them to partake in genteel activities.

2

Virginians Will Dance or Die!

> "It was indeed beautiful to admiration, to see such a number of young persons, set off by dress to the best advantage, moving easily, to the sound of well performed music, and with perfect regularity, tho' apparently in the utmost disorder."
> —Philip Fithian, December 18, 1773

On the 30th of November 1737, to celebrate St. Andrew's Day, a series of diversions "for the entertainment of the gentlemen and ladies" was held on land near Williamsburg owned by William Byrd. As part of the festivities the event coordinators held horse races, foot races, one-handed boxing contests, wrestling matches, and beauty contests for the "handsomest young country maid that appears in the field." Alongside these entertainments were several events representing the vast array of musically-inspired activities available to Williamsburg's citizens. As mentioned in the previous chapter, a contest took place between twenty fiddlers with the best player winning a new violin, followed by a concert performed by all twenty participants. Drums were played during the boxing contest every fifteen minutes to call for new challengers. A number of "songsters" competed in a singing competition, with the best singer receiving a book filled with different ballads. Not expected to take on this challenge with skill alone, each singer was provided with "liquor sufficient to clear their windpipes." Meanwhile, a pair of "handsome shoes" was awarded to the winner of a dancing contest. To cap off the event, a "handsome entertainment" was provided for those gentlemen and ladies who purchased tickets. Included in this entertainment was a musical concert for the guests consisting of "drums, trumpets, hautboys, &c." The following week the *Virginia Gazette* was pleased to announce the event's success, with gentlemen and ladies

2. Virginians Will Dance or Die! 41

experiencing "drums [that] were beating, trumpets sounding, and other musick playing, for the entertainment of the company, and the whole was manag'd with as good order, and gave as great satisfaction, in general, as cou'd possibly be expected."[1]

This 1737 St. Andrew's Day celebration signals the extent to which Virginia was in the early stages of its musical renaissance in the early eighteenth century. Events featuring a multitude of musical activities were just becoming fashionable; indeed, as this festival was only occurring for the second time its organizer felt obligated to explain its purpose, "as such meetings and entertainments are somewhat new," even though its component activities had already become integrated into the daily lives of Williamsburg's elite citizens.[2] In fact, the St. Andrew's Day event was a showcase of the musical abilities genteel individuals were expected to observe and participate in on a regular basis. Singing, playing instruments alone or in public concerts, dancing, and attending formal balls were all part of the expected duties of a gentleman in colonial Virginia, and as the eighteenth century progressed Williamsburg's elite wholeheartedly embraced the new musical activities and marketplace available to them. Building on the previous chapter, which scrutinized the importance of music to genteel society and its reliance on the consumption of English culture and goods, this chapter elaborates on some of the topics previously discussed, showing the various ways in which Virginians' new fascination with music became a part of their lives, especially for those of a high social status. Chapter two also explores the growing complexity of Williamsburg's musical economy during the middle third of the eighteenth century, as Virginians' interest in music and English dancing reached new heights.

In general during the eighteenth century, religion was less important to citizens of the Chesapeake area than it was in New England. The Great Awakening, an approximately ten-year period of religious revivalism that swept the American colonies around the 1730s, did not permeate society in this area of the country as it did in the northern areas. In Virginia the wealthy citizens, not the church, determined what was popular in their cultural pursuits, and as they desired to emulate their British counterparts they focused more on secular activities than religious. The Williamsburg elite held that the musical culture of Europe "represented the triumph of civilization over savagery," and not as the devilish hobby some in the more religious northern colonies believed.[3] Though they did not embrace religious-based music as wholeheartedly as their fellow colonists in New England, Virginians did participate in new musical religious activities that developed in the eighteenth century.

Much of the early singing heard in the American colonies was in the form of psalmody, or the public singing of psalms in church. Due to the inexperience and lack of musical talent of many parishioners, singing schools were developed to teach basic singing abilities to musically-challenged congregations, with the first appearing in New England around 1720. Typically prospective students received notice that a new singing school would soon be opening when it was advertised in their local paper or printed on distributed broadside advertisements, and if interested they could sign up for one or two classes a week for a month or more. These schools educated their pupils via the use of printed music books on how to properly read the music and sing along with what was printed in the tune-books, with the music sometimes originating from the singing master himself but often from a variety of other sources. If printed song books were unavailable students sometimes wrote the music they were to learn to sing in blank manuscript copybooks, with the added benefit that the master now had access to completed music books on the next stop of his teaching circuit. Frequently singing classes culminated with a "singing lecture," a type of choir concert accompanied by a sermon from the local church, or a "singing assembly," which was the same concert without the sermon.[4] These singing schools became enormously popular, especially in the New England area, but not necessarily just for the music. Similar to young people using formal dances as a way to socialize with the opposite sex, so too did singing school students "make new friends, exchange notes, flirt, walk home together after lessons, and, in general, enjoy themselves."[5]

Though more prevalent in New England, Williamsburg also developed singing schools to educate parishioners in proper vocal techniques. In 1752 John Tompkins taught a class "for a dollar entrance" at William and Mary College and Bruton Parish Church to "all persons inclinable to learn a true method of singing psalms."[6] It would appear as well that these singing schools successfully taught congregations how to sing, at least on some occasions. In one incident Philip Fithian attended a church near Williamsburg and was surprised when the attendants started singing psalms as there were "voices singing at the same time, from a gallery, entirely contrary to what I have seen before in the colony, for it is seldom in the fullest congregation's [sic], that more sing than the clerk, & about two others!" According to Fithian, a "singing master of good abilities has been among this society lately & put them on the respectable method which they, at present pursue."[7]

As singing schools became more popular and spread throughout the colonies, so too did the demand for new musical psalm books shipped from overseas or published in America so congregations did not have to sing the same songs over and over again.[8] In the *Virginia Gazette* it was common to see books of psalms listed for sale among others consisting of theatrical plays like *The Beggar's Opera*, instrument instruction manuals, and secular song books like the previously mentioned *American Syren*.[9] For example, in 1773 Williamsburg's Printing Office advertised four columns of books for sale at their store. Sandwiched between philosopher David Hume's published essays and a history of King George III the ad listed a copy of *Harmonia Sacra, or a choice Collection of Psalm and Hymn Tunes*.[10] Books consisting of lessons in church organ and choir music by John Alcock of St. Paul's Cathedral in London, as well as other important religious composers, were found side-by-side with popular composer Handel's works in the possessions of Williamsburg musician Cuthbert Ogle following his death.[11]

The vast majority of music sung in Williamsburg, however, was not for religious but rather secular purposes, consisting of songs popular in Britain and elsewhere in Europe. When learning to play an instrument, a skill required by the genteel of Virginia and desired by many others, young girls had a choice of a keyed or string instrument such as the guitar, harpsichord, or piano. Alternatively they could choose the art of singing as their instrument, after learning proper vocalization techniques. Often these young ladies learned to sing as well as play an instrument, and used these skills in conjunction when entertaining visitors or family. The pressure and social necessity of these vocal musical acts required not only proper singing instruction but guidance on how to perform before audiences of one's peers. This was particularly important for young women. If a girl could sing, especially popular songs enjoyed by Europeans, she might be asked to perform in public for the enjoyment of her social equals.[12] In October 1763 then twenty year-old Thomas Jefferson wrote to his friend William Fleming, recounting meeting a Miss Jenny Taliaferro at a social gathering. Not only did Jefferson find Miss Taliaferro pretty, but he was also "vastly pleased with her playing on the spinnette and singing."[13] The ability to master both instruments allowed Miss Taliaferro to elevate herself in the eyes of polite company, thus increasing her social status.

Though considered an essential part of a young genteel woman's education in Virginia, not all enthusiastically pursued the skill of singing even if society demanded it. Philip Fithian was quite impressed with a seventeen-year-old girl named Jenny Washington and her various musical abilities, including her skill in singing. Fithian noted Washington was much more musically inclined than most girls he observed, writing, "She sings likewise to her instrument, has a strong, full voice, & a well-judging ear; but most of the Virginia-girls think it labour quite sufficient to thump the keys of a harpsichord into the air of a tune mechanically, & think it would be slavery to submit to the drudgery of acquiring vocal music."[14] Others were equally unimpressed with the singing of some Virginia girls, who apparently sang solely because society demanded this skill of them. An anonymous writer to the *Virginia Gazette* wrote an article commenting on "the absurdity, folly, and inconsistency, of various fashionable customs and ceremonies practised in publick and private companies." The writer expressed frustration at "the absurd parade of asking some pouting miss to sing, who will bear teazing [sic] for a full hour before she complies, and then in a most wretched squall, she disturbs your ears for an hour; for when once set off she rattles away like the clack of a mill, while all the company are under the necessity of praising this screaming devil for the very torture she had given them."[15] Whether or not this tirade accurately reflected the singing ability of most girls, Virginia's genteel society required citizens not only to request a performance, but to listen patiently and praise the girl for her singing. The importance of experiencing musical entertainment—and conducting oneself in accordance with the rules of gentility—overrode the quality of the performance itself.

Perhaps due to such newspaper accounts, many individuals desired to master their instruments to better emulate Europeans with access to the highest quality musical education, thus creating a strong market for music masters and helping to diversify an already complex labor marketplace for individuals who could assist Virginia's elites. Performing a piece correctly marked an individual as having truly mastered the genteel arts, and their peers generally recognized when they had achieved a certain level of mastery. Not only was Philip Fithian impressed with young Jenny Washington's singing abilities, but also noted she "understands the principles of musick, & therefore performs her tunes in perfect time, a neglect of which always makes music intolerable, but it is a fault almost universal among young ladies in practice."[16] Despite this criticism of young girls' ability to keep musical time, thus throwing off the tempo during performances and rendering them "intolerable," most genteel youths received some form of musical training, often under instruction from a music master. Frequently these masters were Europeans who had come to America to escape the competition of fellow musical teachers in their homelands, a national identity that increased their prestige in the eyes of Americans who believed the masters possessed direct knowledge of the newest musical trends embraced by the European elite, subsequently increasing the speed at which those trends could be adopted in Williamsburg.[17]

Wealthy individuals hired music masters to come to a plantation or other residence primarily in order to instruct the children, though adults were taught as well. Visits from these musicians were usually "looked upon as a welcome relief from the monotony of rural life" as they provided entertainment and activities for the plantation families. Due to the social necessity of mastering an instrument and singing, country plantation owners in Virginia sometimes pooled their resources and hired a single music master, requiring him to travel from house to house, sometimes in a carriage sent by the planter, according to a schedule.[18] An additional benefit of this sharing system was that each family in a locality would learn the same songs as others in the community, enabling them to participate in group musical activities later on and ensuring all families became familiar with modern European music trends, prohibiting one family from gaining a cultural monopoly and developing a common musical repertoire in which all could participate. Though generally a safe if somewhat tedious occupation, unfortunate accidents did sometimes happen to these traveling musical professionals. It was reported in 1773 that music master Mr. Francis Russworm of Nansemond County, Virginia, "who played such a sweet fiddle, and was a worthy good-tempered man," had accidentally drowned when crossing a river on a ferry.[19]

Traveling teachers would generally remain at each house for two or three days, giving daily lessons to the children on the plantation. These music lessons often superseded general education, as planters viewed the ability to partake in genteel culture as just as important as reading and writing. Philip Fithian often had his regular classroom instruction interrupted by the arrival of a Mr. Stadley, the music master hired to teach the children at Nomini Hall. Fithian described Stadley approvingly as "a man of sense, & has great skill in music," though he also noted plantation owner Robert Carter had to teach his daughter Nancy some musical skills as Stadley "does not understand playing on the guitar."[20] Both girls under Fithian's tutelage were excused from his lessons every Tuesday and Thursday, as Priscilla worked with Stadley to learn the fortepiano and harpsichord, while Nancy practiced her guitar lessons with Robert Carter.

Not all music masters traveled from house to house in Virginia, however, particularly in more urban areas. Many professional teachers decided to instead set up shop in Williamsburg, utilizing advertisements in the local paper to notify students of their prices and accessibility. These masters provided convenient access for wealthier residents in town to receive a necessary musical education. Music masters who established themselves in Williamsburg were intimately involved in all aspects of Virginia's musical industry, including acquiring and fixing instruments, giving music lessons, and performing in the theater and other social venues. They would have regularly interacted with Williamsburg's elite in various music-related situations, and been familiar with which musical trends currently held the attention of those at the top of society.

A Mr. John Singleton advertised in 1752 to inform "gentlemen and others" that he taught the violin in the city for a pistole (a Spanish coin valued at approximately eighteen shillings, or just shy of a pound, in 1752—approximately $120 in today's value), provided he had at least six students. Singleton also promised to be willing to travel to the nearby cities of York, Hampton, and Norfolk should there be demand.[21] While Cuthbert Ogle resided in Williamsburg he advertised his willingness to teach "gentlemen and ladies to play on the organ, harpsichord or spinet; and to instruct those gentlemen that play on other instruments, so as to enable them to play in concert" and likewise would travel "upon having encouragement" to do so.[22] It is unknown, however, if Ogle ever gave any music lessons in Williamsburg as he died less than a month later, leaving his music-filled estate for future scholars to study and analyze.[23] Francis Russworm, the unfortunate music master who drowned crossing a river on a ferry, might have been better off had he remained at the Williamsburg home where he opened a music education school in 1771. At this school Russworm taught "the young gentlemen in and about Williamsburg" how to play on the violin as well as both common and German flutes.[24] At times these schools were not focused around music specifically, but used potential lessons as a selling point to attract new students. Near Norfolk, Virginia, an E. Armston, who sometimes went by the name Gardner, ran a "large and convenient house proper to accommodate young ladies as boarders." At this school he taught these girls how to paint, stitch, read, and "other embellishments necessary for the amusement of persons of fortune who have taste." Armston also promised, if the girls desired, to "engage proficient in musick and dancing."[25] Not all of Williamsburg's music masters set up permanent establishments in and around the city, however. Instrumentalists who were part of traveling theater groups also frequently advertised their teaching skills in local papers when their companies visited larger cities for an extended period of time, setting up temporary shops or completing lessons in the students' households.[26]

Arguably the most well-known music master living in Williamsburg during the latter half of the eighteenth century was Peter Pelham, Jr. Pelham's family moved to the colonies when he was about five years old, and Peter eventually received his musical education from Charles Theodore Pachelbel, son of the famous composer Johann Pachelbel. After serving as the organist of Trinity Church in Boston for a number of years, Pelham eventually was chosen as organist of Bruton Parish Church in Williamsburg after assisting in the first organ's installation, which was not acquired until 1755. While living in town for nearly fifty years Pelham was extremely active in the musical community, taking on students learning the organ and harpsichord, tuning, building, and repairing instruments, conducting performances of theater companies, soloists, and choirs, and organizing or sometimes playing in concerts.[27] In fact, Pelham supervised and helped play the music for the first Williamsburg performance of the famous eighteenth-century play *The Beggar's Opera* on June 3, 1768.[28] Pelham served as Bruton Parish Church's main organist, occasionally accompanied by students from William and Mary in the singing of psalms, until he moved to the new Virginia capital of Richmond in 1802. Pelham apparently did not restrict himself to strictly psalms and religious music during his time as Williamsburg's organist, as in 1769 Anne Blair, who lived near Bruton, wrote that she heard music from such composers as Handel and Vivaldi emanating from the church windows. Much of Pelham's printed music probably came from song books imported by Williamsburg's merchants, though he most likely also acquired some from Cuthbert Ogle's collection, as he helped appraise Ogle's extensive musical library following his fellow music master's death in 1755.[29]

Music masters developed a high demand and prestige because they remained surprisingly rare in colonial America. Though occasionally a town acquired a master like Pelham to teach lessons, as late as 1763 only twelve to fifteen music masters taught in all of the thirteen colonies, according to historian Daniel Mendoza.[30] Despite their rarity, many pursued other occupations because a master's pay was generally insufficient to serve as a sole source of their income. In Pelham's case, friends and patrons helped him secure various positions in the city, including supervising the printing of treasury notes and serving as the clerk for Virginia Governors Fauquier and Botetourt, which involved taking applications for tobacco inspections and issuing passes for ships.[31] He also served for a time as Williamsburg's jailer, which allowed him on occasion, according to some reports, to bring inmates to Bruton Parish Church to help him pump the organ pedals during performances.[32]

Though some masters took non-music-related jobs like jailer or tobacco inspector, others chose to expand their expertise beyond the teaching of lessons. By the time music masters began circulating throughout Virginia in the latter half of the eighteenth century, enough of a diverse musical industry existed for someone in town to occasionally need their talents. In the 1750s frequent theatrical performances were held in Williamsburg, requiring musical talent to accompany the performers. It was common for music masters to play in theater orchestras or organize public concerts and dances. Others copied music for potential students to purchase, or they sold instruments on the side. The best way for these teachers to make a full-time living through music was to work for a theater group or a church, and this demand increased as the century progressed.[33] In 1773 James Miller and John Buckner advertised that they were looking to hire an organist in St. Mary's Parish, located in Caroline County, Virginia, as long as the person was "properly qualified," obviously trying to avoid hiring a musician without proper experience and talent.[34] Peter Pelham's career reflects another such employment opportunity. As the city's primary music master, Pelham oversaw the playing of sixty-nine different musical pieces for theatrical groups around the late 1760s, allowing him to dedicate his time towards other musical pursuits and earn income from his talents instead of menial labor.[35] This increased productivity represented a dramatic shift from earlier in the century when music masters struggled to make ends meet.

Another way music professionals could earn extra income while still participating in the music industry was to throw a "benefit" concert, which in the terminology of the time meant that it would benefit them personally. Concerts in the eighteenth century were lengthy affairs, sometimes lasting as long as three hours and broken into two or three sections or acts. The musical performances, which consisted of a mixture of vocal and instrumental music, were often followed by meals and balls offered by those hosting the show.[36] Not only could music masters earn a profit from these performances, but they also advertised a musician's skill and increased his exposure to the local elite. Sometimes they even performed these concerts for free with the hope that local gentlemen would be impressed by the talents of the master and either offer to act as their patron by financially supporting the musician in various musical pursuits, or hire him to educate their children. These public performances became an invaluable aid in publicity in an era when extensive advertising was difficult, thus supplementing the ads placed in local newspapers and the handbills distributed to announce upcoming shows.[37]

Winning the patronage of the elite helped musicians and music masters in many ways, for the gentry often comprised the primary or sole audience for concerts in Williamsburg, especially in the first half of the eighteenth century. Tickets for those events were costly enough that only those with the most money and of the highest social status would desire or be able to attend. Even if a farmer, merchant, or someone else of lower status had been able to afford a ticket, their clothing and mannerisms would have set them apart from their fellow audience members, immediately identifying them as out of place. It is also likely a common merchant would have little desire to attend a formal subscription concert, as they would have had little opportunity to familiarize themselves with the songs being performed. The music played at these concerts was the same classical music being imported and sold in song books by composers like Vivaldi and Handel. Educated and wealthy individuals, raised and taught that this music was their European heritage, were much more familiar with the famous composers of the time than the average person, which in turn strengthened the social boundaries separating the genteel from the common folk by creating a type of musical turf to which the elite had primary access.[38] Advertisements in the *Virginia Gazette* emphasized that boundary by addressing gentlemen, ladies, or both, indicating the performance would be genteel. One advertisement for a local concert performance was placed in the *Gazette* in October 1768. This "concert of instrumental musick," performed at the courthouse in King William, would cost five shillings per ticket (around $25 in today's money). Those interested in attending could purchase the tickets at multiple locations, including the new printing office in Williamsburg. Geared towards the elite of Virginia, the ad emphasized the concert was taking place "at the particular request of several ladies and gentlemen," and the performance itself would be conducted by "gentlemen of note, for their own amusement."[39] This ensured attendees not only was the concert desired by the gentility, but as those same individuals performed the music all qualities of the show met the qualifications of being sufficiently elite.

The fact that music masters and professional musicians worked for money prevented them from being seen as gentlemen in the eighteenth century. Despite this, their social rank remains difficult to categorize as they had a unique ability to teach fashionable music and necessary social skills to the Virginia gentry who employed them. Due to their importance at elevating family members' social status, music masters who lived temporarily at plantations inhabited a curious social position with their employers. Although considered hired help, their knowledge of musical culture granted them unique access to elite society. In addition to utilizing a family's carriage for transportation between plantations, masters often joined families for meals and concerts, though not just as performers. On multiple occasions, Mr. Stadley (the master employed by a group of planters outside Williamsburg) performed on the violin, harpsichord, and flute for the family, sometimes accompanying his student Priscilla Carter. On one occasion, Philip Fithian and Ben Carter performed a sonata for the family, earning "not only Mr Stadleys approbation, but his praise: he did me the honour to say that 'I play a good flute.'"[40] Fithian expressed honor at this compliment perhaps in acknowledgment of the master's musical expertise both in America and across the Atlantic. If they were not considered gentlemen, music masters and musicians might best be considered on the same social rank as storekeepers or skilled craftsmen.

In fact, due to a lack of professional musicians in the colonies during this era, concert organizers often filled out the ranks of players during public performances using amateur performers. As music masters took on pupils consisting of gentlemen and ladies or their children, they gained access to musical talent they could use for concerts.[41] In these cases, a sharp divide occurred between the genteel amateur musicians and the professionals who recruited them regarding the matter of getting paid for the performance. A concert held in Fredericksburg in 1766 announced "several of the best hands in Virginia will assist" the music master leading the concert, bringing three violins, one tenor, one bass, two flutes, one hautboy, one horn, and one harpsichord to play in the show. Following the performance, the advertisement promised those purchasing a ticket for a mere seven shillings, six pence would be treated to supper, liquor, and a ball "as long as the ladies stay."[42] These "gentlemen amateurs" had no societal qualms about performing in public, but as historian Helen Cripe indicates it was a strict social rule that, no matter their level of skill, they could never be seen taking any form of compensation for their performances. Instead, they had to voluntarily donate their time, and only perform because they enjoyed themselves.[43] Hence in the *Virginia Gazette* ad for the King William concert the "gentlemen of note" made sure to announce they were only performing "for their own amusement." This refusal to accept compensation for their performances represented the gentlemanliness of Williamsburg's male elite. True gentlemen avoided physical labor as much as they avoided any compensation resembling a wage, all of which they viewed as beneath them. Gentlemen instead engaged in scholarly activities, such as reading or debating law and politics; pursuits of the mind rather than the body. The Reverend Hugh Jones, writing his thoughts on the people of Virginia as he traveled through the

"Joseph Haydn Playing Quartets," painted sometime before 1790 by an unknown artist. This painting depicts popular eighteenth-century composer Joseph Haydn supervising a group of gentlemen amateurs attempting to play a piece of music in a string quartet while various audience members listen in the background. Small concerts like this one were quite common in Williamsburg as society required gentlemen like Thomas Jefferson to perform in public. Original painting is located at the StaatsMuseum in Vienna, Austria.

colony, succinctly summed up this work philosophy, commenting that, "The common planters leading easy lives don't much admire labour, or any manly exercise, except horse-racing ... this easy way of living, and the heat of the summer makes some very lazy, who are then said to be climate-struck."[44] Instead, many plantation owners supervised their slaves and hired workers while refusing to do any of the physical work, leaving themselves free to pursue less physical pastimes, such as learning new instruments and volunteering to play in concerts as "gentlemen amateurs."

One additional way in which Virginians' desire for music manifested itself was the growing importance of dancing masters as the century progressed. In a twist from the usual desire to separate themselves from those beneath them, in the mid-seventeenth century the genteel of England began to appropriate a dancing style similar to that of the peasant ranks. This dancing style, sometimes referred to as "country dances," was generally accompanied by one or two fiddles, playing without additional instruments, and the musicians generally sat in a chair with the end of the violin placed against the chest rather than under the chin. The music played during these country dances was "adapted from the country folk." In the eighteenth century, however, with the requirements of gentility and refinement, elites increasingly strove to distinguish their dances from those of lower ranks by adopting new styles of genteel dancing, while at the same time participating in the less formal "country" style. While country dances retained their appeal, elites expanded their repertoires by learning minuets, cotillions, jigs, hornpipes, and reels. Despite memorizing this array of more formal dances, Williamsburg's ladies and gentlemen eagerly embraced the less rigorous country dances and continuously integrated them into their balls and other festivities.

The physical placement of the participants varied in these folk dances, as compared to the somewhat rigid formality of the more refined type. Whereas traditional dances had couples pairing off in a circle or small group, country dances instead positioned couples facing each other in long rows with men on one side and women on the other, referred to as "longways for as many as will." Due to this arrangement, as many couples as possible could participate in the dance, and beginners were encouraged to join in the fun as most of the movements were executed by those at the beginning of the columns. Such a dance allowed newcomers time to observe the head couple before they were required to participate themselves, which made this style of dance "a social, participatory affair."[45] One of the most famous of the "longways for as many as will" dances is known as the "Virginia Reel," taught to many elementary school children today in the United States as a popular eighteenth-century dance performed by Virginians. This dance involves long rows of participants on two sides facing each other, men on one side and women on the other. The lead dancers in both columns move towards the center of the columns to meet each other, where they either bow, clasp hands, or turn around each other. After repeating this process two or three times, with varying changes and returning to their places, the male and female heads of both rows sashay down the middle to the end of the line, then back to the front, at which time they split off to the sides so a new couple is now at the head of the group, with the process repeating until the song ends. Though a fun dance for groups and an interesting story about early American dancing, the history of the "Virginia Reel" is unfortunately not true. Music historian

2. Virginians Will Dance or Die! 53

"A Kentucky Wedding" by Howard Pyle, 1882. This drawing of an eighteenth-century American wedding shows gentlemen and ladies at a country dance organized in the "longways for as many as will" style with men in one column and women in another. Note only one couple is participating, allowing newcomers to observe and learn the dance moves. Also note the singular fiddle player in the background, who appears to be a slave or servant, a common practice at the time. The location of Pyle's original drawing is unknown, but the image appeared in Charles Carleton Coffin's 1883 book *Building the Nation: Events in the History of the United States from the Revolution to the Beginning of the War Between the States*. Image courtesy of Ian Schoenherr.

Kate Van Winkle Keller notes in her book *Dance and Its Music in America* that no record exists of a dance having movements similar to the "Virginia Reel" until 1765, and that record is a single printing from London of a dance known as "Roger of Coverly." Though movements similar to those described above appeared in England following that printing, and the "longways for as many as will" format was extremely popular in the 1700s, the dance and its specific movements we know and teach today to young students as the "Virginia Reel" did not appear until 1849.[46]

Of course, no country dancing could have taken place without the accompanying fiddle music. According to historians Joy Van Cleef and Kate Van Winkle Keller, music for these dances was "drawn from the vast reservoir of popular tunes which were as well known as the dances themselves in England and the English colonies." These songs were generally simple songs, easy to remember and hard to forget, playable on any kind of instrument or they could be sung if no instruments were available. Most importantly the songs were popular in England, making them a necessary part of Virginian society in their pursuit of Britishness. They were also extremely catchy, and therefore frequently played at balls and dances.[47] Other dances, like the minuet, required far more complicated training in the steps, for these dances asked couples to work as partners rather than allowing them to learn from other dancers on the spot.

Because dancing was an extremely important activity in England, often performed by not just the upper class of society but by the royals themselves, Virginians eagerly sought the same skills as those across the Atlantic. Dancing may have been popular throughout the American colonies, but historians suggest that elite Virginians especially embraced this activity. According to historian Mary Newton Stanard, "There is abundant evidence that dancing was by far the most generally popular amusement in the colony. Wherever there was 'company' there was dancing. Everybody danced."[48] In 1755 John Kello, in a letter written to London from Hampton, indicated that in Virginia, "Dancing is the chief diversion here."[49] Ben Carter, one of Philip Fithian's students, was concerned on one occasion that he had no one to accompany him to a dance. Fithian had no such worries however, noting "blow high, blow low, he need not be afraid; *Virginians* are of genuine blood—They will dance or die!"[50] The Reverend Andrew Burnaby, when describing the women of Virginia, noted, "They are immoderately fond of dancing, and indeed it is almost the only amusement they partake of." Despite their fondness, Burnaby was less than impressed with their dancing skills, observing that "they discover want of taste and elegance, and seldom appear with that gracefulness and ease, which these movements are calculated to display."[51] Regardless of their skills, it was expected that the women of Virginia dance with modesty. When Fithian described Jenny Washington, the same girl who impressed him with her singing and music-playing abilities, he also commented positively on her dancing, noting that even though she just recently began dancing lessons "she moves with propriety when she dances a minuet & without any flirts or vulgar capers, when she dances a reel or country-dance."[52]

Considering how important these balls and dances were to the citizens of Williamsburg, it was imperative they had the proper instructor to teach them the intricate movements involved in the great variety of dances that existed. Like music masters, dancing masters were generally Europeans plying their trade in the colonies. Rather than focusing simply on dance techniques, however, these masters had a far greater responsibility: to teach Virginians how to be ladies and gentlemen. They offered lessons in fencing as well as dancing, as both involved intricate footwork and body movements.[53] Many dances in the eighteenth century were extremely elaborate and similar to dancing found in the theater, requiring precise movements that would be observed by many social peers and must appear as if they were accomplished easily and with grace.[54] Most likely such complicated dance moves were taught to students without the benefit of music, even though most dancing masters had the ability to play the violin or another instrument. However, hiring an instrumentalist to accompany the teacher would have been an added expense which would have cut into any small profit earned, and having the master perform required too much coordination. The physical movements of the participants took precedence at these sessions over the music involved, thus frequently removing its integration. Actual playing of music would have been unnecessary anyway, and perhaps a distraction to the master's instructions. Instead the dance steps would be learned by using vocal commands and the clapping of hands to create a beat.[55]

Several dancing masters set up classes in Williamsburg and advertised in the *Virginia Gazette* for not only students, but more importantly their parents with their hopefully heavy pocketbooks. In 1737 William Dering, a portrait painter as well as a dancing master known for his talent on the French horn, gave notice that he opened a dance school at William and Mary where "all gentlemen's sons may be taught dancing, according to the newest French manner, on Fridays and Saturdays."[56] Note that Dering emphasized to potential clients that their children would be learning not only the newest and most popular dances, but those originating in France, as copying European styles held great importance to the Virginia elite. One French dancing master, Le Chevalier dePeyrouny, while living at Mr. Finnie's in Williamsburg, not only taught dancing, but also "the art of fencing" and "the French tongue."[57] Music master Francis Russworm also made himself available to teach dancing, offering to "wait upon young ladies at their own homes, to teach them to dance a minuet after the newest and most fashionable method."[58] Simply opening a dancing school and advertising in Williamsburg was no guarantee of success, however. It would appear William Dering at least did not succeed in Virginia as either a dancing master or a painter, as he and his wife moved to Charleston, South Carolina, in 1749 and sold all of their belongings to settle their debts, and Mrs. Dering had to take in boarders to help pay for their daily expenses.[59]

It is interesting that to effectively teach these genteel activities to their students, teachers were required to personally master each one. Yet, despite the ability to behave impeccably among elite individuals, many of whom lacked the skills of the teacher, their job was considered on par with a tradesman, similar to music masters. Thus dancing masters could never acquire the status they were helping others achieve. Not all dancing masters in Virginia were necessarily credible, however. An Irish servant man named Thomas Hoy ran away from his master in Prince George County, and in addition to being an alcoholic "pretends to teach dancing."[60] Yet another indentured servant named Stephen Tenoe was giving dancing lessons in the Williamsburg area, and apparently stealing the money he was paid instead of giving it to his master Jones Irwin. Potential students were warned to avoid paying Tenoe, and were able to attend the lessons without payment until the end of the year when they could pay Irwin directly for their instruction.[61]

Dancing masters were also hired by local plantation owners around Williamsburg and traveled from house to house, similar to music masters, following well-established though long and circuitous routes. During the times in Williamsburg between court sessions and meetings of the general assembly, when demand for dancing lessons was at a low point, dancing master Charles Stagg traveled from the tidewater area of Virginia north across the York and Rappahannock Rivers to the peninsula known as the Northern Neck, giving lessons at plantations along the way. From there he went northwest to Caroline County near Fredericksburg, then south near Richmond and down the James River to William Byrd's plantation at Westover, in between Richmond and Williamsburg. Stagg likely made additional stops along the way during this lengthy tour that covered most of the well-populated areas of Virginia in the 1720s.[62] This extensive travel showed not only the demand for dancing masters at the plantations surrounding Williamsburg, as Stagg apparently had plenty of work to keep him occupied, but also the amount of effort the master himself was required to exert to earn a living. Establishing a physical business in Williamsburg was not sufficient at that time as a low population for most of the year led to a lack of customers, and dancing masters knew the Virginia elite with their deeper pockets were on their country plantations away from the city; if the students would not go to the teachers, the teachers had no problem going to them.

The favored dancing master of Robert Carter at Nomini Hall was a man named Francis Christian. Similar to Charles Stagg, Christian traveled extensively around the Northern Neck and Williamsburg regions of Virginia, stopping in the towns of Port Royal and Fredericksburg and fre-

T   *H E S E are to give Notice to all Perſons who em-*
ploy Stephen Tenoe *as a Dancing Maſter, that the ſaid* Stephen Tenoe *is my Servant, and hath been for near Two Years paſt; and that all Sum and Sums of Money due for teaching (by him) to dance, is due and payable to me the Subſcriber : And I do hereby forewarn all Perſons from paying him any Money, giving him Credit, or dealing with him, the ſaid* Tenoe, *on any Account whatever, until he has diſcharg'd himſelf from all Obligations due to me ; which ſhall be publickly advertiſed, when accompliſhed. And I do inform all Gentlemen and Ladies, that want to learn to dance, or that have Children to be taught, that he ſhall conſtantly attend his Schools at the ſeveral Places following, viz. at* Hampton, *at Mr.* Francis Hayward's, *at* York Town, *and at* Williamsburg : *All thoſe who have a mind to enter, may apply to me at* York Town, *and the Entrance Money ſhall remain in their Hands 'til the Year is fulfilled, except Sickneſs or Death ſhould prevent ; and then the ſeveral Scholars to be paid for, in Proportion to the Time they have been taught. Dated* April 3d, 1739.   Jones Irwin.

A *Virginia Gazette* ad which appeared on April 6, 1739. Dancing Master Stephen Tenoe, an indentured servant to Jones Irwin, was giving dancing lessons in and around Williamsburg and keeping the profits for himself rather than forwarding the money to Irwin. Irwin implored his customers to continue their dancing lessons with Tenoe, but to hold their payments until the end of the year when Irwin could collect the money himself.

quenting the Bushfield, Stratford, Wakefield, Sabine Hall, Mount Airy, and Gunston Hall plantations, in addition to George Washington's home of Mount Vernon.[63] By the time he began teaching at Philip Fithian's temporary home, Christian had been a dancing master in Virginia for about twenty years; in one of his earliest jobs he had received twenty pounds to teach Priscilla and Mary Rootes of King and Queen County.[64] Similar to the lessons of the children's music master, Francis Christian's dancing lessons were important enough to the children's education that they were regularly dismissed from Fithian's classes, sometimes for multiple days.[65] The children were, unsurprisingly, not always enthusiastic about attending these lessons. On one occasion Robert Carter's son Bob claimed he could not attend Christian's classes due to having no stockings or shoes. Perturbed, Carter sent someone to the store to obtain shoes for Bob, and while waiting for them to arrive he took the boy to his study and had him "flogg'd severely for not having given seasonable notice, & sent him instantly to the dance."[66]

While staying at the plantation houses, dancing masters did not simply teach the students dance lessons, but also would have family members attend and lead informal group dances. In September 1720 William Byrd visited the Rappahannock River plantation known as Corotoman, home of Robert Carter I, the grandfather of Robert Carter III, Philip Fithian's future employer. During his stay Charles Stagg, the dancing master from Williamsburg mentioned above, visited along with an unnamed captain and his daughter. While there Byrd and Stagg danced a minuet with Robert's wife Anne Carter and the captain's daughter. After an early afternoon dinner the group danced again, this time "French dances and country dances," before ending the night with punch and card games.[67] Over fifty years later a similar scene occurred at Robert Carter's grandson's house. Following one morning of dance instruction at Nomini Hall, Fithian noted Christian requested people to dance, after which "there were several minuets danced with great ease and propriety; after which the whole company joined in country-dances, and it was indeed beautiful to admiration, to see such a number of young persons, set off by dress to the best advantage, moving easily, to the sound of well performed music, and with perfect regularity, tho' apparently in the utmost disorder." Following an afternoon meal, the group again returned to the house's dancing room where Fithian observed Christian's teaching style. He described the teacher as "punctual, and rigid in his discipline, so strict indeed that he struck two of the young misses for a fault in the course of their performance, even in the presence of the mother of one of them! And he rebuked one of the young fellows so highly as to tell him he must alter his manner, which he had observed through the course of the dance, to be insolent, and wanton, or absent himself from the school."[68]

Though statistically more likely, it was not a prerequisite for dancing masters to be male. Following the death of Charles Stagg in 1735, Williamsburg's preeminent dancing master at that time, a woman William Byrd refers to as Madam La Baronne de Graffenreidt, also known as Mrs. Barbara Degraffenreidt, hoped "to succeed to part of his business in town," taking over Stagg's dancing lessons for the city's well-to-do. Byrd, a prominent citizen, had no problems with her taking over this role, even recommending Degraffenreidt to his friend Sir John Randolph, noting "she really takes abundance of pains and teaches well." Being a woman, there were possible moral implications involved as well, but Byrd reassured Randolph "were you to attack her vertue [sic] you would find her as chaste as Lucretia."[69] An endorsement by someone as prestigious in Virginia as Byrd indicates that women who acted as dancing masters were not necessarily frowned upon; others would have taken his acceptance as an indication that the upper levels of society approved of this teaching method and anything learned via this arrangement would not hurt their genteel credentials. Though again uncommon, women performing this service continued right up until the outbreak of the American Revolution. On August 17, 1775, Sarah Hallam, a one-time actress in the Williamsburg theater scene, advertised she intended to open a dancing school for young ladies at Mr. Blovet Pasteur's building on Nicholson Street and "therefore hopes the gentlemen and ladies will be kind enough to favour her with their daughters." Hallam appeared quite confident in her abilities to teach dance, noting "she flatters herself she shall be able to give entire satisfaction, as no care or pains on her part will be wanting." The school was open on Fridays and Saturdays for an entrance cost of twenty shillings, plus a four-pound annual fee.[70]

A dancing master's ability to teach the proper manners of the genteel may have been as important as the dancing itself. Masters taught students how to stand or sit erect with the chin held up. In portraits, genteel subjects would be seen with their heads turned or perhaps inclined, but their chins would always remain raised from their chests. At formal entertainments in the company of those they wished to impress, these subjects had to maintain their erect postures even when sitting, having their heads and chins up with their shoulders held back to maintain a rigid pose. When seated the legs needed to be motionless, and should never be crossed as it was considered disrespectful. The stance of the genteel was similar to that of ballet dancers, and when walking down the street they were taught to keep chins and torsos up, while never ambling or sauntering on a public street.[71] George Washington addressed these movements as well, writing in his *Rules of Civility*, "When you sit down, keep your feet firm and even, without putting one on the other or crossing them" and "Run not in the streets; neither go too slowly nor with mouth open; go not shaking your arms; kick not the earth with your feet; go not upon the toes nor in a dancing fashion."[72] By combining proper body movements and posture to the intricate steps involved in dances, dancing masters provided some of the necessary tools the gentry needed to make their way in elite society.

One way Virginia's gentility could showcase their newly-learned dancing skills and proper manners was at organized dances. To accommodate Virginians' love of dancing, regular balls or formal dances were frequently held in Williamsburg, some of which offered financial opportunities for the organizers, thereby further expanding the colony's music-related economy. Not just anyone could show up and attend balls and dances, even those held in the more populous city of Williamsburg. Many advertised upcoming private balls by word of mouth between friends and acquaintances, intentionally selecting the desired participants. Starting in 1737, however, the *Virginia Gazette* advertised some dances as open to the public, though many of these set ticket prices high enough that they effectively eliminated many of the lower and middle ranks from attending. This allowed those who considered themselves to be genteel to ensure only social equals were present at a dance, even if it was theoretically a public affair. Because they could charge for admittance, music masters regularly organized balls in Williamsburg which were held in the ballroom at the governor's mansion, occasionally in a private home, or at the Apollo Room of the Raleigh Tavern.[73] In 1763 Thomas Jefferson, then single and infatuated with a girl named Rebecca Burwell (nicknaming her Belinda in his writings), attended a ball at the Raleigh Tavern with his love interest, describing himself "as merry as agreeable company and dancing with Belinda in the Apollo could make me."[74]

Other upper tier citizens, perhaps especially those experiencing financial difficulties, profited from the gentry's desire to dance. Mrs. Barbara Degraffenriedt, possibly counting on her bid to become a dancing master two years earlier to bolster her genteel credentials, listed the first tickets ever advertised in the *Virginia Gazette* for a Williamsburg ball, appearing in February 1737. Her husband Christopher, owner of a plantation on the James River, had experienced financial difficulties, and the couple's townhouse, which was adjacent to the governor's palace, made it an ideal place to hold dances.[75] Selling tickets served as an additional source of revenue to help the couple support themselves, in addition to supplying a product currently in demand in Williamsburg. Over the next two years, Mrs. Degraffenriedt held multiple balls, with varying sorts of entertainment. The dances advertised by the couple in the *Virginia Gazette* were hardly the first they had hosted, however. As early as 1720, William Byrd II attended a ball held by Christopher Degraffenriedt in Williamsburg where Byrd "danced four dances and ate some plumcake."[76]

It is unclear exactly how Christopher and Barbara Degraffenriedt advertised their earlier dances as the *Gazette* did not arrive until 1737. Presumably they relied on word of mouth or playbills to advertise tickets to their upcoming events, but considering they began placing ads in the newspaper the first year it appeared they apparently believed they required more advertising. Though Mrs. Degraffenriedt did not list the ticket price in some of her advertisements, in others she indicated an entry fee of five shillings (over $30 today), which most likely was the price for all of her entertainments. In her final advertisement in April 1739, she offered not only a room at her house for a dance, but also "musick, candles, and liquors," all for five shillings.[77] Though the only *Gazette* advertisement offering her ballroom for rent, it seems likely she rented this party space to anyone who could afford it given her family's financial distress.

Mrs. Degraffenriedt was hardly the only person in Williamsburg selling tickets to musical events. During the same time period Mary Stagg, widow and co-founder of the first Williamsburg theater with her recently deceased husband, dancing master Charles Stagg, held regular dancing "assemblies" at the capitol building. Tickets for these events were sold for half a pistole each (approximately £35 or $50 in today's currency), making this a prohibitively pricey event for many of lower status, and earning a substantial income for Stagg. Her agenda of excluding the lower ranks was hardly hidden, as Stagg addressed one *Virginia Gazette* advertisement "To the gentlemen and ladies" of Williamsburg. Later in the same ad she not only again repeated her appeal to "those gentlemen and ladies," but notified them if they would "favour her with their company, [they] are requested not to pay any money at the door," apparently giving them free entry simply to spend time with her in public and theoretically increasing her social standing.[78] Stagg sold tickets to these gatherings from her own home, usually on the night before an event or sometimes at the door; she often held two of these dancing assemblies on back-to-back nights in Williamsburg. Additionally, dancing was not the sole form of entertainment at these events. Raffles were held at several of them where "several valuable goods will be put up to be raffled for," including on one occasion "a likely young Negro fellow." At this same assembly at the capitol it was advertised participants could witness "several grotesque dances, never yet perform'd in Virginia."[79] When reading this description it is tempting to imagine that when Mary Stagg referred to "grotesque" dancing it involved some form of hideous and disturbing body movements, and indeed that image may contain an element of truth. In the eighteenth century "grotesque dancing" was a category of theatrical dancing based off the

Italian Commedia dell'arte (Comedy of Art) which involved buffoon or comedic-type characters moving in unusual and athletic ways. The name of the dancing style specifically arose as it was the exact opposite of the French noble or formal dances such as the minuet, therefore it was called "grotesque."[80] A week before Mary Stagg held her ball advertising "several grotesque dances," a family of gymnasts arrived in Williamsburg. The *Virginia Gazette* praised them as "a man and his wife, and with them two children, who perform the agility of body, by various sorts of postures, tumbling, and sword dancing, to greater perfection than has been known in these parts for many years, if ever."[81] Though she does not mention it specifically, it seems quite likely Stagg acquired the services of this talented family to perform the physically-demanding "grotesque dances" at her upcoming party.

A decade later, starting in the 1750s, it became extremely common for the wealthier citizens of Williamsburg to advertise tickets for sale to balls or other entertainments held in town as musical commerce expanded in the colony. Anne Shields sold tickets for "a ball for the entertainment of gentlemen and ladies" at the city courthouse.[82] Richard Coventon, proposing "to have a ball for my scholars," also sold tickets to a courthouse ball to "such gentlemen and ladies who are pleased to favour me with their company."[83] Rather than posting notices for individual balls, Alexander Finnie notified "the ladies and gentlemen" that he would hold a ball once every week at the Apollo Room of the Raleigh Tavern, at least while the general assembly and court were in session.[84] Henry Wetherburn followed the same pattern as Finnie and simply notified he would be having a ball at his residence every Tuesday evening "during the sitting of the general assembly." As the frequency and popularity of these dances increased, music became more and more integrated into not only the Virginia economy, but also the lives and culture of Williamsburg's citizens.

Beyond Williamsburg's borders, balls and dances held in plantation societies were so elaborate that they represented enormous financial investments by their hosts and generated gossip and excitement for all involved. Apparently these plantation dances appealed greatly to Thomas Jefferson, who laid out what he considered to be a perfect life to his friend William Fleming, describing "the cleverest plan of life that can be imagined. You exchange your land for Edgehill, or I mine for Fairfields, you marry S-y P-r, I marry Rebecca Burwell, join and get a pole chair and a pair of keen horses, practice the law in the same courts, and drive about to all the dances in the country together."[85] Apparently a life of marriage and traveling from dance to dance in the Virginia countryside sounded idyllic to Jefferson, though he was hardly the only one enamored with such an idea. Upcoming balls and dances were a constant source of conversation for Philip Fithian at Nomini Hall. With the holidays approaching, he wrote, "Nothing is now to be heard of in conversation, but the balls, the fox-hunts, the fine entertainments, and the good fellowship, which are to be exhibited at the approaching Christmas."[86] With balls approaching, the young people living at the house could scarcely think of anything else. Robert Carter informed his boys "concerning their conduct this day, & through the course of the ball—He allows them go to; to stay all this night; to bring him an account of all the company at the ball; & to return tomorrow evening—All the morning is spent in dressing."[87] It was not unusual for these balls held at local Virginia plantations to last several consecutive days, with the participants staying at the house hosting the dance. Fithian noted a ball being prepared by a Squire Lee that would last four or five days, and to which the entire family was invited.[88] On one occasion a ball was hosted at Nomini Hall, Fithian's temporary home, and he observed when a chariot arrived bearing "four young misses to be ready for the dance which happens here tomorrow." The next morning he wrote the dance was taking place with "great spirit & neatness" with a play following the music, and on the third day "all our company continue," showing no signs of leaving after three days on the plantation.[89]

Dancing was also frequently integrated into other celebratory events in addition to holidays and organized balls. In April 1720 William Byrd II, the wealthy planter living close to Williamsburg, attended a christening and noted in his diary, "We danced a little before dinner and then I ate some bacon and fowl. After dinner we danced and were merry and at night some danced and some drank and we were all pleased till 10 o'clock and then the company went home and we went to bed."[90] On another occasion Byrd and several other guests participated in a birthday party on the boat of a Captain Randolph where "after dinner we danced and toasted all the healths consequent to the good agreement of the Governor and Council ... we were very merry."[91] Virginians would use any event or celebration they could to utilize their dancing skills, some of which required great financial outlays on the hosts' part.

The gossip generated by these elaborate plantation dances demonstrates why an organizer might be so willing to spend enormous sums of money on the event. Information about which dances were performed, who was there, how they were dressed, and the instruments played all reflected the hosts' gentility and that of the gathered guests. These affairs offered ideal situations during which Virginia's elites got to practice their own refinement and cultivate their ability to perceive it in their peers. Virginian society put great stock in the quality of these dances as the smallest details could either meet or fail societal criteria established overseas and embraced in America. The order of the dances itself was quite important, and generally followed a strict regimen. Balls usually began with a slow and stately dance requiring more extensive dancing lessons like the minuet, or perhaps a march, frequently performed by the host, whether the governor, another important official, or the owner of a plantation. This first dance had the potential to be a double-edged sword, as most attendees would watch the participants, judging every move they made for a mistake and critiquing their clothing, hairstyles, and physical appearances. On the other hand, the first dance was a statement of one's social status, and being invited to join the host in full view of everyone raised the profile of the participant in the eyes of their fellow dancers, as long as no mistakes were made. William Byrd noted in his diary that at one governor's ball in Williamsburg, the same one mentioned in the first chapter which he nearly missed due to his cold, his wife had the honor of opening the festivities by performing a French dance with the governor. Apparently no social mistakes were made, as Byrd gave no indication he was displeased with the performance.[92] Livelier country dances often followed these opening dances including cotillions involving four couples (an early predecessor of the modern square dance) and reels, which frequently closed out the night.[93] At one ball Fithian noted "the company danced after candle-light a minuet round, three country dances, several reels."[94] On another occasion his young charge Priscilla reported to the family that she and her companions "had an elegant dance on the whole" and that "Mr. Christian the master danced several minuets, prodigiously beautiful; that Captain Grigg (Captain of an English Ship) danced a minuet with her; that he hobbled most dolefully, & that the whole assembly laughed!"[95]

Aside from which dances were performed, it was also common to gossip of the ball's participants, how they were dressed, and their social status. Recounting the same Williamsburg ball where his wife had the privilege of dancing with the governor, William Byrd commented that the governor himself was "very gallant to the ladies and very courteous to the gentlemen," though one individual, only referenced as Colonel Smith's son, "made a sad freak."[96] At one dance Robert Carter's wife and daughters reported to the family that the previous night they observed "there were upwards of seventy at the ball; forty one ladies … that the company was genteel." Getting into specifics, the ladies reported, "About seven the ladies & gentlemen begun to dance in the ball-room—first minuets one round;

2. Virginians Will Dance or Die! 65

second giggs; third reels; and last of all country-dances; tho' they struck several marches occasionally—the music was a French-horn and two violins—the ladies were dressed gay, and splendid, & when dancing, their silks & brocades rustled and trailed behind them!"[97] By recounting their experiences from the dance, family members mentally participated in these events even if unable to physically attend, and the description of individuals and their dancing prowess played an integral role in one's social status and how others in the same plantation system viewed them in regards to their gentility.

On another occasion the family at Nomini Hall attended a ball presented by a Mr. Ritche at Hobbs's Hole near present day Tappahannock, Virginia, where Fithian yet again went into great detail about the dance:

> About sunset we left the ship [*The Beaufort*], & went all to Hobbs's Hole, where a Ball was agreed on ... the ball room—25 ladies—40 gentlemen—the room very long, well-finished, airy & cool, & well-seated—two fidlers [*sic*]—Mr Ritche (merchant with much influence in that area) stalk'd about the room—he was director, & appointed a sturdy two fisted gentleman to open the ball with Mrs Tayloe—he danced middling tho.' There were about six or eight married ladies—at last Miss Ritche danced a minuet with [*missing*] —— she is a tall slim girl, dances nimble & graceful ... soon after her danced Miss Dolly Edmundson—a short pretty stump of a girl; she danced well, sung a song with great applause, seemed to enter into the spirit of the entertainment—a young spark seemed to be fond of her; she seemed to be fond of him; they were both fond, & the company saw it—he was Mr Ritche's clerk, a limber, well dress'd, pretty-handsome chap he was—the insinuating rogue waited on her home, in close hugg too, the moment he left the ball-room—Miss Aphia Fantleroy danced next, the best dancer of the whole absolutely—and the finest girl—her head tho' was powdered white as snow, & crap'd in the newest taste—she is the copy of the goddess of modesty—very handsome; she seemed to be loved by all her acquaintances, and admir'd by every stranger.[98]

When Fithian made note that the dance was presented by a Mr. Ritche, a "merchant with much influence in that area," it increased the importance of the event due to his prestige. It is also interesting to note how Fithian goes into great detail about which participants opened the ball, their skills at dancing and singing, the social interactions between the guests, the order of dances, and the clothes worn by attendees, including a wig "powdered white as snow, & crap'd in the newest taste." Fithian's detailed account shows not only how important the dance itself was, but the intricate elements that went into a successful event. The endless dancing and singing lessons young girls were forced to endure now paid off when society watched and judged them at these gatherings. Dances had to be presented in a certain order, and ladies in particular had to wear the newest, finest fashions lest they be judged by their peers. The desire to possess these new fashions, many of which were presumably based on European styles, would have led to ever increasing financial expenditures on clothing as the eighteenth century progressed, further contributing to the growing expenses tied to musical activity.

These observations were hardly unique to Philip Fithian, and others could be quite critical of what they observed. Nicholas Cresswell, a British farmer exploring Virginia in the mid–1770s, also observed a ball near Alexandria, making sure to note in his journal "Here was about 37, ladies dressed and powdered to the life, some of them very handsome and as much vanity as is necessary." Following this small compliment, Cresswell dives into his critiques by writing, "All of them fond of dancing, but I do not think they perform it with the greatest elegance. Betwixt the country dances they have what I call everlasting jigs. A couple gets up and begins to dance a jig (to some Negro tune) others comes and cuts them out, and these dances always last as long as the fiddler can play. This is sociable, but I think it looks more like a Bacchanalian dance than one in a polite assembly. Old women, young wives with young children in the lap, widows, maids and girls come promiscuously to these assemblies which generally continue till morning."[99] This scathing review of the female dancers at the Alexandria ball show how important proper dance training and decorum were at genteel events, especially for women, lest an observer label the participants as promiscuous based on their movements. As Cresswell noted in his journal, the one or two fiddlers performing these country dances generally played a simple section of music over and over again until either a set dance pattern was completed, or more generally until they felt they had sufficiently performed the piece or were simply exhausted. This repetition allowed numerous groups of dancers an opportunity to participate in the festivities before the end of a song.[100]

Plantation owners also found ways to ensure their neighbors held subsequent dances after the current one finally ended. In fact, some of them integrated a way to identify the next host into the current ball's entertainment. Cresswell observed a unique ritual at the same dance near Alexandria. In the eighteenth century, Virginia plantation owners formed a tight community, and as such, similar to the residents of Nomini Hall, it was common for dances to be held in a rotation with each planter taking a turn at hosting. In the case of this ball near Alexandria, a cake was made every year, which was cut into small pieces and handed around the room. At the same time participants took a ticket out of a hat "with something merry wrote on it." The male who drew "the king" from the hat had to host the ball the following year, while the female drawing "the queen" had

2. Virginians Will Dance or Die! 67

to make the next cake.[101] With the frequent gossip and observations taking place at these events, it is easy to imagine that each year participants would increasingly try to outdo each other's presentation, spending larger amounts of money to not appear cheaper than their neighbors.

As attendees so closely catalogued these specific details of balls and dances, participants had to be constantly aware of their behavior and maintain the poise and dignity expected of the gentility. These dances "were elaborately staged performances, with guests serving as both performers and audience," as historian Richard Bushman has explained. "People did not attend such events to relax, but to present their most beautiful, gracious, and pleasing selves." Each guest had to think about how they were performing at the dance, and how others were observing them. This meant a gentleman could not be seen fumbling with his buttons like a rustic person, while a lady may have to delay or even cancel an appearance if her hair was not done right, as it was sure to generate talk behind her back. An example of exactly this delay occurred on February 5, 1711, when William Byrd's wife Lucy Parke spent the day preparing for the governor's ball to celebrate the queen's birthday, which was to be held in Williamsburg on the following day. Concerned about her appearance, Lucy insisted on plucking her eyebrows, though for some reason Byrd opposed this grooming method. They "quarreled about her pulling her brows," at which point she "threatened she would not go to Williamsburg if she might not pull them." Declining to let Lucy's concern about her appearance cancel their participation in the ball, Byrd refused and, in his own words, "got the better of her and maintained my authority." Lucy apparently accepted this pronouncement with good grace as later that day "the women prepared to go to the Governor's" while Byrd talked with his brother. Lucy's eyebrows must not have been as hideous as she feared, as this was the same ball mentioned above where the governor honored her with the opening dance.[102] At times the pleasure participants received from the dancing itself was secondary to the idea of others watching, judging, and admiring the dancer.[103] Even the dancing itself was quite competitive among the participants, who closely watched and judged others for mistakes, sharing their observations with fellow attendees. Sometimes even the playing of the fiddler became competitive with the dancers, to see who had more endurance on the dance floor.[104]

As a host, a great deal of thought was given as to decorations and food which would certainly be judged by guests of the dance. Most formal entertainments took place in private residences around Williamsburg, and the owners obtained expensive objects to represent their gentility, such

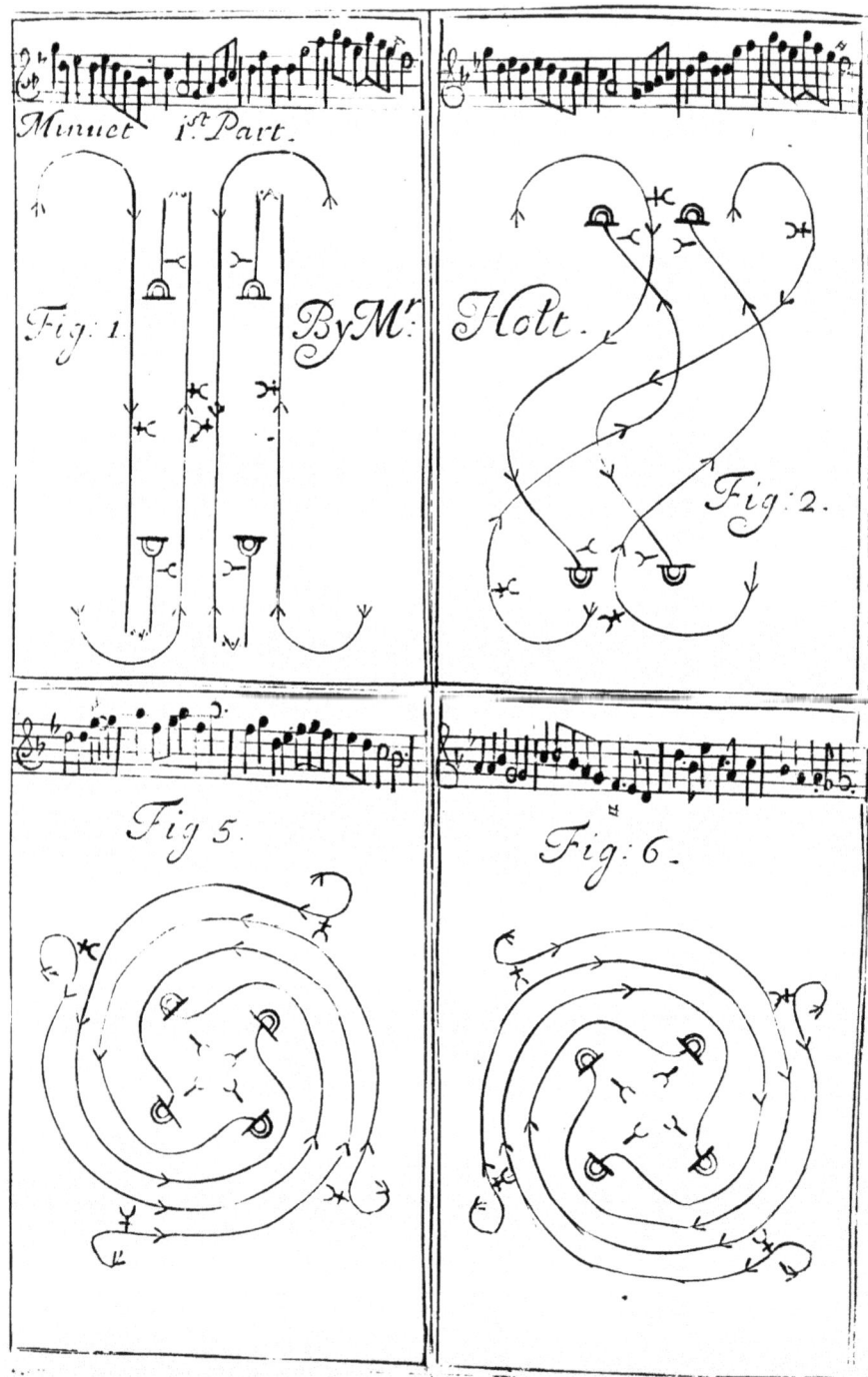

as carved tables and chairs, and glass, pewter, and silver serving instruments for food and alcohol.[105] If participants judged the food or décor to be inadequate, they had no problem expressing their displeasure. In 1760 George Washington attended a ball in Alexandria hosted by some local merchants. At this ball, he noted, "music and dancing were the chief entertainment." However, he was less than pleased with the food provided, though it was presented in a separate room allocated specifically for refreshments. Washington only noted there was a "great plenty of bread and butter, some biscuits, with tea and coffee, which the drinkers of could not distinguish from hot water sweetened." He also wryly observed no table cloths or napkins were provided, forcing guests to use pocket handkerchiefs instead, and that "no apologies were made." Due to the inadequacy of this dance's food and décor, Washington amusingly dubbed it "The Bread and Butter Ball." He even specifically named the organizers, seemingly to hold them accountable for the poor production of the dance, as following those names he mentioned a doctor who "would claim no share of the merit of it."[106] If a host proved inadequate at hosting a formal dance with all the genteel accoutrement, the criticism could be quite harsh indeed.

As the eighteenth century progressed, Williamsburg's most elite citizens needed new venues to support their musical needs, and as a result, the musical economy grew far more complex and diverse, permitting new kinds of individuals to benefit from it. To be like the British, Virginians needed to act like them, and that included partaking in those music-related ventures which were considered mandatory among the European genteel. To achieve this societal parity plantation owners and Williamsburg's citizens hired European music and dancing masters to teach them the proper instrument playing and dancing techniques. They also learned how a genteel individual acts, stands, and walks, movements which further separated them from those of the lower stations in America. After learning how to distinguish themselves from those beneath them, and to prove themselves just as good as their European counterparts, Virginians began increasingly participating in popular European musical activities such as concerts and

Opposite: **This diagram of dance movements, part of a minuet, appeared in E. Pemberton's 1711 publication** *An Essay for the Further Improvement of Dancing.* **Based on the complicated movements associated with just one section of this minuet, it is easy to see why it was necessary to hire a dancing master to learn these types of dances, and also why simple, easy to learn country dances may have appealed to those not willing to dedicate the time and effort to memorize complicated dance routines. Image courtesy of the Library of Congress.**

formal balls. Though these events had existed previously and were quite popular, starting in the eighteenth century enterprising individuals discovered people were willing to pay high fees simply to attend a ball geared towards the genteel, in order to ensure they were classified in that same social group. Not all were able to participate in these expensive events, however, and those without the financial resources of their social superiors needed their own source of musical fulfillment. Despite the newfound and growing economy catering to the wealthy and upper crust, music was a universal language in Virginia, and Williamsburg's citizens and visitors alike integrated their love of singing and dancing into daily life in a variety of ways.

3

Casual Music and Common Folk

"You must very often drink very much, and when you have drank very much you must appear very great; that is, you must swear a very good round hand, and sing a very good baudy song. You must be expert and ready at giving an ingenious toast or sentiment; by ingenious, I mean that it must be smart and witty; by smart and witty, I mean that it must be smutty and fulsome. This is life."
—Hector, *Virginia Gazette*, January 29, 1767

In August 1769 Miss Anne Blair wrote a letter to her sister Martha Braxton describing an incident which had occurred on the streets of Williamsburg. On one summer night the Dawson family was enjoying the company of friends at the Blair house on Duke of Gloucester Street, the main road running through town. By 10 p.m. the coach had arrived to carry the Dawsons home, but with "every one appearing in great spirits, it was proposed to set at ye steps and sing a few songs w'ch was no sooner said than done." As the Blair and Dawson families, and presumably servants and other visitors to the house, joined in the spontaneous sing-along on the front porch, they noticed "a candle & lanthorn was observed to be coming up street; (except Polly Clayton censuring their ill taste, for having a candle such a fine night) no one took any notice of it—till we saw, who ever it was, stopt to listen to our enchanting notes—each warbler was immediately silenced; whereupon the invader to our melody, call'd out in a most rapturous voice, Charming! Charming! Proceed for God sake, or I go home directly." This mysterious stranger who had stopped at the Blair house to listen to the spontaneous group singing was none other than Virginia Governor Botetourt, out for an evening stroll. Upon hearing the governor's voice and recognizing him, the entire group jumped to their feet and invited him into the house, though he refused, proclaiming "he would set on the steps too," subsequently joining the group for the next half hour.[1] Though it is unknown if Governor Botetourt participated in any further singing, or if it resumed at all, considering the praise he lavished on the group it is a safe guess that the party enjoyed more casual music that night in some form or another.

Not all musical acts experienced by Virginians were as formal as those mentioned in the previous chapters. In fact, they could sometimes be spontaneous and quite informal, much to the delight of those required to attend frequent and elaborate concerts, balls, dances, and celebrations. As demonstrated by the incident involving Governor Botetourt and the two singing families, music played an integral role in the life of all of Williamsburg's citizens, and occurred frequently in situations which were not planned, did not require tickets, and were not evaluated by every participant to discuss and gossip over the trivial details in the following weeks. This was simply music for the sake of music, and it was used to celebrate happy occasions as well as sad, to make political statements or comment about everyday life, or simply to be bawdy for the sheer entertainment value. Whereas chapters one and two emphasized the music of Williamsburg's elites and the various forms in which dancing and concerts became an integral part of their lives and economy, this chapter looks at the "common folk," those who sang and danced because they wanted to, regardless of their place on the social ladder, and not necessarily because society told them it was required. The common Virginian, those not attending the formal plantation dances and private balls at the governor's mansion, danced and heard music frequently at taverns, harvest feasts, holidays, funerals, country dances, and everything in-between. Slaves, forcibly transported from Africa, brought African instruments and musical heritage with them, and over subsequent generations integrated that music into their lives in America. Playing music, singing, and dancing were essential parts of life in Williamsburg, and those festive activities made frequent appearances in the everyday lives of all Virginians regardless of sex, religion, social status, or ethnicity.

Williamsburg's musical marketplace and its associated dances, concerts, and performances came about and flourished due to the necessities of those wealthy individuals at the pinnacle of society. Despite this fact, the origins of many of the songs and music popular in the eighteenth century derived not from the few elite at the top of the social hierarchy, but from the many below. In the 1600s, when early America was a loose scattering of villages with small populations, European settlers arrived in growing numbers from such various countries as England, France, Holland,

Scotland, and Ireland, to name just a few. Some of these colonists, as mentioned in chapter one, brought a great variety of instruments with them. Many others, especially those with lesser financial resources, did not own instruments, and if they had owned them in Europe may not have been able to ship them overseas, or perhaps may have sold them to afford passage to the New World. All newcomers, however, arrived with one vital musical resource—their voices. As they arrived in Virginia and the other colonies, immigrants carried with them a vast repertoire of music passed down from earlier generations. This music is generally referred to as "folk songs." Historian H. Wiley Hitchcock refers to this type of music as "the 'pop songs' of the day—a living music of everyday use by all."[2] By the eighteenth century these songs were familiar to the vast majority of Americans and sung on the streets, at celebrations, and in taverns and private homes. More important than where they were sung was who sang them: everyone. Taking a stroll through Williamsburg one could hear these popular songs being sung by merchants, members of the House of Burgesses, craftsmen, and planters working in their fields, not for anyone to establish their genteel credentials or boost their social positions, but simply for the joy of hearing the music.

Despite the popularity of this music, or perhaps because it was so well-known it was unnecessary, hardly any of these folk tunes were written down in the form of sheet music. Instead this music had been passed down orally from person-to-person, with parents singing to their children, who in turn sang the same songs to their children, and so on. Another important factor which played a role in the lack of written folk music was the literacy rate among immigrants, especially those from Ireland, England, and Scotland. Many of these newcomers to Virginia and elsewhere, especially in the 1600s, could not read and write, making it impossible for them to transcribe song lyrics, let alone any sort of musical notation.[3] Those illiterate immigrants incapable of writing down their favorite songs did have certain advantages over the genteel of society who specialized in learning and playing the highbrow European music of composers like Mozart and Handel, however. Social standards for members of Virginia's elite dictated music be played exactly as written to the best of one's ability; only then could an individual prove their refinement matched those of the Europeans they desired to copy in every way. The originators of folk music, on the other hand, had no such rigid guidelines and could therefore exhibit a greater amount of creativity and flexibility when participating in musical performances, casual or otherwise. As these songs held great personal meaning to many of those who sang them, the lyrics frequently evolved over time to better fit the circumstances of the performers. As this music gradually made its way across the Atlantic, it began taking on American characteristics with references to local people and places, further increasing its popularity with audiences in Virginia and the other colonies.[4] Due to this local flavor and its inherent creativity, being musically illiterate certainly did not hurt the proliferation of folk music in Williamsburg. Despite lacking the ability to put their cultural music down on paper, these songs continued to grow in popularity as the eighteenth century approached.

Folk music, being as popular as it was, could not exist solely as an oral tradition forever. As noted in chapter one, during the eighteenth century printed music books were increasingly imported and sold in Williamsburg's stores. That was a phenomenon, however, which developed primarily in the latter half of the century, as secular, non-religious music books did not appear in *Virginia Gazette* advertisements until as late as 1751. In fact, in Virginia no known works of printed music in manuscript form have been found before the year 1718. Folk music, however, appeared as popular songs when settlers began arriving in Virginia in the early 1600s, existing in America for well over one hundred years before those songs were written down and sold as sheet music. Though many of the immigrants who brought songs to Virginia lacked the ability to write words or musical notation, plenty of others were quite capable of this feat and proceeded to publish these popular tunes in a variety of forms. By the latter half of the eighteenth century, printed folk music was everywhere, including in the homes of Williamsburg's elite citizens and visitors. Thomas Jefferson owned a large variety of music, including that of genteel European composers, but also numerous country dances, ballad operas, "English, Scotch & Irish Airs" and even "two books of 'Drinking Songs.'"[5] Though no official printed collections of music existed before 1718, folk music did not exist solely in vocal form during the 1600s and early 1700s. As the eighteenth century approached it became more common for song references to appear in diaries and broadsides, large single sheets of paper containing news, song lyrics, or advertisements and commonly being distributed by peddlers on street corners in colonial cities. Many of these broadsides prove the popularity of folk music among the general public as they frequently indicate to the reader that printed song lyrics should be "sung to the tune of" a well-known, popular song which most Virginians would be familiar with due to frequent exposure at parties, taverns, and their homes.[6]

The concept of changing song lyrics to fit popular music was hardly unique to broadsides. As newspapers became more prevalent in the eighteenth century, editors were often desperate for content to fill their weekly four or more pages. Desiring to appeal to their audience, which generally consisted of the gentility and well-to-do, editors especially implored local amateur poets and writers to send in their poems, essays, or other written works to fill what was essentially a "literary corner" of the paper.[7] Many anonymous or pseudonym-using contributors happily obliged, writing poetry, thoughts on current events, and rant-filled letters to the editor for publication. Frequently included among these contributions were song lyrics, presumably created by the writer, or perhaps the anonymous author overheard the lyrics in a tavern or when being sung by friends and family. Often the submitted lyrics contained references to ongoing events either in Virginia, elsewhere in the colonies, or perhaps in Europe, and give valuable insight into the views of Americans at certain periods of time on how they perceived events around the world. The printed lyrics included similar instructions as broadsides on how the song should be sung. In one example, an anonymous writer submitted "A new song" to the *Virginia Gazette* which appeared in the January 20, 1774, edition, just over a month after the Boston Tea Party event where a group of Bostonians boarded a British ship to throw tea into the Atlantic in protest of taxes. The following song, as indicated by the contributor, was to be sung "to the plaintive tune of Hosier's Ghost":

> As near beauteous Boston lying,
> On the gently swelling flood,
> Without Jack or pendant flying,
> Three ill fated tea ships rode.
>
> Just as glorious sol was setting,
> On the wharf a numerous crew,
> Sons of freedom, fear forgetting,
> Suddenly appear'd in view.
>
> Arm'd with hammer, axe, and chisels,
> Weapons new for warlike deed,
> Toward the herbage-freighted vessels
> They approach'd with dreadful speed.
>
> O'er their heads, aloft in midsky,
> Three bright angel forms were seen;
> This was Hampden, that was Sidney,
> With fair Liberty between.
>
> 'Soon, they cry'd, your foes you'll banish,
> Soon the triumph shall be won,
> Scarce shall setting Phebus vanish,
> Ere the deathless deed be done.'

> Quick as thought the ships were boarded,
> Hatches burst, and chests display'd;
> Axes, hammers, help afforded;
> What a glorious crash they made!
>
> Squash into the deep descended
> Cursed weed of China's coast,
> Thus at once our fears were ended;
> British rights shall ne'er be lost.
>
> Captains! once more hoist your streamers,
> Spread your sails, and plow the wave!
> Tell your masters they were dreamers
> When they thought to cheat the brave.[8]

This reference to events in Boston shows that Virginians were well aware of the political turmoil taking place elsewhere in America, and writing lyrics for popular songs was one way in which they could address their feelings about the actions of their fellow colonists.

Though appearing in printed form through broadsides, newspapers, and eventually music books, folk songs were most popular when sung at a variety of celebrations. At these events diverse crowds could gather together, sometimes consisting of the genteel, other times common farmers or laborers, and even an intermingling of the two groups, united by the festivities and their love of music. Some of the most popular locations for these gatherings were colonial taverns. In the 1700s coffeehouses and taverns became the most frequented social gathering places in towns and cities, with numerous visitors spending a large amount of time inside engaging in conversation, games, and social interaction with their peers. Separating the taverns from the coffeehouses, however, were the types of activities taking place in the establishments. As compared to coffeehouses, much of the social interaction in taverns consisted of dancing, playing instruments, and singing, and was fueled by alcohol. Early in the eighteenth century, Virginians of every sex, social status and age, including children, regularly drank alcohol and in large quantities. William Logan, traveling through Virginia in 1745, commented in his journal on, "The vile practice of giving children, as well those of all other ages, rum in a morning as soon as they rise, continues here. I saw a child of ab' 3 years old drink

Opposite: **The first page of music to the popular eighteenth-century song "Hosier's Ghosts." This sheet music appeared in Mr. Burk Thumoth's publication** *Twelve Scotch, and Twelve Irish Airs with Variations Set for the German Flute Violin or Harpsichord* **published in London around 1760. When an anonymous writer submitted song lyrics to the** *Virginia Gazette* **following the Boston Tea Party, he informed the reader to sing the lyrics to this popular music, which he referred to as "Hosier's Ghost."**

a common glass of raw rum, & the parents encouraged it reckoning it wholesome."[9] One colonial authority estimated the average person drank four gallons of hard liquor per year. The most common drinks were distilled liquors such as rum, whiskey, gin, and brandy, all of which contained a similar amount of alcohol as today, approximately forty-five percent. Fermented drinks like beer were also popular, as what was known as "small beer," only containing one percent alcohol, could be brewed in the home. For the citizens of Williamsburg, however, hard cider was the drink of choice, having an approximate ten percent alcohol content.[10]

The vast quantities of alcohol Virginians consumed fueled the singing enjoyed by tavern patrons in Williamsburg. As mentioned in chapter one, during the eighteenth century a divide gradually grew where those of different social status frequented their own taverns, with the gentility adopting certain locations and those from the lower end of society gravitating towards their own sites. Though music, dancing, and singing were common at most taverns regardless of the clientele, the songs experienced by common folk were, at times, much more unstructured, risqué and vulgar than what the more refined gentlemen frequently heard. Singing in taverns often occurred spontaneously, started either by the customers or perhaps a visiting musician or theatrical performer well-versed in popular music. Oftentimes they had no musical accompaniment and relied solely on their voices. Due to the quantities of liquor involved, it is easy to imagine the quality of the singing would have left something to be desired, though most of the patrons probably had little concern for their melodic skills during those moments. Frequently the song lyrics would have been quite sexual for public spaces, at least by modern standards.[11] Hector, the pseudonym-adopting contributor to the *Virginia Gazette*, sarcastically commented on the content of tavern songs and how Williamsburg's citizens should act when visiting these locations by noting, "You must very often drink very much." After getting drunk, tavern patrons should "sing a very good baudy [sic] song. You must be expert and ready at giving an ingenious toast or sentiment; by ingenious, I mean that it must be smart and witty; by smart and witty, I mean that it must be smutty and fulsome." Hector also advised when visiting multiple taverns, "you must keep it up all night and morning in drinking, swearing, and singing."[12] By drunkenly singing smutty songs filled with swearing and other vulgarities, the customers at these taverns helped use common folk songs to establish their own place in Williamsburg's social hierarchy.

While being particularly bawdy and lowbrow in taverns, common folk songs also appeared regularly at some of the plantation dances

3. Casual Music and Common Folk

"Barroom Dancing" by John Lewis Krimmel, drawn approximately 1820. This drawing shows a typical late 1700s/early 1800s tavern scene and the activities patrons would find in that sort of establishment. An individual on the right is drunkenly spraying liquor around the room, while a couple tries to dodge the liquid. Another couple in the back is engaged in amorous pursuits, while a black fiddle player entertains a dancing couple for the amusement of onlookers. Image courtesy of the Library of Congress.

attended by Williamsburg's elite, with alcohol playing an important role in these private homes as well. Nomini Hall tutor Philip Fithian described one party he attended hosted by Thomas Lee at Stratford Hall, home of American Revolution soldier "Light-Horse Harry" Lee and future birthplace of Confederate General Robert E. Lee. This event started with the traditional formal dances in the ballroom consisting of minuets and reels, though it soon devolved into a drunken lowbrow party. Fithian noted that many of the attendees did not participate in the dancing as they had split up into different rooms either playing cards, "drinking for pleasure," "toasting the sons of America," or "some singing 'Liberty Songs' as they call'd them, in which six, eight, ten or more would put their heads near together and roar, & for the most part as unharmonious as an affronted...." As the end of the entry is missing, it is unknown what comparison Fithian intended to make with the out-of-tune and off-key drunken singers, but considering how much respect Virginia's genteel gave to those with singing talents, it was likely an unflattering assessment. One of the participants, in Fithian's mind at least, appears to have been one of the worst vocal offenders, as he wrote, "Among the first of this vociferators was a young Scotch-Man, Mr Jack Cunningham; he was nimis bibendo appotus (Author's note: Roughly "intoxicated by drinking too much" in Latin); noisy, droll, waggish." Though offended by his musical style and butchery of songs, the tutor did not mind Mr. Cunningham personally, commenting he was "civil in his way & wholly inoffensive." Philip Fithian was quite glad to escape this singing tragedy, as when he returned home to his warm bedroom he wrote in his journal, "Better this than to be at the ball in some corner nodding, and awaked now & then with a midnight yell!" As this experience indicates, even at genteel activities designed to be elaborate and fashionable affairs, alcohol combined with love of casual music turned even the classiest Virginians into noisy and loudmouthed singers.

While taverns and private dances provided one venue where casual singing could be integrated into social activities, theatrical performances were another activity which enthusiastically succumbed to the allure of popular eighteenth-century songs. Williamsburg developed a thriving theater scene as the 1700s progressed, which is further examined in chapter four, however it is important to briefly note the influence folk music had on the performances that eventually arrived on the stage. Much of the music accompanying the plays at the Williamsburg playhouses, especially in the first half of the century, originated from popular folk songs known to the average spectator. This made performances accessible to all layers of society, thereby increasing their popularity and ticket sales. As the theater became more established and the ability to write musical composition more prevalent, composers increasingly included their own musical works in their plays, but many of those tunes still retained the sound and style of popular folk music. In William Shield's popular eighteenth-century play *The Poor Soldier*, for example, Shield only composed two of the seventeen songs appearing in the show, with the other fifteen being arrangements of well-known folk songs, some of which are even still around today, including "The Rose Tree," which is more commonly known now as "Turkey in the Straw." This folk music, recognizable to audience members from every level of society, was extremely popular and frequently requested, and when performed on stage received enthusiastic applause and demands for encores.[13]

The popularity of folk songs not only influenced what was heard in

3. Casual Music and Common Folk

the theater, but at public concerts as well. The performers themselves, however, were not always so passionate about focusing on casual songs, as they desired to showcase their abilities to perform the highbrow European music sought after by the gentility in the audience. Depending on the crowd in attendance, however, they may not have had much of a choice. In a letter to Lord Kames of Edinburgh in June 1765, Benjamin Franklin described his observations of common folk in one particular audience: "I have sometimes at a concert attended by a common audience plac'd myself so as to see all their faces, and observ'd no signs of pleasure in them during the performance of much that was admir'd by the performers themselves; while a plain old Scottish tune, which they disdain'd and could scarcely be prevail'd on to play, gave manifest and general delight."[14] As Franklin observed, many musicians and other performers had no choice but to play folk music, regardless of their preferences, as those songs were popular and many audiences in the eighteenth century loved them.

In addition to singing, love of folk music also greatly influenced country dances around Williamsburg. These were not the formal minuets, cotillions, or even "longways for as many as will" country dances adopted by the gentility at formal balls, but rowdy gatherings of common folk to dance, drink, have fun, and celebrate various occasions like the end of a harvest or a wedding. Group dancing at public social occasions had been a part of life in Europe for centuries, and made its way across the Atlantic via the immigrants settling in the New World.[15] Virginians frequently converted funerals into drinking parties with all neighbors invited, a practice which got so out of hand that some of those on their deathbeds requested that the drinking be controlled at their own funerals. At one particular funeral "five gallons of wine, three gallons of brandy, a steer, and three sheep were consumed," an impressive amount of gluttony for a single event.[16]

Attending these functions, as well as participating in the festivities, was not just a part of life for the common folk of Virginia, but almost a social necessity, where those who abstained from the frivolities could be frowned upon by their neighbors and family. The Reverend Devereux Jarratt described one such incident in his recollections of living just outside Williamsburg. He commented that upon going to visit his brothers and their wives on a local plantation his visit was cause for celebration:

> Everyone seemed overjoyed at my coming ... nothing was thought too good for me, which their houses afforded, and they wished to entertain me, in the most agreeable manner. It was in the season of autumn, when the cellars, in that quarter, were generally stored with good, sound cider. These were set open with great liberality. But, by

the bye, this was no great temptation, as you know I am not very fond of spirituous liquors. But they knew I had been very fond of company and merriment, and wished to entertain me with frolic and dance. This proposal I rejected, and told them my reason for so doing. This was a disappointment they did not expect, and they soon discovered there was a great alteration in me, and that my mind was turned to religion. This, I suppose, might put some damp on their spirits, though they allowed that all people ought to be better than they were—but they thought I had overshot the mark, and carried matters quite too far. 'We all ought to be good, say they, but sure there can be no harm in innocent mirth, such as dancing, drinking and making merry, &c.'[17]

As Jarratt observed while visiting his brothers, drinking and dancing were expected of visitors at these Virginia celebrations. Even though the reverend's family admitted they should probably improve their ways, Jarratt's excuse to bow out of the festivities was frowned upon, even if that reason involved something as serious as a religious conversion.

Under the peer pressure associated with country dancing and drinking, even a man of religious conviction would have a hard time sticking to his principles. Jarratt only lasted five days against the temptation, though he placed the blame for his surrender squarely on "the influence of my brethren, and their strategems to take me in." Due to this influence he "was insensibly, and at unawares, drawn from my integrity, in the course of one week." According to Jarratt, his brothers conspired to drag him into a drunken dance when he went to visit his Uncle Clopton. Upon returning from this trip, one of his brothers "had contrived to gather a considerable company of people, of different sexes and ages, for the purpose of drinking cider and dancing, as liked them best. I was surprised, when I rode up, to see such numbers, both within and without doors. Without, the tankard went briskly round, while the sound of music and dancing, was heard within." Resisting for a while, Jarratt soon succumbed to peer pressure but only "with reluctance," as he described it. Soon he gave up the struggle, reaching the conclusion that "I might as well give a loose to my passions, and get what little happiness I could in sports and sensual gratifications." Though he apparently had fun at his brother's dance, the negative influence of his family caused such distress Jarratt abandoned his religion "for two or three months."[18] The influence of family and friends and their insistence on group participation in dancing and drinking at country parties may have gotten most attendees to join in the fun, but there were always potential negative side-effects as well.

As opposed to the formal dances held by Williamsburg's elite where only those with an invitation or enough money could participate, most anyone could attend country dances and public festivities regardless of social status. At times this could lead to an interesting intermingling between genteel ladies and gentlemen and drunk, frequently vulgar tradesmen and farmers.[19] Even if these common folk could somehow attend a formal dance, they would not know how to handle themselves and act the proper role in such a setting, leading to the scorn and mockery of other participants. As one father explained to his son, "An awkward country fellow, when he comes into company better than himself, is exceedingly disconcerted. He knows not what to do with his hands or his hat, but either puts one of them in his pocket, and dangles the other by his side; or perhaps twirls his hat on his fingers, or fumbles with the button. If spoken to, he is in a much worse situation, he answers with the utmost difficulty, and nearly stammers."[20] Though commoners were incapable of attending social functions above their station, it was perfectly acceptable for those above them to attend country dances and public events where everyone could act as befit their social level without the judgments of one's peers.

It was certainly a good thing the dance attendees did not concern themselves with how others at the festivities perceived their actions. As in colonial taverns and at other events such as funerals, graduation days, and fairs, to name a few, alcohol played a large role in the celebrations around Williamsburg. Following the consumption of large amounts of hard cider, liquor, and beer, inebriated celebrants began to sing, shout out toasts to individuals, their colony, the king or queen, or anything else to justify more drinking, and then began to dance, throwing propriety to the wind in ways the genteel could not do at their formal, sophisticated balls. In July 1774, Nicholas Cresswell, a wealthy farmer who traveled to Virginia and Maryland in 1774 to explore life in America, was aboard the schooner *John* on the St. Mary's River near Charlottesville, Virginia, when a small boat approached and invited Cresswell and the captain to a barbecue. Attending the feast "under a large tree," Creswell found himself "highly diverted" when "a great number of young people met together with a fiddle and banjo played by two negroes, with plenty of toddy, which both men and women seem to be very fond of. I believe they have danced and drunk till there are few sober people amongst them."[21]

On another occasion Nicholas Cresswell was near Alexandria when he observed a celebration being held by the local Virginians, which they called a "reaping frolic" or "harvest feast." Cresswell described the crowds as "very merry, dancing without either shoes or stockings and the girls without stays, but I cannot partake of the diversion."[22] A "stay" in the eighteenth century was similar to a corset, designed to pull in the waist and lift the bosom. The primary role during this century, however, was not to manipulate the figure of the woman but rather her posture, as it forced the wearer to maintain an erect, upright, proper bearing taught by dancing masters and fitting for the genteel. It is easy to imagine then the derision Virginia's elites may have had for these country folk, seeing them dance with no shoes or stockings, and the women not keeping a proper posture, while ironically at the same time those lacking genteel accoutrements were most likely much more comfortable and carefree than dancers at a formal gathering.

Music, of course, played a vital role at country dances and other casual entertainments even though much of what the crowds heard is unknown today. Due to the musical illiteracy of the performers, little of the music was ever written down or published in any form, similar to the vocal songs which made their way across the Atlantic. Of course, even if the musicians had the capability to write down their musical pieces, the structure of informal dances would have made the prospect quite difficult. Rather than the set and pre-written music from composers like Mozart and Haydn which frequently appeared at formal balls, the folk songs used in informal country dances lacked the same rigidity and structure, allowing them a flexibility unavailable when performing published works. Instead the musicians were able to lengthen or shorten songs, repeat certain segments or skip over others, or change entire sections all based on the response of the crowd, leading to a sense of uniqueness for each and every dance. An additional challenge to writing down this folksy, impromptu music was that the types of instruments involved did not necessarily stay consistent. Though fiddles remained the primary source of instrumentation, due to the often sudden, non-organized manner in which country dances developed whatever instruments were on-hand generally sufficed, even if those instruments only consisted of voices. Due to the lack of consistency between songs, in the rare instances dance music was written down it generally appeared as more of an outline of what to play, leaving the performer to fill in the blanks and modify the music during the dancing as the situation dictated.[23]

Shunning the more formal types of dances held at genteel balls such as minuets and cotillions, participants at informal parties and casual gatherings instead primarily engaged in less structured and more spontaneous country dances, many of which were eventually co-opted by the upper crust at their invite-only events, including those based on the always popular "longways for as many as will." However, according to the Reverend Andrew Burnaby, one style of dance afforded guests an especially unique experience as "these dances are without method or regularity." Appearing "towards the close of an evening, when the company are pretty well tired with country dances, it is usual to dance jiggs."[24] Jigs did not follow any sort of defined structure, separating this dance from most others which had fixed starting and finishing points. This distinction is especially true for formal dances requiring the expertise of a dancing master to learn the complicated steps, making the jig almost the antithesis of stuffy, rigid dancing, and perhaps increasing the appeal to Williamsburg's lower sorts due to its inherent rejection of formality. At the beginning of the jig, a group forms a circle and "a gentleman and lady stand up, and dance about the room, one of them retiring, the other pursuing, then perhaps meeting, in an irregular fantastical manner. After some time, another lady gets up, and then the first lady must sit down, she being, as they term it, cut out: the second lady acts the same part which the first did, till somebody cuts her out. The gentlemen perform in the same manner." As Burnaby describes this scene, there are no set dancers and no set dance moves; instead a couple dances around the room while everyone observes, creating their own impromptu movements, sometimes together and sometimes apart. When someone in the crowd feels it is time to add a new partner, ladies and gentlemen alike, they interject and "cut out" one of the dancing pair, with the onlookers presumably playing a role in judging whether enough time had passed for a "cutting out" to occur and giving verbal approval or disapproval when a new dancer attempted to join. Burnaby correctly notes in his journal that the jig with its chaotic, barely regulated movements was "a practice originally borrowed, I am informed, from the negroes."[25] Most Virginians who danced the jig in and around Williamsburg were well aware it was derived from traditional African dancing, a detail which did not seem to bother anyone as it presented them with a change from formal dances.[26] In fact, African music and dancing imported by slaves, who were forcibly brought to the American colonies, played an important role in Williamsburg among the elite, common folk, and the slaves themselves.

In 1619 the first African slaves to step foot in America debarked from the ship the *White Lion*, arriving with little fanfare. John Rolfe, Pocahontas's husband until her death in 1617, briefly commented on the incident in his journal by noting, "About the latter end of August, a Dutch man of war of the burden of 160 tons arrived at Point Comfort. The commander's name was Capt. Jope ... he brought not anything but 20 and odd negroes, which the governor and Cape Merchant bought for victuals (whereof he was in great need as he pretended) at the best and easiest rate they could buy." These slaves, traded to the colonists for victuals, or food for the starving crew, did not usher in a new era of black slavery; this event was fairly unique early in the seventeenth century, as by 1625 there were still only twenty-three Africans living in Jamestown.²⁷ At this time the practice of indentured servitude, the pledging of a person to serve another for a set amount of time in exchange for land, passage to the New World, or future income, was the prevalent form of labor in the colonies. Still, despite taking another half century for the institution of slavery to become the predominant system of labor in America, the Jamestown incident represents the first step towards the eventual enslavement and importation of millions of Africans, all with their own musical history and heritage.

Music, whether it appeared as dancing, singing, or playing of instruments, was integral in the lives of Africans in their homeland. Richard Jobson, an Englishman who traveled to Africa in the early 1600s to explore the Gambia River, published a book in which he remarked, "There is, without doubt, no people on the earth more naturally affected to the sound of musicke than these people; which the principall persons do hold as an ornament of their state, so as when wee come to see them, their musicke will seldome be wanting ... as they use singing of songs unto their musicke."²⁸ Jobson's observation that the Africans he encountered used music in matters of state for visiting dignitaries represented just one of many events in which tribes incorporated musical activities. Music, singing, and dancing accompanied work rituals, religious ceremonies, marriages, funerals, agricultural rites, reenacting historical events, and gatherings involving chieftains.²⁹ Olaudah Equiano, a one-time Virginia slave who purchased his own freedom in 1767, published an English-language autobiography in 1789, and at one point described some of the musical rituals he observed while still living in Africa:

> We are almost a nation of dancers, musicians, and poets. Thus every great event, such as a triumphant return from battle, or other cause of public rejoicing, is celebrated in public dances, which are accompanied with songs and music suited to the occasion. The assembly is separated into four divisions, which dance either apart or in succession, and each with a character peculiar to itself. The first division contains the married men, who in their dances, frequently exhibit feats of arms, and the representation of a battle. To these succeed the married women, who dance in the second division. The young men occupy the third; and the maidens the fourth. Each represents some interesting scene of real life, such as a great achievement, domestic employment, a pathetic story, or some rural sport; and, as the subject is generally founded on some recent event, it is therefore new. This gives our dances a spirit and variety which I have scarcely seen elsewhere.³⁰

According to Equiano, music appealed to all Africans, young and old, male and female, and was used through singing and dancing for any "great event," whether it be victory in battle or something as simple as musically recounting a "pathetic story." Music was everywhere in Africans' lives.

3. Casual Music and Common Folk 87

The majority of slaves sent on the arduous and often deadly Atlantic crossing came from a variety of West African tribes, and slave traders frequently forced those from different tribes into the same ships to prevent uprisings. This meant many of the Africans being transported did not know their fellow captives, and at times did not even speak the same language. One of the things they did share, however, was a musical background from their homeland.[31] Even if the songs and languages were not the same, music was used in the same way and for similar things by most West African tribes, giving these captives at least one commonality between them. Though familiar with African music, the vast majority of slaves would have never heard European or American music before their capture. Imagine their confusion then when, even before the slaves reached their new homes in a strange land filled with bizarre people, they heard and saw the ship's crew dancing and playing music of a variety never before experienced, being performed on instruments they had perhaps never seen. It was not uncommon for American and English sailors to dance while on their ships to improve their moods and to exercise, and captains placed a high value on crew members with musical talent to provide the background music for this dancing.[32] Seeing the sailors cavorting about on the deck would be confusing enough, but often the slaves themselves were forced to participate as they were considered extremely valuable property. It was believed by forcing the captives to sing and dance on the journey, sometimes by resorting to whips, it gave them exercise, a little bit of sunlight, and perhaps cheered them up in some way, keeping them healthier and more likely to survive the otherwise brutal conditions. In an account of the slave ship *Hannibal*, one crewmember remarked regarding slaves, "We often at sea in the evening would let the slaves come up into the sun to air themselves, and make them jump and dance for an hour or two to our bagpipes, harp and fiddle, by which exercise to preserve them in health."[33] In 1700 Thomas Starks of London ordered the captain of the ship *Africa* to "Make your negroes cheerful and pleasant makeing [sic] them dance at the beating of your drum, etc." While crewmembers often carried western instruments such as fiddles and bagpipes to accompany this mandatory exercise, many slavers also acquired African instruments and forced the slaves themselves to play the music to which their fellow captives had to dance.[34] By the time the Africans arrived in Virginia, many were well-acquainted with American- and English-style music and dancing.

Upon arriving in America, slaves disembarked from the ships and went to an auction house to be sold to individuals, most of whom were plantation owners, who bid on them based on their age, sex, and physical condition. Plantation life was generally an unpleasant existence involving backbreaking labor from sunup to sundown, usually six days a week, though of course conditions varied from place to place, with certain owners being much more flexible and lenient with their slaves. At these expansive farmsteads just outside of Williamsburg, knowledgeable they most likely would never return to Africa, both newly-arrived slaves and those born in America over successive generations gradually began creating a new culture, mixing certain aspects of their African homeland with the lives they now lived in Virginia, and music played an integral role in crafting this new identity.

One way in which African music remained a part of slaves' cultural identity was through their singing. While toiling away in plantation fields under the hot southern sun, slaves sang songs either to each other or collectively, a ritual predating their enslavement and perhaps comforting them to a small extent as they remembered their homelands. One fundamental element of African singing which found its way to the colonies was the "call-and-response" singing style, where one person would sing a snippet of song and the rest of the group would join in on the chorus. The timing of this singing method intentionally had the solo singer begin interjecting their next lines before the chorus had finished their respective section. To the slaves this represented a greatly-prized and respected musical complexity learned from their ancestors; to their owners it appeared to be confusion and disharmony, reinforcing their beliefs that their black workers were inherently inferior to whites as their western music did not have this overlapping style. Additionally, western music generally had a set starting and stopping point, while the African music did not, instead continuing until the singers' task was completed, which was a fair amount of time for field workers, and again confused their white overseers. As for the words themselves, to the masters the lyrics were nothing more than meaningless mispronunciations filled with trivial content, while in reality these songs contained not only stories of lives before their captivity, but religious and gossip-like stories of people they had met in their new homes. The songs also frequently included sad references to their own living conditions or subtle critiques of their masters.[35] As whites generally dismissed these songs as inferior and unimportant, they also gave slaves a venue to express certain feelings and thoughts with their fellow captives in relative safety, while also preserving an extremely important piece of their culture.

In addition to the vocal music they integrated into their daily lives,

3. Casual Music and Common Folk

slaves also fashioned instruments native to their homeland to play in their free time. In his autobiography, Olaudah Equiano recalled the instruments he experienced while still in Africa: "We have many musical instruments, particularly drums of different kinds, a piece of music which resembles a guitar, and another much like a stickado. These last are chiefly used by betrothed virgins, who play on them on all grand festivals."[36] Equiano's memories cover just a small portion of the vast array of instruments available in Africa. During his explorations of the continent, Richard Jobson commented:

> They have little varietie of instruments, that which is most common in use, is made of a great gourd, and a necke thereunto fastned, resembling, in some sort, our bandora; but they have no manner of fret, and the strings they are either such as the place yeeldes, or their invention can attaine to make, being very unapt to yield a sweete and musicall sound, notwithstanding with pinnes they winde and bring to agree in tunable notes, having not above six strings upon their greatest instrument.

This instrument, most likely a relative to the banjo, was not the most impressive in Jobson's mind however:

> I would acquaint you of their most principall instrument, which is called Ballards made to stand a foot above the ground, hollow under, and hath upon the top some seventeene woodden keyes standing like the organ, upon which hee that playes sitting upon the ground, just against the middle of the instrument, strikes with a sticke in either hand, about a foote long, at the end whereof is made fast a round ball, covered with some soft stuffe, to avoyd the clattering noyse the bare stickes would make: and upon either arme hee hath great rings of iron: out of which are wrought pretty hansomly smaller irons to stand out, who hold upon them smaller rings and juggling toyes, which as hee stirreth his armes, makes a kinde of musicall sound agreeing to their barbarous content: the sound that proceeds from this instrument is worth the observing, for we can heare it a good English mile, the making of this instrument being one of the most ingenious things amongst them: for to every one of these keyes there belongs a small iron the bignesse of a quill, and is a foote long, the breadth of the instrument, upon which hangs two gourdes under the hollow, like bottles, who receives the sound, and returnes it againe with that extraordinary loudnesse.[37]

Most African instruments were not as elaborate or complicated as the one Jobson described above with its seventeen keys, mallets, jangling arm bands, and gourds to amplify the sound. While exploring the continent, European visitors most frequently encountered percussion instruments, including a variety of drums ranging from ten or twelve inches to ten or twelve feet, often made from the trunks of trees and using skins for the drum heads. Other percussion instruments included anything capable of producing sound by striking it, including bells, gongs made of iron, rattles, hand and thumb pianos, and xylophones. Wind instruments consisted of small flutes including one similar to the Pan flute, horns and trumpets made from elephant tusks and animal horns, and long pieces similar to clarinets. Stringed instruments included lutes made of gourds and covered with skins, harps, and fiddles using horse or cow hair for strings.[38] As noted in chapter one, the banjo was one type of these African stringed instruments and arrived in the colonies via the slave trade, eventually becoming the predecessor to the modern guitar.

Probably the most important stringed instrument slaves adopted and mastered while living in America was the violin, or fiddle, due to its importance in genteel society. As the violin is an extremely complicated instrument to learn how to play, let alone master, it is unclear exactly how slaves learned this particular skill. After all, Virginians paid music masters to visit their homes so their children could acquire at least a bare minimum of playing ability, with no guarantees of mastering an instrument. It is highly unlikely, however, that slave owners would have paid any amount of money for white music masters to come teach music lessons to their workers, let alone given them time off from their field duties in order to attend these lessons, though this practice inevitably happened on rare occasions as a slave with musical talent could be a financial investment. To complicate the learning process, most music books did not appear until the latter half of the eighteenth century, and even if a slave somehow did acquire one of these guides they would have lacked the music-reading abilities, and general literacy skills, to use the book effectively. Though most Africans had at least some background in music from their homeland, and instruments in America bore a passing resemblance to those they were familiar with, the fiddle and other instruments were different enough they would not necessarily be intuitive to learn.

Instead, slaves taught each other, with a select few learning either through observation or perhaps hands-on lessons if they were lucky, then taking those skills back to their fellow captives to pass on what they had learned.[39] There were at least a few avenues open to slaves to receive rudimentary music lessons, even if their masters did not provide those lessons directly. As previously mentioned, wealthy Virginia plantation owners like Robert Carter had multiple instruments in their homes, and house slaves were constantly exposed to music, both through hearing it played as well

Opposite: "Musical Instruments from the Gold Coast," drawn by Jakob van der Schley approximately 1750. Schley's work depicts some of the instruments which could be commonly found in Africa, including a trumpet made of horn, castanets, various percussion instruments including different types of tambours (a type of drum), an early guitar, flutes, and bells. Image courtesy of the Library of Congress.

3. Casual Music and Common Folk

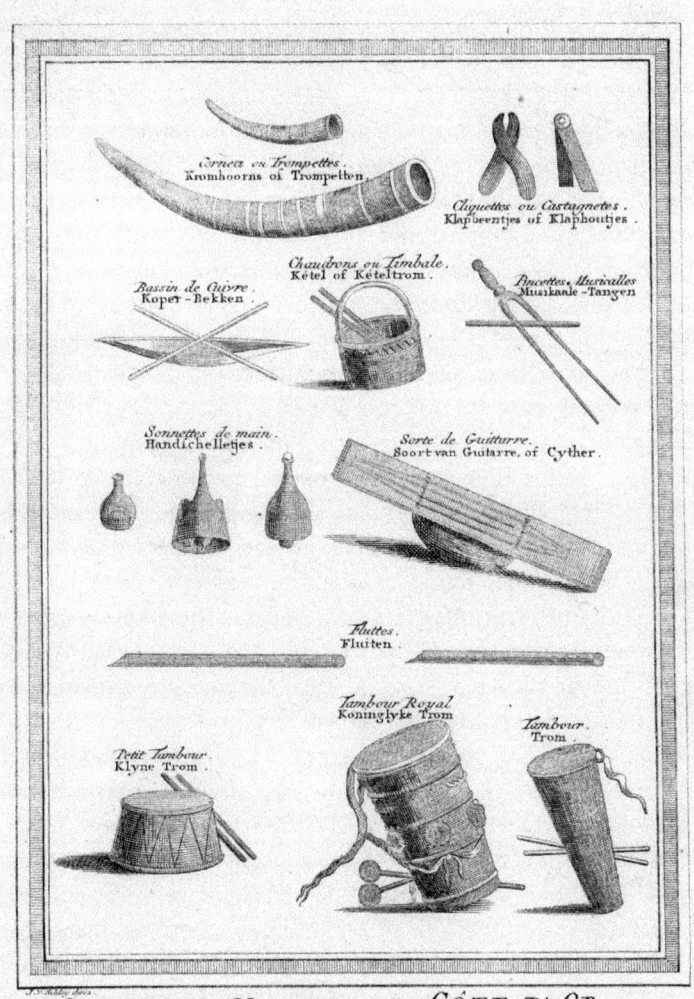

as observing musicians during performances. It was possible then to begin copying what they had seen during these informal concerts, using their small amount of free time to experiment on the numerous instruments available in the house. Some slaves were also present when music masters arrived at the plantation homes and could watch the children receive their music lessons. In those instances it would be inevitable that the observers would learn a thing or two from the music masters, even if they were not directly playing an instrument during the lessons. Some slaves also accompanied white students when they attended classes at the College of William and Mary in Williamsburg. As they did not have separate living quarters, these personal attendants would have often stayed with the students in their quarters and likely attended classes with them, including music and dancing lessons, giving them yet another opportunity to absorb music theory.[40] Taking these lessons and applying them to instruments like the fiddle in their spare time, servants slowly developed musical talent which they then passed on to their fellow slaves.

The violin was one of the most important instruments in Virginia, for slave and master alike, because it played an integral role in the social life of the genteel. By the second half of the eighteenth century it became more common for slaves to learn to play the violin for their masters' entertainment. A slave named Simeon Gilliat frequently played at the governor's palace in Williamsburg, and eventually became the official fiddler at state functions held in the town. Performing at these functions meant Gilliat needed to appear similar to a member of the gentility, and subsequently dressed in a powdered wig, "an embroidered silk coat and vest of faded lilac, silk stockings, and shoes with large buckles."[41] Jefferson himself mentioned the skills of black musicians, noting, "In music they are more generally gifted than the whites with accurate ears for tune and time," making them a valuable addition to genteel entertainment.[42] As part of the musical economy of eighteenth-century Williamsburg, some situations required neither professional musicians nor gentlemen amateurs, instead necessitating enslaved blacks who excelled as musicians. One such activity was the highly popular and frequent organized dance, a common pastime of the gentility.[43] White music masters and other professional musicians did not perform at these types of dances as it was considered beneath their social status, instead focusing their attentions on formal concerts and plays. As popular as it was, the violin was the most frequent instrument played by slaves at these dances and balls.[44] In many areas of the American colonies slaves were forbidden from playing all but stringed instruments due to fear of an uprising, as horns, trumpets, and drums were "regarded

3. Casual Music and Common Folk

as too suitable for signaling and calling to arms," as historian Gilbert Chase has explained. Fiddles, on the other hand, were considered non-threatening, presumably due to their quieter sound as compared to horns and drums. This was not a hard and fast rule, in the Williamsburg area at least, as some trusted house slaves were granted permission to expand their musical repertoires to perform with a variety of instruments such as French horns at private dances and balls, with the income going to their masters.[45] In addition to Simeon Gilliat, the official slave fiddler in Williamsburg, Governor Botetourt also frequently requested the skills of Landon Briggs, a slave flutist who performed with Gilliat at official state functions.[46]

Slaves even, from time-to-time, received some forms of compensation for their services at these balls and dances. On one occasion William Byrd II attended a ball at the governor's mansion in Williamsburg, where the governor made a bargain with his servants that if they avoided drinking at his party, a common occurrence and one difficult to control, he would allow them to "be drunk" the following day. According to Byrd, "They observed their contract and did their business [at the party] very well and got very drunk today."[47] In 1670 one slave fiddler, owned by Captain Richard Bailey of Accomac County, earned a small payday at an impromptu country dance due to his involvement in a dispute between two families, both of whom desired to utilize his fiddling skills. Bailey's sister-in-law, a Miss Elizabeth Parker, accompanied by Mr. Samuel Doe and his wife, went to the home of the Reverend Thomas Teakle to visit Teakle's daughter while he was away on business, bringing the young fiddler along on the visit. Finding the reverend gone, it was decided to hold an impromptu dance, at which point someone returned to Bailey's plantation to fetch the slave's fiddle. During the ensuing dancing, a James Fairfax arrived at the home to retrieve the musician, but Elizabeth Parker convinced Fairfax she had rightfully borrowed him from her sister, his owner, Ursula Bailey. At this point, realizing the musician's worth, and despite his status as a slave, Parker pulled out her purse and gave the boy a Spanish piece of eight (worth about six shillings, or around $40 today), and even convinced Fairfax to stay for the dance.[48]

As evident from this example, slaves with musical abilities were in high demand in Virginia. Between 1736 and 1780 more than sixty references to enslaved musicians appeared in the *Virginia Gazette*, forty-five of whom, an impressive seventy-five percent, were violinists or fiddlers.[49] Only two such advertisements appeared before 1740, with the rest occurring in the decades following 1750, indicating either that more slaves learned musical abilities as the century progressed or that those who knew how to play an instrument rose in value to their owners and potential buyers. Indeed, slave advertisements often highlighted an individual's instrument-playing abilities as a selling point in the paper. In 1755, when Edward Dial died, the *Virginia Gazette* listed that his estate included a "valuable negroe slave, about 28 years of age" who, among other qualities, "plays well on the violin."[50] Another slave, about eighteen to twenty years old and recently arrived from London, was advertised as having "every qualification of a genteel and sensible servant," including having "been in many different parts of the world," knowing how to shave and dress hair, and of course his ability to play the French horn. This instrument also came with the slave when he was purchased.[51] It is important to note that when this seller listed the slave as "genteel" he did not mean the slave himself was genteel; rather it implied the servant was intelligent, loyal, and knew how to act in polite company, contributing to the gentility of the slave's future owner. Other times a purchaser advertised his desire to buy a slave who could play an instrument, such as when William Fearson sought "to buy or to hire, an orderly negro or mulatto man, who can play well on the violin."[52]

Advertisements for runaway slaves in the *Virginia Gazette* likewise included information about musical abilities alongside a list of a slave's physical characteristics. Mentioning these skills in the paper also indicated how much musical talent added to the value of a slave as they could be utilized in balls and dances for Williamsburg's elite. In 1752 Virginia Governor Dinwiddie himself posted an ad in the *Virginia Gazette* for two runaway slaves. The first, a "negroe man slave" named Guy and owned by a George Purcell, had escaped from a jail and the advertisement noted Guy "plays on the violin." The second "negroe man slave" in the ad, listed as Dick and belonging to William Hutchings, was identified as "a strong active fellow, and can play on the fiddle."[53] One runaway slave boy was even good enough at the instrument that the advertisement listed him simply as "Fiddler Billy."[54]

Though the violin was overwhelmingly the most popular instrument for slaves to play, fiddling was not the only musical skill listed in these advertisements. A slave about eighteen years old named Pompey was listed as having the ability to play the French horn, and another named Tom was valued for "his fine dancing."[55] Yet other slaves were not wanted simply for their playing abilities, but for the value of the instruments themselves. A slave named Billy ran away from John Tayloe in Prince William County, and stole the violin which he was given to play. A thirty-two-year-old slave named Sambo not only could play the fiddle, but also made them, a valuable skill the slave's owner would not want to lose, hence the ten-pound reward owner Mark Jackson offered for his return.[56]

Aside from singing and using instruments imported from their homeland, many slaves also integrated African-style music and dancing into their lives in America. Similar to white "common folk" in Virginia, blacks in the colony did not have any sort of rigid genteel standards to live up to, permitting them a freedom and flexibility to their dances which was forbidden to many of those from the upper part of society in Williamsburg. These social interactions and expressions of African heritage were important enough that even after a hard day of labor working in the fields, those slaves with a small bit of physical freedom would sometimes exert themselves even more to attend a dance. John Smyth, a European visitor to America, wrote his thoughts on slaves and noted in one instance:

> Instead of retiring to rest, as might naturally be concluded he would be glad to do, he generally sets out from home, and walks six or seven miles in the night, be the weather ever so sultry, to a negroe dance, in which he performs with astonishing agility, and the most vigorous exertions, keeping time and cadence, most exactly, with the music of a banjor (a large hollow instrument with three strings), and a quaqua (somewhat resembling a drum), until he exhausts himself, and scarcely has time, or strength, to return home before the hour he is called forth to toil next morning.[57]

Though in Smyth's account a slave participated in a dance following a day of work, it was quite common for these gatherings to occur on Sundays, the one day most workers did not have to toil in the fields. Since this was the only day in which the slaves had free time, and they were not admitted to most churches, planters sanctioned blacks using Sundays to do as they pleased, including recreational and musical activities.[58] While observing one slave dance, Nicholas Cresswell commented on this trend when noting the gathering took place on a Sunday as these were "the only days these poor creatures have to themselves."[59] Philip Fithian also observed the pleasure slaves and servants derived from Sundays, writing, "A Sunday in Virginia dont [sic] seem to wear the same dress as our Sundays to the northward—generally here by five o-clock on Saturday every face (especially the negroes) looks festive & cheerful—All the lower class of people, & the servants, & the slaves, consider it as a day of pleasure & amusement, & spend it in such diversions as they severally choose."[60] The pleasures, amusements, and diversions Fithian referred to often involved slaves gathering together to play music, sing, and dance using African instruments, songs, and dance moves. Cresswell described one of these events in 1774:

> Mr. Bayley and I went to see a Negro Ball. Sundays being the only days these poor creatures have to themselves, they generally meet together and amuse themselves with dancing to the banjo. This musical instrument (if it may be so called) is made of a gourd something in the imitation of a guitar, with only four strings and played with the fingers in the same manner. Some of them sing to it, which is very droll music indeed. In their songs they generally relate the usage they have received from their masters or mistresses in a very satirical stile [sic] and manner. Their poetry is like the music—rude and uncultivated. Their dancing is most violent exercise, but so irregular and grotesque. I am not able to describe it. They all appear to be exceedingly happy at these merrymakings and seem as if they had forgot or were not sensible of their miserable condition.[61]

Note how dismissive Cresswell is of the Africans' music, referring to it as "rude and uncultivated," hinting that the banjo was barely a musical instrument, and calling their dancing "violent ... irregular and grotesque." This is just one example of how Americans dismissed the music of their slaves, while simultaneously adopting certain aspects of it and the talents of the slaves themselves into their own musical world.

"The Old Plantation," painted approximately 1785–1790 by John Rose of South Carolina. This painting depicts a gathering of slaves on a plantation performing what appears to be some type of dance. Two musicians are visible on the right, one playing a hollow gourd instrument similar to a banjo, and the other holding two sticks to play on a percussion instrument. These African-style dances were quite popular with slaves as they integrated music from their homeland into their new enslaved lives in America. The original painting is located in the Abby Aldrich Rockefeller Folk Art Museum in Williamsburg.

Despite a common cultural derision towards African music, many whites in and around Williamsburg began to slowly integrate many of its characteristics into their own musical activities, as well as intermingling with slaves at their own dances. Philip Fithian noted an instance where his employer's enslaved people "collected themselves into the schoolroom, & began to play the fiddle, & dance." Catching two of his white students, Ben and Harry, dancing to the music, he immediately dispersed them, believing it taboo to fraternize with the enslaved workers. The two students apparently ignored his rebuke, however, as five days later he caught them again in the school room with "several negroes ... playing on a banjo & dancing!"[62] It would appear that Ben and Harry had enough fun dancing to the African music that it was worth taking a chance at being caught to join in the festivities. While attending a barbecue near Charlottesville in 1774 Nicholas Cresswell seemed less bothered than Fithian by white people interacting with black fiddle players. Remarking on the party he noted that "a great number of young people met together with a fiddle and banjo played by two negroes." This interaction between black musicians and white dance participants apparently did not bother him in the slightest as he commented, "I am sorry I was not able to join them."[63]

A desire to join in with slaves playing African-style music on African-inspired instruments perfectly symbolizes the growth of casual music in the eighteenth century. Music was important to all demographics, regardless of age, sex, ethnicity, or social status. Williamsburg's professional music scene expanded in large part due to the wealthy needing instruments and musical talent to make themselves as European as possible. However, this expansion only indirectly influenced the music of common folk who had less disposable income and less societal pressures demanding strict musical standards, leaving them with the ability to craft their own music culture. Without a rigid structure to define exactly how music should be played and how dancers should move, Virginians, especially those at the lower parts of society, integrated music into many of their activities, including harvest feasts, funerals, birthdays, and other celebrations, as well as enjoying a bawdy tavern song or two along with their alcoholic drinks, which fueled many of these occasions. Slaves frequently held their own dances with liquor and African music from their homeland, and used songs from their past mixed with lyrics from their present to pass the time while doing field work. Slave owners, in turn, adopted African-inspired dancing and instruments, and even used the slaves themselves to perform at their formal dances. In short, music was everywhere in and around Williamsburg and used by everyone, regardless of their place in society. During the eighteenth century Williamsburg even acquired a venue where citizens from all social levels, excluding blacks, could see and hear much of this music in a public forum: the theater.

4

The Vibrant Stage of Williamsburg's Colonial Theaters

> "When at a play we observe the stage darkened, we are naturally struck with terror, and the soul is alarmed with the expectation, of some astonishing event."
> —Anonymous, *Virginia Gazette*, August 14, 1752

In April 1771, Colonel Hudson Muse of Middlesex County wrote to his brother Thomas Muse of Maryland, telling him of his travels through the Virginia countryside. In this letter he wrote of visiting Williamsburg and being detained in the city for eleven days. To make the best of a bad situation, Muse "spent the time very agreeably, at the plays every night" where he was entranced by the performance of Sarah Hallam, one of many performers from traveling theater companies that regularly visited Williamsburg, thinking her "super fine." The playhouse in town was "crowded every night, & the gentlemen who have generally attended that place agree there was treble the number of fine ladyes that was ever seen in town before." Aside from finding the selection of attractive women so overwhelming "for my part I think it would be impossible for a man to have fixed upon a partner for life" as it would be difficult "to have fixed on one," Muse somehow managed to pry his eyes away from the ladies and focus on the shows put on by the Williamsburg entertainers. So impressed by the performances he saw, Muse vowed at the end of the month, "I intend down again, & perhaps shall make out such another trip, as the players are to be there again, and its an amusement I am so very fond of."[1] Hudson Muse's appreciation for the variety of theatrical performances shown on the Williamsburg stage reflected the growing enthusiasm for American colonial theater, originating in the heart of Virginia at its capital.

As a complex musical culture spread throughout Virginia over the course of the eighteenth century, more people became acquainted with fashionable plays and pieces of music popular in Europe. By observing these plays and the musical acts that accompanied them, the American gentility brought themselves culturally closer to Europeans experiencing the same shows. If a theatrical act was good enough for Britain's elite, Virginians wanted to appreciate it on the same intellectual level. As the century progressed and the Williamsburg theater experienced periods of intense activity, the citizens of Williamsburg enjoyed many theatrical entertainments that came directly from London, appearing shortly after a London premiere. Whereas early in the eighteenth century a European play might have taken years before it could be performed by an American company, by the 1770s Virginians frequently heard the same scripts and songs from across the Atlantic within months of their debut, an impressive feat considering oceanic travel times. Williamsburg's audiences now demanded the speedy arrival of new entertainments, no longer content to experience out-of-date theatrical performances. Gentlemen and ladies in Williamsburg also learned the songs heard in newly-arrived plays as one aspect of keeping up with fashionable culture. While many heard these pieces in small gatherings, such as performing them in households or as groups of gentlemen amateurs in local taverns for concerts, Virginians increasingly felt the need for larger venues where an assembled public audience could experience new musical fashions.

Even before the arrival of the Williamsburg playhouses, the colony of Virginia was no stranger to the theater and its theatrical presentations. In fact, the very first known performance by a troupe of actors in the relatively new American colonies occurred in the city of Pungoteague in what is now Accomack County, then known as Accomac County, on the eastern shore of the colony. On August 27, 1665, Cornelius Watkinson, Philip Howard, and William Darby performed the play "ye Bare and ye Cubb" (*The Bear and the Cub*) at an unknown location in the city. The content of this play is no longer known, but for whatever reason its production must have been quite frowned upon, as the king's attorney John Fawsett summoned them to court to answer for their actions. During the first examination the judges apparently felt they could only render a proper verdict if they personally watched the play in question, as they ordered the three men to reappear in court the following month wearing the clothing they wore during the performance "and give a draught of such verses, or other speeches and passages, which were then acted by them." Upon viewing the performance in the December 1665 court session the judges

4. Williamsburg's Colonial Theaters 101

realized the charges against *The Bear and the Cub* and its performers, whatever they may have been, were overblown as they found the three men not guilty and ordered their accuser Edward Martin to pay all of the court costs.[2] By the beginning of the next century, however, Virginians had moved away from arresting performers and began to embrace a newfound love of the theater, becoming the only colony besides Maryland to never pass legislation banning theatrical performances.[3]

During the eighteenth century three separate playhouses appeared in Williamsburg, each used primarily for musical and theatrical acts, although they also featured other types of entertainment. As Hudson Muse's visit confirmed, these playhouses became the most popular locations in town, especially during the second half of the century, when many visitors and local citizens purchased tickets and spent their evenings listening to the newest European plays or concerts. The frequency of performances and size of these types of theaters also allowed common citizens to pay for the experience of hearing music that had primarily been accessible only to those Virginia elites capable of visiting Europe or importing

Theaters of Williamsburg

KEY
1 First Theater (1716–1730s)   3 Douglass Theater (1760–1770s)
2 Second Theater (1751–1757)   4 Bruton Parish Church

This map, covering the years 1716–1770s, shows the approximate locations of the three Williamsburg theaters, as well as prominent landmarks like the governor's mansion, the Palace Green, the capitol building, and Bruton Parish Church. Note the theaters' proximity to both the governor's mansion and the capitol, providing easy and convenient access for the Williamsburg elite. Map courtesy of Rachel Harper.

the latest music from overseas. The popularity of these venues was in part due to the creation of traveling entertainment troupes that moved up and down the East Coast and spent months at a time in Williamsburg putting on nightly shows. Through the popularity of playhouses and the groups that utilized them, music spread to a larger percentage of the Williamsburg population than ever before, and further helped expand the growing musical marketplace.

The first theater built in Williamsburg, indeed, the first theater built anywhere in the American colonies, was located near the governor's palace just to the east of the Palace Green that ran north to south in the city. William Levingston, a merchant from New Kent County, Virginia (mentioned in an earlier chapter as teaching dancing classes at William and Mary), built the theater in 1716. Levingston rented the site where the theater was eventually located, along with two other lots, for "Yearly one rent of one grain of Indian Corn," with the Trustees of the city stipulating that he must build on each lot "one good dwelling house or houses of such dimensions," indicating as part of the rental agreement he was required to build either a single decent-sized house or multiple smaller houses equivalent in size.[4] The Trustees included this stipulation in an effort to increase the size of Williamsburg and encourage growth through mandatory building construction. Seeking a partnership for his new venture, Levingston formed an agreement with his indentured servant Charles Stagg, a dancing master in Williamsburg, and his wife Mary Stagg. This newly-formed group subsequently petitioned Governor Alexander Spotswood for the "Sole privilege of acting comedies, drolls or other kind of stage plays within any part of ye sd colony." As part of this agreement Charles and Mary Stagg would act in plays performed on the stage, as well as teaching others how to act, as long as they remained in Virginia; they would also grant Levingston the power to approve any plays in which the Staggs acted. Levingston constructed the playhouse itself to give them a location to perform these services.[5] Notices were sent to England, at Levingston's expense, to recruit actors and musicians to come to Virginia and perform in plays, compensated at the same rates as local performers.[6]

Though not known for certain, the playhouse was probably completed by 1718, as part of Levingston's stipulations for acquiring the lots required that buildings must be erected within two years or he would forfeit the land. As the lots stayed in his possession, it would seem he completed his end of the bargain.[7] Additionally, in June 1718 Governor Spotswood wrote to the Board of Trade that to celebrate King George I's birthday he had given "a publick entertainment at my house, all gent'n that would come were admitted." Unfortunately Spotswood was perturbed that eight counselors not only failed to attend his party due to a disagreement over funds spent on the governor's palace, but also did not attend "the play w'ch was acted on that occasion."[8] Though not indicated, presumably this play would have been put on at Levingston's playhouse, located almost immediately next to the governor's residence. This letter also indicates how the genteel, and specifically politicians, of Williamsburg valued theatrical and musical entertainments and integrated them into their celebrations, even early in the eighteenth century.

What is known for certain, however, is that the first Williamsburg theater was up and running by 1721, as Levingston mortgaged five lots, including his playhouse, to Archibald Blair for a period of five hundred years.[9] By 1721 the area around the theater had been enlarged to include a stable, a house, a detached kitchen, and a bowling green, indicating at least some initial commercial success for Levingston's venture. Measuring eighty-six and a half feet long by thirty feet on a brick foundation, the playhouse was a good size and featured a shingled roof and five windows for light and ventilation. Inside, plastered walls and wood floors ran the length of the structure.[10] The theater's completion represented a cultural step forward for Williamsburg's citizens, as they now had a central gathering place, open to multiple social classes, to partake in new forms of musical commerce that had been previously relegated to private homes or taverns catering to particular social groups.

Though seemingly designed to hold theatrical presentations, Virginians could hear music just as frequently emanating from the new playhouse near the Palace Green. Almost every play in the eighteenth century utilized music, whether accompanying actors during a song or dance, or as an interlude between acts; music often appeared by popular demand. Indeed, without musical performances many patrons would have been reluctant to spend their money to see these shows.[11] As the *Virginia Gazette* was not published until 1736, it is difficult to ascertain how many performances appeared, or even the names of specific plays, at the first Williamsburg playhouse. Regardless, historian John Molnar has speculated that the 1705 comedy *The Tender Husband,* along with its accompanying songs, may have been one of the early plays performed. Written by Sir Richard Steele, this play focused on a Captain Clerimont, who disguises himself as an artist to court a woman named Biddy, painting her picture under the watchful gaze of her aunt. While working on the portrait, he claims he knows of a fellow painter who eloped with his model and subsequently wrote a sonnet for her; the enamored Clerimont claims he knows this particular song by heart. As Biddy desires to hear this song, he sends for his servant, who has a good singing voice, at which point the script simply declares, "Here it is sung."[12]

The fact that we know so little about the first playhouse should not diminish our appreciation for its early appearance in the city. Despite the appeal of plays such as *The Tender Husband* containing multiple musical pieces, by 1727 Levingston had lost the land in Williamsburg and relocated to Spotsylvania County.[13] Additionally, although others subsequently used the building for public performances, by 1732 the playhouse was only used sporadically. William Hugh Grove of England observed while traveling through Virginia that even while the town ran two successful dancing schools, "There was a playhouse managed by Bowes, but having little to do is dropped."[14] It would appear then that by Grove's visit in 1732 the first theater was rarely, if ever, in use for theatrical performances or any other sort of entertainment, at least to his perceptions. One cause of the playhouse's decline was lack of advertising. Before William Parks, first publisher of the *Virginia Gazette,* arrived in Williamsburg in the 1730s no one was able to print newspaper advertisements promoting upcoming performances. Additionally at this point in the early eighteenth century there were no professional theater companies touring through Virginia, making the theater less of an organized performance space and more of a convenient location for casual and intermittent theatrical acts.[15]

Regardless of the reason for its eventual closure, the first Williamsburg playhouse had just about outlived its usefulness by the 1730s. The students of William and Mary put on the only known performances at the theater following William Grove's 1732 visit to town. In September of 1736 the "young gentlemen of the college" took out ads in the *Virginia Gazette* that they would demonstrate the acting, singing, and dancing skills learned at the school to perform *The Tragedy of Cato, The Busy-Body, The Recruiting-Officer, The Beaux-Strategem,* and *the Drummer; or the Haunted House* over a series of evenings.[16] Even this early in the eighteenth century those presumably wealthy individuals sending their children to William and Mary recognized the value of an education in the musical arts, and by having them demonstrate their abilities in a public venue it assured them they were receiving a good value for their money. At this point it appears the residents of Williamsburg had not yet fully embraced the love of theater that would grip their society in the later years, as the only other known mention of the first playhouse was in 1745, when a notice indicated the structure was to become a new courthouse. Based on the advertisement, the theater had fallen into a state of disrepair, as it required new shingles, paint, windows, doors, flooring, plastering, and carpentry inside.[17] It would not be long, however, before the theater returned to Williamsburg, as the musical culture that had been slowly growing up to this point reached a crescendo.

Though it is unclear if the first theater's slow fall into disuse related to Williamsburg residents' initial lack of enthusiasm, by 1751 signs of renewed theatrical interest had begun to appear. Alexander Finnie, owner of the Raleigh Tavern, posted an advertisement in the *Virginia Gazette* in August 1751 notifying the readership that a theatrical company from New York intended to perform. This troupe, run by Walter Murray and Thomas Kean, went by the name of the New York Company of Comedians. Historian John Molnar has noted although known for their theatrical productions, the troupe regularly featured musical acts as well, as indicated by advertisements in New York papers, as well as use of an amateur orchestra during a performance of *The Beggar's Opera* in Maryland.[18] Though Finnie desired to bring Murray and Kean's troupe to Williamsburg, at this point the first playhouse had been converted to a government building and no suitable location existed for performances. To provide adequate space, Finnie proposed to hastily build a theater during the two months before the company arrived. Searching for a method to pay for this ambitious project, Finnie initiated a subscriber system wherein "those gentlemen and ladies" purchasing a subscription for one pistole (approximately $120 today), payable at the Raleigh Tavern, were "entitled to a box ticket, for the first night's diversions," in addition to extra tickets for future performances. Finnie promised the newspaper's readers that the building would be ready in time for October's court.[19] This was an important deadline for Finnie, as well as reassurance to not only the performers but those considering investing their money in this project. With the commencement of the October court Williamsburg's sleepy population of approximately one thousand individuals would explode to around five or six thousand.[20] This meant an influx of potential customers and their spending money. Most importantly, however, these particular customers represented the social and financial elite of Virginia. These individuals would be looking for nightly entertainment, much of it music-based, and were willing to pay for this diversion. Those entrepreneurs willing and able to provide these amusements stood to make a tidy profit during court season, as well as having the opportunity to interact with Virginia's social elites, potentially increasing their own standing in Williamsburg due to their proximity. Finnie's proposal appears to be successful, as a few days after running his *Gazette* ad, on September 2, 1751, he purchased two lots for £40 on the east side of Williamsburg, almost immediately behind the capitol building off of Eastern Street, to build the new theater.[21] This places the site of the second theater approximately where Christiana Campbell's Tavern stands today on the eastern side of the capitol building. Similar to the first theater's location near the governor's mansion, the new playhouse's proximity to the capitol also afforded wealthier patrons convenient access to performances during their time in town attending to government business.

Subscription sales for the new playhouse lagged, but Finnie pressed on with construction. On September 26 the *Virginia Gazette* announced the company's first performance in Williamsburg would be "the tragical history of King Richard the Third," accompanied by "a grand tragic dance; compos'd by Monsieur Denoier, call'd The Royal Captive, after the Turkish manner, as perform'd at his majesty's opera house, in the Hay-Market."[22] Despite the announcement of the plays to be performed on opening night, rumors began to swirl throughout town that due to time restrictions on building the playhouse, the theater troupe would not be performing after all. John Blair, president of the Virginia Governor's Council, wrote about his doubts that the actors would make it to Williamsburg in his diary on October 6, commenting "Hear ye actrs are dispersed presid will nt come."[23] Despite these rumors the Company of Comedians did indeed arrive in town for the theater's premier performance. Though sources suggest the hasty construction of the building left much to be desired, by the time of opening night it featured a stage, boxes, a pit, and a gallery.[24] A *Gazette* advertisement on October 17 set the prices for the show with boxes available for seven shillings, six pence, pit seats for five shillings, nine pence, and a gallery view for three shillings, nine pence.[25] This set the ticket prices at approximately £16–£32, or $25–$50, in today's money—rather substantial sums that would most likely prohibit many lower and middle rank patrons from attending performances. The more genteel the audience, and the more they could generally charge for ticket prices, the higher the prestige of the theatrical company. Williamsburg's gentility gladly paid high admission prices for shows that elevated their social status, as part of their required duties as members of the elite included attending the theater.

Though charging a somewhat steep price for tickets to their performances, in Williamsburg the New York Company of Comedians struggled financially, perhaps due to lackluster ticket sales or due to the cost of the hastily-built theater. The actors may also have lacked the European credentials the Williamsburg gentry valued, considering them not genteel enough to justify attending performances. Whatever the reason for their financial difficulties, they could not afford to advertise in the *Virginia Gazette* other than the two occasions mentioned above, so instead they handed out playbills on the day of the performance in Williamsburg.[26] Three days after their first show, an ad appeared notifying the public that due to "a greater expence [sic] than they at first expected in erecting a theatre in the city of Williamsburg," as well as needing funds to "procure proper scenes and dresses," the company hoped to sell a share of the theater itself to "those gentlemen who are lovers of theatrical performances," with larger donors receiving a greater percentage of the returns. The Company was apparently suffering from rather severe financial distress by this point, as they asked those who purchased shares to provide the money immediately.[27] Despite this last ditch effort, and following the performance of several more plays in and around the Williamsburg area, Murray and Kean's troupe eventually disbanded, to soon be replaced by a much more successful traveling act that offered more appeal to the genteel sensibilities of eighteenth-century Virginians.

Soon after the New Yorkers' departure, a new troupe arrived in Virginia directly from London, one that directly appealed to the cultured Williamsburg elite. In June 1752 the vessel *The Charming Sally* arrived in Yorktown bearing Lewis Hallam, his actress wife, and a company of ten actors, also known as the Company of Comedians, though emphasizing their origins as London rather than New York.[28] It was common at that time for theatrical troupes to label themselves as a "Company of Comedians," but rather than just being a specific title it was also intended to describe the talents of the performers; therefore it would not have been unusual for audiences to see a Company of Comedians from New York and a Company of Comedians from London performing around the same time but with different actors and shows. Great anticipation surrounded this new theatrical troupe's arrival, as the *Virginia Gazette* noted they were "daily expected here."[29] It is likely Virginians looked forward to this group of entertainers as Lewis Hallam came from an important British theatrical family, active in London's theater scene. In fact Lewis's brother William Hallam managed the Goodman's Fields Theatre in that city, where patrons saw and experienced the same plays and music Lewis would be bringing to Williamsburg, giving the American audience the feeling of being connected to their European counterparts.[30] Another part of the excitement stemmed from the fact this London-based company advertised European-style qualities appealing to Williamsburg's elites in their pursuit

BY AUTHORITY.

By the AMERICAN Company.

At the THEATRE in WILLIAMSBURG, this present WEDNESDAY (the 20th of JUNE) 1770.

The Clandestine Marriage.

Lord OGLEBY by Mr. HALLAM.
Sir JOHN MELVIL by Mr BYERLEY.
LOVEWELL by Mr. PARKER.
STERLING by Mr. MORRIS.
Serjeant FLOWER by Mr. DOUGLASS.
BRUSH by Mr. HENRY.
CANTON by Mrs. HARMAN.
TRAVERSE by Mr. ROBERTS.
TRUMAN by Mr. WOOLLS.

Mrs. HEIDELBERG by Mrs. DOUGLASS.
FANNY by Miss RICHARDSON.
BETTY by Mrs. HENRY.
CHAMBERMAID by Mrs. HALLAM.
Miss STERLING by Miss HALLAM.

To which will be added a MUSICAL ENTERTAINMENT, called

THOMAS & SALLY: Or, The Sailor's Return.

The SQUIRE by Mr. WOOLLS.
The SAILOR by Mr. HENRY.
DORCAS by Mrs HARMAN.
SALLY by Miss HALLAM.

The Doors will be opened at 6, and the Play begin precisely at 7 o'Clock.

TICKETS to be had at the POST OFFICE, of Mr. *PATRICK GALT*, near the Capitol, and of Mr. *JAMES RUSSELL*, at Doctor *ANDERSON*'s Shop. BOXES 7s. 6d. PIT and GALLERY 5s.

N. B. *No Person can, on any Pretence whatsoever, be admitted at the Stage Door.*

of Britishness. The company bragged in the *Gazette*, "The scenes, cloaths, and decorations are all entirely new, extremely rich, and finished in the highest taste, the scenes being painted by the best hands in London, are excell'd by none in beauty and elegance."[31] This entire description succinctly summarized many of the qualities upper crust citizens desired, including brand new goods from London that embodied "beauty and elegance," both highly desirable to this group. To emphasize the refinement of their shows they ensured that "ladies and gentlemen may depend on being entertain'd in as polite a manner as at the theatres in London, company being perfect in all the best plays, opera's, farces, and pantomimes, that have been exhibited in any of the theatres for these ten years past."[32]

Many of the company's advertisements mirrored those for polite entertainments found in London—a connection the city's genteel would not miss. This ensured customers that the shows performed were both acceptable for their social class, and that a portion of the audience consisted of their peers, preventing them from mingling with the lower sorts. Even the new and rich sets and costumes were designed by "the best hands in London," automatically making them fashionable, and therefore desirable, in the eyes of Williamsburg's elites. By importing not only the newest European music and plays to Virginia, but also the latest and most tasteful fashions, the Company of Comedians offered a venue where citizens could pretend they were indeed in London, or at least participating in the exact same entertainments of the same caliber experienced in Europe. The sights and sounds of these plays fully immersed customers in the world in which they wished to live.

After traveling overland from Yorktown to Williamsburg, Lewis Hallam likely rented one house for the entire troupe's residence, as he later did while living in New York. Though the general public likely anticipated the company's appearance, some government leaders in Williamsburg, Governor Robert Dinwiddie in particular, expressed concern. The previous group, the Murray-Kean Company, had gotten into trouble in the colony

Opposite: **A playbill from the American Company's June 20, 1770, performance of** *The Clandestine Marriage* **at the third Williamsburg playhouse. Playbills such as these were commonly handed out at performances or on the streets to advertise upcoming shows. It is possible the American Company also took out an ad in the** *Virginia Gazette* **for this show, but the surviving pages of the June 14, 1770,** *Gazette,* **the issue in which an ad would most likely appear, are either ripped or ink-stained, making large sections illegible. This playbill then is one of the few surviving items documenting which shows were seen on this date. The original playbill is housed in the collections of the Colonial Williamsburg Foundation.**

for "'loose behaviour'" and "'the disturbance they had like to have occasioned in private families.'"³³ In a letter to a friend and member of the Virginia Assembly, Dr. George Gilmer of Williamsburg wrote that due to the Assembly's failure to pass an act "suppressing ordinaries and players," Governor Dinwiddie and his Council wrote an order that "no player should act here; which is likely to prove the utter ruin of a set of idle wretches." Referring to Hallam's Company of Comedians, Gilmer estimated the governor's order would cost the troupe £1000, well over $130,000 today, in lost revenue and other expenses.³⁴ The Governor's Council wrote the order "to prevent unlawful playing of interludes" within two miles of Williamsburg, though luckily for Hallam the Virginia House of Burgesses rejected the council's proposal.³⁵ As a result, Hallam's players arrived to find some in town keeping them under a watchful eye.

The company still needed the governor's permission to put on their shows, and though Dinwiddie initially rejected the petition, Hallam and his actors continued to prepare for their debut. The first step was to purchase the theater used by the Murray-Kean Company on the east side of Williamsburg. Hallam paid Alexander Finnie £150 for the building, as Finnie planned on also selling the Raleigh Tavern and heading to England. According to historian Hugh F. Rankin, despite having a gallery, boxes, and a pit, the second theater in town at this point was "little more than an empty barn-like structure" with poor acoustics.³⁶ The inadequate construction distorted speaking and singing voices, permitting only those patrons closest to the stage to understand the dialogue or lyrics. Though the theater was located just to the east of the capitol building, Williamsburg was small enough at the time that the building bordered the forest, close enough that years later, according to Lewis Hallam, Jr., the actors shot wild game "from the doors and windows of the playhouse."³⁷

Despite these obstacles, Lewis Hallam and his company slogged on with their renovations and preparations for their first upcoming performance as the theater needed to reflect the refined ambiance they had advertised for their patrons. By the time of their opening night the *Gazette* reported that the troupe had "altered the play-house at Williamsburg to a regular theatre, fit for the reception of ladies and gentlemen, and the execution of their own performances."³⁸ In addition to upgrades to the boxes, pit, and gallery sections, a balcony had also been added for wealthier customers to get a better view of performances and subsequently pay higher ticket prices for the luxury of being further separated from those of the lower sorts whose seats remained closer to the stage. Williamsburg's elite would not have wanted to associate with those considered beneath them by sharing a physical space, as their social status partially stemmed from their ability to physically and financially distance themselves from those they considered below them in rank. More expensive ticket prices would have been a small price to pay for this necessary geographic separation.

Even though we lack the specifications for Hallam's renovations, we can surmise the interior layout of the second Williamsburg playhouse based on other eighteenth-century theaters. Though lacking financial accounts, Hallam must have invested a significant amount of money into the local economy upgrading the theater to the modern London standards patrons expected. Props and scenery would probably have been rather crude by modern standards, but considering the dim lighting from multiple chandeliers holding whale-derived spermaceti candles, called hoops, providing the primary illumination on the stage, few would have noticed the difference between high- and low-quality scenery. These candles were less likely to run and drip, thereby preventing costumes from being ruined by wax falling from the ceiling. Sconces on the walls held additional candles made of tallow, which had a tendency to drip and run down onto the floor, providing lighting for audience members.[39] The amount of candles the theater used during one performance would have seemed dazzling and extravagant to most members of the audience, unaccustomed to this ostentatious display. Lighting a multitude of candles after dark in the eighteenth century indicated wealth, as most Virginians could not afford such a luxury. Some playhouses could go through half a box of candles per night. This excess of lighting had two primary effects. For one, those who purchased the more expensive box tickets would appear well-lit in the audience, letting those in the cheaper seats clearly see their social superiors and once again establishing the pecking order in the hierarchy due to their prominent seating placement. Additionally the overabundance of theater lighting made that building one of the brightest in the town on show nights, adding a sense of prestige and wealth to the performances. Not only did this increase the status of the theater, its performers, and the patrons, but Williamsburg itself gained prestige by showcasing an entertainment extravaganza, with word hopefully reaching other towns of the city's wealth and luxuries like the theater.[40]

The stage would have been slightly sloped and about five feet off the ground, with its edge probably lined with iron spikes, most likely to keep audience members a safe distance from the performers. Patron comfort received little consideration, as the primary goal was to squeeze as many customers as possible into the playhouse. Those in the pit and gallery seats sat shoulder-to-shoulder on narrow benches, a mere nine inches wide with twelve inches of leg room, and metal spikes topped short walls to separate those lower status patrons from the wealthier attendees who would most likely be utilizing the box seats ringing the edge of the building, safely separated from their inferiors.[41] Though they oftentimes separated themselves by social status inside the theater, entering the playhouse was a different matter. Early theaters only had one entrance, regardless of where a patron would sit once inside. An eclectic crowd of Virginia's politicians, genteel citizens, merchants, and even farmers waited side-by-side outside these doors to enter together, one of the few social situations bringing these usually separated groups together on equal terms, even if for an extremely short period of time.[42]

As Hallam's Company of Comedians' premiere date approached, and after finally obtaining Governor Dinwiddie's permission to perform, *Virginia Gazette* ads encouraged the ladies of Williamsburg to purchase their tickets early "for their places in the boxes," and make sure to send their servants to the theater early to save their seats "in order to prevent trouble and disappointment."[43] The date of the actual premier is an interesting piece of historical curiosity. In the *Virginia Gazette* on August 28, 1752, Hallam stated the show would be held the following Friday, which should have been September 4, yet he listed the actual date as September 15, 1752.[44] Historian Hugh Rankin points out that while some historians have surmised this was a typographical error on the part of the *Virginia Gazette*, what actually occurred was in 1752 England and its colonies switched from the Julian calendar to the Gregorian calendar. This meant Wednesday, September 2, 1752, was immediately followed by Thursday, September 14, completely omitting the days in-between, and the Company's first performance was indeed on Friday, September 15.[45] Though this switch was presumably a bit jarring to the citizens of Williamsburg, Hallam made no mention of any confusion in the ads he placed in the paper, so customers must have been fairly well-informed that this leap was going to take place.

On September 15, 1752, Lewis Hallam's Company of Comedians held their first performance at the second Williamsburg playhouse, performing *The Merchant of Venice*, touted as "Written by Shakespear [sic]," as well as a farce called *The Anatomist; or, Sham Doctor*. Lewis Hallam performed the role of "Launcelot" while his wife Sarah played the role of Portia. While advertised as a play with multiple speaking roles, these types of productions also integrated a large amount of music, and the *Virginia Gazette* ad listed a Mr. Adcock in the role of Lorenzo "(with songs in character)."[46] It was common to see advertisements for playhouse shows listing various

4. Williamsburg's Colonial Theaters 113

actors or actresses as having singing roles during the show. Colonial audiences would have expected music to be a large part of these performances, and the actors made sure to be at least passable singers to keep viewers happy, and this was especially important for those in leading roles.[47]

An emphasis on quality singing led to several surprising strategies in theatrical troupes like Hallam's. For example, there were instances where certain actors not up to the task of singing their parts could go off stage in order to be replaced by a fellow actor with more skill. At other times a play itself might call for a servant or other sidekick to the main actors to take on the singing roles, as these could then be filled by lesser known but more gifted performers. At times a play's dialogue might explicitly reflect this strategy, having the non-gifted actor apologize for his singing voice, explaining he had a cold or was having an off day, justifying his lousy performance to the audience.[48] A playwright, anticipating that not all actors necessarily had adequate singing skills, also sometimes staged scenes to deliberately keep an actor off stage, or at least not visible to the audience if hiding behind a prop. In the play *The Constant Couple, or A Trip to the Jubilee* during "The Serenading Song," the character Sir Harry Wildair serenades Lady Lurewell through the closed door of her apartment, while only she is visible to the audience. This allowed another actor to step in and sing that part if the lead performer was an inadequate singer.[49]

The leading musician in the town hosting the theatrical troupe generally performed with the group during their performances, and as mentioned in a previous chapter Peter Pelham, eventual organist at Bruton Parish Church, played during Williamsburg's first production of *The Beggar's Opera* in 1768. Though the musician playing with Lewis Hallam's debut is not specifically mentioned in any sources, it was likely Cuthbert Ogle, he of the extensive printed music collection, who played harpsichord to assist the actors in their singing. It is also possible, as Rankin speculates, that music master John Singleton, while not playing the role of Gratiano in the play, joined Ogle on the violin to add to the spectacle.[50] Integrating local music masters into their performances provided yet another source of revenue to local musicians forced to work secondary jobs in order to survive—but these choices by troupes also reflected the fact that in a region as small as Williamsburg, they had little other choice.

The Merchant of Venice was a smashing success according to the editors of the *Virginia Gazette*, performed "before a numerous and polite audience" and followed by "great applause."[51] Though the audience was most likely unaware of it at the time, the play they observed was the beginning of a new musical and theatrical era in Williamsburg. Whereas before the first theater had struggled and eventually fallen into disrepair, and a previous theater group had gone out of business, Hallam's Company of Comedians was just beginning a successful run, and the second Williamsburg playhouse was soon to become the primary source of entertainment for the town's citizens, as well as a commercial success for the city.

It had not taken long for Lewis Hallam to capture the attention, and pocketbooks, of Williamsburg's citizens. The theater filled with large crowds three nights a week, and when Virginia's General Court was in session the troupe sometimes made upwards of £300 per performance, or the equivalent of over $40,000 per night in today's terms.[52] Hallam's successful business venture lasted for eleven months in Williamsburg, before finally relocating the company to New York in 1753.[53] News of the plays performed must have spread by word of mouth through the town, or perhaps handed out as leaflets to individuals in the city, because the only other play advertised in the *Virginia Gazette* during the company's time in Williamsburg was *Othello*, attended by the "emperor and empress of the Cherokee nation," who (as discussed in Chapter 1) assumed the fighting on stage was real.[54] Another possibility is at the end of each performance one actor completed an act called "giving out the play" wherein they would perform a dance or other small entertainment and then announce the next show to the audience. In the London theater the crowd would even sometimes vote with "ayes and noes" for which play they wanted to see on the next night, though it is unknown whether this was practiced in Virginia.[55]

A typical crowd at an eighteenth-century theater displayed an interesting mixture of various social statuses and behaviors. The desired audience, and coincidentally those with the most money who could afford the highest ticket prices, consisted of those "ladies and gentlemen" who generally purchased box seats separated from other areas of the theater. These genteel citizens were perfectly aware that by spending their money on theatrical performances, many seen only recently in Europe, they thereby associated themselves with the entertainments of their English brethren they so desperately wished to emulate. Below these citizens in the pit and gallery area of the theater the crowd represented a different social world entirely. It was not uncommon for rowdy lower status ticketholders in the pit and gallery areas to engage in drunken gambling and prostitution during a performance, activities perhaps encouraged by the smoking and drinking allowed in the playhouse. This rowdiness often led to members of the audience interacting directly with performers on stage, even hurling bottles at actors and musicians. Drunken observers also shouted at the actors, either to criticize their singing and acting abilities or demand encores. Sometimes these demands would even be made during dialogue or other songs that were being performed.[56] At one London performance a man became so intoxicated that "after expressing the greatest admiration [of the play] in the most vociferous terms, jumped from the top of the balcony to the stage, where he broke his arm, and terribly bruised one of the musicians, on whom he fell."[57] In 1773 following a performance in New York the Douglass Company offered a reward "to whoever can discover the person who was so very rude to throw eggs from the gallery, upon the stage last Monday, by which the cloaths of some ladies and gentlemen in the boxes were spoiled, and the performance in some measure interrupted."[58]

It is not hard to imagine then why the genteel desired to separate themselves from this rabble. Safely enclosed in their box seats where they could absorb the culture of the performance in relative peace, they mingled with their peers while safely ignoring the lowbrow antics of the lower sorts literally and figuratively beneath them, even if an occasional egg found its way into their sanctuary. It is somewhat ironic to note that wealthier theater patrons in the eighteenth century spent the largest sums of money in those seats further away from the stage, as they were considered more prestigious, and today those seats closest to the stage generally command the highest costs while the cheaper seats are located in the balcony. Despite their feeling of social superiority, it was also not unheard of for the elite patrons in the box section to cause trouble of their own. During one of the plays performed in 1736 by the students of William and Mary at the first playhouse, one "gentlemen, who, towards the latter end of the summer, usually wore a blue calmet coat lin'd with red, and trim'd with silver, a silver-lac'd hat, and a tupee wig, has been often observ'd by Miss Amoret, to look very languishingly at her the said Amoret, and particularly one night during the last session of assembly, at the theatre, the said gentleman ogled her in such a manner, as shew'd him to be very far gone." Apparently this drunken, longing stare caused enough distress with Miss Amoret she took out an advertisement with the *Virginia Gazette* requesting the anonymous gentleman take the "first handsome opportunity that offers, to explain himself on that subject," though perhaps his attention was not all bad as "she believes he has very pretty teeth."[59] The *Gazette* also reported on one incident at the Drury Lane Theatre in London when "the audience was terrible alarmed by a noise from behind the boxes, occasioned by two gentlemen quarrelling and drawing swords, which produced a rumour of

"The Laughing Audience" by William Hogarth, 1733. This etching, which Hogarth originally made to be printed on a subscription ticket to the Southwark Fair, shows a typical eighteenth-century theater scene in Britain. The wealthier patrons are behaving politely (if lasciviously) in the upper box seats, safely removed from the lower sorts who are demonstrating their uncouthness with broad emotions. Metal spikes separate the rabble from the musicians as they had a tendency to get rowdy during performances. It would have been common to see spikes lining the box seats as well.

fire, and was instantly spread throughout the house: The confusion was general, and many people hurt in attempting to force their way out; a woman in the front row of the first gallery had got one leg over, and was with difficulty prevented, by a man that sat next to her, from throwing herself into the pit."[60]

4. Williamsburg's Colonial Theaters   117

Though lowbrow antics tended to be more associated with European and northern American theaters, the Williamsburg theater proved to be a dangerous spot even when there were not rowdy troublemakers in the audience throwing bottles and food at the stage. In December 1752 one of Lewis Hallam's workers stayed overnight to guard the playhouse when "about 11 o'clock, the play-house in this city was broke open by one white man and two negroes, who violently assaulted and wounded Patrick Malony, servant to the company, by knocking him down, and throwing him upon the iron-spikes, one of which run into his leg, by which he hung for a considerable time, till he was relieved by some negroes: The villains that perpetrated this horrid fact escaped, but a reward is offered for apprehending them, and as the aforesaid Patrick Malony continues dangerously ill of his wounds, it is hoped they will be taken and brought to justice."[61] It is unknown if Malony survived his wounds, or if his assailants were ever captured, but he was certainly not the only person ever wounded on the spikes which lined the orchestra pits in eighteenth-century theaters. In November 1771 an account from Dublin, Ireland published in the *Virginia Gazette* reported, "that a certain theatrical performer there, having some words with one of the carpenters on the stage during the time of rehearsal, suddenly knocked him over the orchestra, and the man falling upon the spikes, was so terribly wounded that he died soon after." In this case at least justice was served, as "the offender was secured, and committed to jail."[62] It is certainly a bit ironic that these spikes, designed to protect the musicians, actors, and genteel in their sections of the theater, were just as likely to injure as to prevent injury.

During the eleven months of thrice weekly plays, this eclectic combination of Williamsburg's citizens experienced a multitude of various theatrical entertainments performed by the Company of Comedians. An evening at the theater provided attendees with a mixture of theatrical acts, singing, dancing, or even acrobatic maneuvers. The sheer variety of acts available to audiences guaranteed they did not grow bored by repeated viewings, thereby encouraging return patrons and additional ticket revenue. It was certainly possible the crowd could grow restless as shows usually contained two individual performances, interspersed with numerous musical and other theatrical acts, lasting between two and five hours total.[63] This format had been firmly established by the middle of the eighteenth century as the expected presentation at English-speaking theaters. Desiring to emulate British entertainment as closely as possible, the companies traveling throughout America stuck with this arrangement during their own shows. Not only were the performers familiar with this structure from their European performances, but their colonial audiences would have also been comfortable with it from either seeing plays while traveling abroad, or simply having read about them in papers. Historian John Molnar breaks a typical eighteenth-century performance down into eight different acts, though even those were sometimes broken up into subcategories:

1. *The opening music*—This varied based upon the year and the particular company;
2. *A prologue*—Appearing before the main act, this was sometimes sung but usually spoken;
3. *The mainpiece*—A play consisting of three to five acts, usually integrating music in some capacity, including singing, dancing, or orchestral music;
4. *An epilogue*—Following the main act, and similar to the prologue it was sometimes sung but usually spoken;
5. *Dance*—Some form of dance, and sometimes advertised as having never been seen on stage;
6. *An afterpiece*—An additional one or two acts that could be a farce, ballad, or other form of opera;
7. *Popular vocal or instrumental music*—This was performed during the intermissions and after the mainpiece;
8. *Specialty acts*—A variety of acts, sometimes consisting of individual or group dancing, often a dance involving all of the performers, or a performance of instrumental or vocal music.[64]

An example of how long these shows could be occurred on May 18, 1768, when the Virginia Company of Comedians showcased the play *The Constant Couple, or A Trip to the Jubilee.* Between the first and second acts a Mr. Parker gave a prologue in the character of a country boy. Following the second act a group of performers demonstrated a dance called the Coopers. Then the play had its third act, after which Mr. Parker sang a cantata. During the fifth act of this rather lengthy production, a Miss Yapp and Mrs. Osborne danced a minuet. Even following this final act in the play a Mr. Godwin played the hornpipe for the audience. However, not believing the audience would be content with a five-act play interspersed with musical and dancing numbers, the Company also added a farce called *The Miller of Mansfield* to the night's entertainment, though the *Virginia Gazette* made no mention of the number of acts or musical performances in this additional production.[65] For those citizens willing and able to purchase tickets to these theater shows, they apparently expected and received a great quantity of entertainment for their money.

By far the most popular forms of theatrical entertainment audiences would have experienced in the latter half of the eighteenth century were ballad operas.[66] As described by historian Ron Byrnside, these acts differed from modern operas, instead sharing similarities to current Broadway musicals, with a mixture of solo songs, some simple and some more elaborate, duets or group songs, dances, musical performances, and spoken dialogue.[67] In the early 1750s while Hallam's company resided in Williamsburg, one of the favorite acts performed at the theater involved the singing of ballads. Several types of vocal music eventually made their way from various parts of Europe to America, but the oldest was probably the ballad. Hundreds of these types of songs circulated through Britain around the time emigration began in earnest in the 1600s. Some of these songs dealt with actual historical events, others believed to have been based off true events were unconfirmed, and some simply told the stories of fictional characters.[68] As many operas focused on comedy or farce, some of the songs were deliberately ridiculous, such as "The Tragical History of the Life and Death of Billy Pringle's Pig" from *The Mayor of Garrat*. All of the ballads appeared in English, generally written simply as text without accompanying music. It was generally accepted that a written ballad would be set to one of several popular tunes commonly known at the time of publication. Even after the 1760s it was rare for music to be written specifically to accompany a ballad.[69] For example, the song "A Soldier and a Sailor" appeared first in the comedy *Love for Love* in 1695, and was repurposed as "A Fox May Steal Your Hens, Sir" in *The Beggar's Opera*, in addition to various other operas. Being written in English and set to common, well-known music added a level of accessibility to songs performed in the theater, encouraging Williamsburg patrons to attend as they could easily relate to the pieces heard during shows as they had most likely heard and sang them in their own homes.

Many ballads were distributed through the use of broadsides, the printed sheets of paper containing news, advertisements, or other written information. Ballad texts were frequently sold on broadsides, and the person hawking the sheets was often a singer, attracting the attention of customers by singing some of the ballads he was selling. Some of the ballads sold in this manner were written by writers or journalists with a keen ear for what appealed to the populace at the time the songs were written, while others were traditional ballads known to many people through frequent exposure over the years. The distributed ballads were "traditionally sung by a single unaccompanied voice" and were sometimes performed at home for family and friends. Other times these ballads would be performed in public commercial venues such as the Williamsburg theater, where around 1770, for example, audiences experienced the song "Dear Pretty Youth" from William Shakespeare's *The Tempest*. During a ballad performance the singer was supposed to remain free from the emotions of the song, telling a story in a detached manner. The performer would close her eyes, raise her head, and maintain a neutral facial expression, not smiling, laughing, frowning or crying. When the song finished, a short pause would follow, whereupon the singer would relax and repeat either the last line of the ballad or the song's title, presumably followed by either applause or jeers depending on the crowd's reaction.[70]

The first known ballad opera performed in the colonies, *Flora, or Hob in the Well*, appeared in Charleston, South Carolina, in 1735 and made its way to Williamsburg via Hallam's Company of Comedians. Though *Flora* was popular, probably the most famous, and most influential, ballad opera to appear in the eighteenth century was *The Beggar's Opera*, which included the ballad "My Heart Was So Free," among others. The music for this extremely well-known eighteenth-century song had originally appeared in the 1706 comedy *The Recruiting Officer*. Poet, actor, and flutist John Gay appropriated the musical arrangement and simply changed the words to write his song "My Heart Was So Free." Though completed in 1728, no existing records indicate *The Beggar's Opera* was performed in the colonies before 1750, and it did not appear in Williamsburg until June 1768 when Bruton Parish Church organist Peter Pelham assisted with the musical acts. Despite this delay, word had traveled across the ocean about the play's "combination of tunefulness, novelty, gibes at Italian opera, political satire, and parody of the social order, which appealed to all varieties of taste," according to historian John Molnar.[71] On one occasion in 1732 William Byrd II, the prosperous plantation owner, was traveling through Virginia when bad weather forced him to spend a few days with a Mrs. Fleming. Lacking entertainment, their discussion soon turned to the theater, where he discovered she had an interest in comedies. Though it would not appear on an American stage for another eighteen years, the house happened to have a copy of *The Beggar's Opera* on hand, which Byrd volunteered to read to the household. Having spent a large portion of his life in London, Byrd was quite familiar with this play and its success on the European stage. He remarked in his diary that the play's popularity, in his opinion, was not necessarily due to its wit or humor, though he believed those aspects "sparkled." Instead its success derived from "political reflections that seemed to hit the ministry," as well as it had captivated the interest of the Duchess of Queensbury. Apparently in Byrd's opinion the political satire and backing of a royal were enough of an influence to popularize the play, and its humor was a side benefit. Having explained the history of this relatively new production to his audience, Byrd proceeded to read three acts, leaving the remainder to Mrs. Fleming and another gentleman, who "read as well as most actors do at a rehearsal. Thus we killed the time and triumphed over the bad weather."[72] Situations like these would have been more and more common as published ballad operas made their way across the Atlantic and slowly trickled into the homes of Virginians desperate for European entertainment.

Though earning substantial amounts of money performing ballad operas and other acts in Virginia, Hallam's Company of Comedians also repeated some of the mistakes of the Murray-Kean Company before them. By the time the troupe left Williamsburg for New York, actors William Rigby, Charles Bell, John Singleton, and William Adcock owed large unpaid debts to local merchants. Although some debt was to be expected when members of traveling theatrical groups remained for some time in one location, during which a certain financial exchange developed, near the end of their stay these debts proved troubling. With their expensive lifestyles (some of the debts belonged to wig maker Edward Charlton, wigs being a mandatory accessory for the genteel in eighteenth-century Virginia), the actors frequently spent far more money than they had earned. Forced to decide between letting his actors serve time in a debtors' prison and dissolve his troupe, or paying off the debts of his employees, Lewis Hallam chose to deed the second Williamsburg playhouse as collateral to settle their debts. If the actors did not pay back what they owed by October 10, 1753, he would lose possession of the theater. Unfortunately for him, not a single actor repaid their debts, and the playhouse once again changed hands.[73]

During the years following the London Company of Comedians' departure the second playhouse sat unoccupied by theatrical troupes for long stretches; no performances were advertised in the *Virginia Gazette* until 1768, and by then a third theater had been constructed. Sources suggest that similar to the first theater, however, it is likely various parties utilized the second structure for gatherings, plays, or concerts even if they did not formally advertise the events during that fourteen-year stretch. During the General Court in October 1755, for example, a mechanical contraption designed by Henry Bridges of London was displayed in the Williamsburg theater, variously referred to as the "Piece of Mechanism,

The Microcosm, or The World in Miniature." This device consisted of a multitude of moving parts, many of which incorporated an array of musical works. According to its description in the paper, "the inward contents are as judiciously adapted to gratify the ear ... for it plays with great exactness several fine pieces of musick." Also on the machine were "the nine muses playing in concert on divers [sic] musical instruments, as the harp, hautboy, bass viol, &c," plus "Orpheus in the forest, playing on his lyre, and beating exact time to each tune; who, by his exquisite harmony, charms even the wild beasts." When the entire machine was in operation "upwards of twelve hundred wheels and pinnions are in motion at once; and during the whole performance it plays several fine pieces of music, on the organ and other instruments, both single and in concert, in a very elegant manner."[74] Tickets could be purchased to see this marvelous contraption for five shillings, or half that for children. Though overall ticket sales are unknown, considering the scarcity of professional musical entertainment at this time in Williamsburg, it is conceivable there was much anticipation for this display and many citizens would have gladly paid the admission price. Despite Hallam's theater being used for occasional performances and showcasing mechanical gadgets, by 1757 the building had been converted to a private residence, and the citizens of Williamsburg needed a new location for their entertainment needs.[75]

Lewis Hallam, Sr., never returned to Williamsburg, as after touring America the company relocated to Jamaica where he died. While living in that country his widow Sarah married David Douglass, who reorganized the company and returned to the colonies in 1758.[76] Still billing themselves as "A Company of Comedians from London," or the Douglass Company, only four of the original troupe members remained, including Sarah Hallam, her two sons Lewis Jr., and Adam Hallam, and Mrs. Charles Love.[77] Sometime before October 1760 the traveling company had returned to Williamsburg when local merchant William Allason purchased two tickets to a performance, held at a brand new third playhouse David Douglass built upon his troupe's arrival in Virginia. Curiously the *Virginia Gazette* made no mention of this performance, nor did it offer editorial comments following the show. Historian Hugh Rankin speculates either the town was so crowded due to the General Courts that advertising was unnecessary, or the company was struggling financially and could not afford to take out any advertisements.[78]

A third possibility was that Douglass's reputation preceded him, making advertising unnecessary as the Williamsburg elite would have been aware of his arrival and impending performances. His wife Sarah, after all, was the widow of Lewis Hallam, a familiar character in the theater world and owner of the second playhouse in town. Not only would this have given Douglass some well-needed credibility in the city, but Sarah was most likely familiar with the city's elites and could introduce them to her new husband. Though undoubtedly useful, David Douglass luckily did not need to rely solely on Sarah's connections, as before arriving in Williamsburg his Company of Comedians completed a tour of the northern American colonies. Through the connections made at these previous stops, the new theater owner acquired letters of introduction from influential persons, including one letter of recommendation from Maryland Governor Horatio Sharpe to Virginia's Governor Francis Fauquier which most likely granted Douglass access to the upper echelons of Williamsburg society, his primary future audience at his playhouse.[79]

David Douglass built the third, and final, theater in Williamsburg's colonial era just to the southeast of the capitol building at the eastern end of Duke of Gloucester Street. This convenient location allowed visiting plantation owners, politicians, and other important members of society in town on government business to easily walk to the theater to take in a performance and relax at the end of a day filled with emotionally exhausting political maneuverings. Due to the importance of Virginia's elites spending their money at the theater during the 1760 session of the General Assembly, Douglass rushed to have the building up and running by the beginning of October. This ambitious timetable was certainly feasible as he was no stranger to theater construction upon his arrival in town, having previously built three theaters in Annapolis, Philadelphia, and Jamaica. However there is no way to know for certain how Douglass's Company of Comedians financed the playhouse's construction, as unfortunately the 1760 issues of the *Virginia Gazette* no longer exist. Despite this lack of information it is a safe assumption he instituted a subscriber system similar to Alexander Finnie's during construction of the second Williamsburg theater, whereby the owner of the building provided an assortment of theater tickets to those who invested money in the enterprise, a common practice at the time.[80]

Regardless of the money's origins, Douglass certainly put a great deal of expense, time, and effort into the theater's construction. When completed the third Williamsburg playhouse's size rivaled some of the great theatrical structures in Great Britain, eclipsing the Georgian Theater in North Yorkshire, and comparable to the 1768 Edinburgh Theater. Measuring seventy-two feet east to west paralleling Duke of Gloucester Street and forty-four feet heading north to south, the two-story building's appearance was most likely not awe-inspiring, as its plain clapboard siding probably made it resemble a large barn or warehouse-type structure. Carl Lounsbury of the Colonial Williamsburg Foundation speculates this plain design occurred "in response to ambivalent moral attitudes toward theatrical performances and the lingering concerns about censorship and licensing of companies."[81]

Despite its rather plain exterior, the interior of the theater would have many of the same luxuries as Finnie's theater from ten years prior. Initially Douglass built box seating for the wealthiest patrons, a pit for slightly cheaper seats, and a gallery for the cheapest tickets. His Company did well enough in Williamsburg that by 1771 the gallery seating was converted to box seating to increase ticket revenue, as the vast majority of the patrons were those wealthy individuals in town for government business or well-to-do merchants who could easily afford pricier seats. The boxes, being the most expensive section, were most likely painted rich colors, a sign of wealth at the time, or perhaps upholstered in some fashion. After all, those paying the highest prices needed to be aware they were not only paying for the performance, but for the status those seats conveyed to the rest of the crowd. Similar to the second theater, however, the third playhouse also had only one entrance conveniently facing north towards the capitol building, forcing those of varying social levels to intermingle outside, at least to some extent, before entering through the common entrance whereupon they would be directed towards their separate seating areas, again establishing the expected and preferred social hierarchy.

It seems likely that, similar to Alexander Finnie's second theater, metal spikes were utilized to separate the box seats from those in the pit and gallery, providing a buffer zone for the different social groups in attendance. More spikes probably separated the orchestra pit right in front of the stage from the pit audience, protecting the musicians during a performance from an oftentimes raucous crowd. Numerous spermaceti and tallow candles illuminated the structure, greatly increasing the cost of operating the theater, but at the same time increasing its prestige and gentility in the consumers' eyes. Douglass routinely commissioned scene painters in London to create theatrical sets which could be transported from theater to theater, including Williamsburg, adding to the grandeur of his shows and creating the impression for his audience that the acts they were seeing closely resembled those in Great Britain, a necessity for the genteel audience members. One building improvement over previous theaters which Douglass implemented was a ventilator in the ceiling, designed to pull out some of the heat and smoke from the burning candles and crowd, a surely welcome addition in the opinions of the audience members, especially as even during the October court sessions Virginia could be quite hot and humid and any lessening of an oppressive atmosphere in the theater would have been very much appreciated.[82]

It appears that during the troupe's time in the city their behavior exceeded that of the previous theater groups, as Governor Fauquier, his council, and "near one hundred of the principal gentlemen of Virginia" wrote a letter vouching that Douglass's group had made it a "constant practice to behave with prudence and discretion in their private character, and to use their utmost endeavours to give general satisfaction in their public capacity."[83] Douglass's Company of Comedians remained in Virginia from October 1760 until May 1761, though presumably the group did not just stay in Williamsburg, but toured other areas of the colony like Fredericksburg and Norfolk. In October 1760, while attending the General Assembly in Williamsburg, George Washington attended the theater on more than one occasion and noted in his ledger that he had spent £7 11s 3d to "By [sic] Play Tickets at Sundry times."[84] He also purchased "Play Tickets in March" of the following year for £2 7s 6d while the Douglass Company was still in town.[85] Armed with the document from Governor Fauquier the new Company of Comedians headed for New York, and the citizens of Williamsburg were once again left without a resident theater troupe.

Sometime in early 1763 the company returned for a brief stint in Virginia. Since the group once again took out no ads in the *Virginia Gazette*, the primary source of information on their whereabouts at this time comes from George Washington's ledger, in which he records the purchase of play tickets in April and May for multiple theater performances. Unfortunately he does not record the specific plays he saw, just that he bought the tickets amounting to £2 1s 3d over five shows.[86] By the fall of that year Douglass's company again left Williamsburg and renamed itself the American Company. This troupe did not return to the town until 1770, by which time a competing theatrical company had arrived on the scene, and the third playhouse was entering its final years of use.

The years between 1763 and 1768 represented a comparatively stark time for the theater in Williamsburg, perhaps reflective of the broader economic depression that hit the colonies following the Seven Years' War. The playhouse, for the most part, sat empty and had no official performances. To entertain themselves citizens had to rely on the private balls and dances frequently held in town, or listened to gentlemen amateurs give concerts in local plantation houses or taverns frequented by the genteel. In January 1767 William Verling, a former member of the American Company, arrived in Williamsburg and put on two performances of the "celebrated *Lecture on Heads,* so much admired and applauded by all who have heard it performed" at 6 p.m. "in the great room of the Rawleigh [sic] Tavern."[87] This was a one-man play popular in the colonies at the time, and its production strongly implies Verling was the only member of the company in town, as otherwise he presumably would have teamed up with fellow actors for performances.

Then in March 1768 a simple statement in the *Virginia Gazette* notified the public that for the first time in almost five years, "On Thursday next the theatre here will be opened."[88] By this time the paper had taken to referring to the third playhouse as "the old theatre," though it was only nearing eight years old. A newly formed theater troupe calling themselves the Virginia Company of Comedians and led by William Verling utilized the structure. With the permission of "the worshipful ... mayor of Williamsburg" George Wythe, the first play performed at the theater on Monday, April 4 was *Douglas,* followed by a farce called *The Honest Yorkshireman.* Specifically advertised in the *Virginia Gazette* and highlighted as part of the show was "a dance by Mr. Godwin."[89] Considering the numerous displays of talent during a single night's entertainment, as demonstrated by the multiple acts and musical performances in *The Constant Couple,* we can assume those purchasing tickets got their money's worth. Between March and June of that year Verling's company put on numerous plays, dances, and songs at the Williamsburg playhouse, to the delight of those in town who had not seen these types of performances in years. As was his habit, George Washington attended some of these shows, apparently taking a group of individuals on May 2nd consisting of "Colo. Bassett Colo. Lewis and Mr. Dick." Altogether Washington spent £1 7s 6d for this group to attend the theater, and apparently was pleased enough with the performances to attend again on May 5th.[90] Thomas Jefferson also attended the May 2nd performance, paying five shillings for a ticket and returning for the May 6th show.[91] As prominent citizens of Virginia, Jefferson and Washington's appearances at the theater surely added to the respectability of any performances they attended, further increasing ticket sales.

The Virginia Company of Comedians left Williamsburg in June 1768 in typically dramatic fashion, for some of the actors apparently aided the escape of a slave named Nanny who, as reported in the *Gazette* by her owner Jane Vobe, "it is supposed that she has gone off with some of the comedians who have just left this town, with some of whom, as I have been informed, since she went off, she had connections, and was seen very busy talking privately with some of them."⁹² Some of Verling's troupe may have also run off with the wife of a local religious figure, as the Reverend Isaac Gilberne of Williamsburg wrote to Landon Carter in July 1768 remarking on his wife's sudden elopement, who, as he was "credibly informed," kept company "every night with some strolling players."⁹³ Based on the dates of Gilberne's spouse's disappearance, these "strolling players" were presumably members of the Virginia Company of Comedians, who had conveniently left town at almost exactly the same time as his wife. Still other performers left Williamsburg deeply in debt and wanted by the courts. Charles Parker and Christopher Bromage were arrested and detained for their debts while living in town, and actors David Jefferson, Frederick Spencer, and William Burdett had legal suits going through the court system in York County. George Walker, another performer, actually sued three of his fellow actors for unpaid debts, some of whom were already being sued by merchants living in Williamsburg for the same reason. As for William Verling, by the time he left town at least five individuals had sued him individually for money he owed them and the courts issued an order that he appear in person before them. By the time of the order's issuance, however, Verling had left the city and failed to make his mandatory court appearance, forcing the judges to levy his estate for £21, approximately £1,400 or over $2,000 in today's money.⁹⁴ Whereas Verling's Company of Comedians brought drama to the stage, they certainly added a sense of drama to their departure from the city as well.

Verling's troupe disbanded the following year and most likely never returned to Williamsburg, especially considering the debts and controversy surrounding their exit.⁹⁵ Over the next three years David Douglass's American Company visited town, usually during the fall court sessions, performing on numerous occasions, and it was during this time period that Hudson Muse wrote to his brother that he attended the playhouse eleven times in eleven days. The final theatrical performance by any theater company in Williamsburg before the American Revolution was *The Fashionable Lover*, taking place sometime in May 1772. The *Virginia Gazette* touted the "industry of the American Company" for this show as the paper claimed this play had only been so far performed in London for not "above ten days."⁹⁶ Before being abandoned for good, one final theatrical act utilized the playhouse in November 1772. A Mr. Gardiner used the theater to demonstrate "a magnificent piece of machinery" with sea monsters, ships, forts, and armies, all accompanied by music. At the end of this "Mr. Gardiner will extend himself between two chairs, and suffer

By AUTHORITY.

At the THEATRE in WILLIAMSBURG, on Monday the 23d of this instant (November) Will be exhibited, by Mr. GARDINER, A CURIOUS SET OF FIGURES, richly dressed, four feet high; they are to appear on the stage as if alive, and will perform a tragic performance, called

BATEMAN AND HIS GHOST.

LIKEWISE A SET OF WATERWORKS, representing the SEA, and all manner of SEA MONSTERS sporting on the waves. With the taking of the

HAVANNAH,

with ships, forts, and batteries, continually firing, until victory crowns the *British* forces; with the appearance of the two armies. To which will be added, a magnificent piece of MACHINERY, called

CUPID's PARADISE,

representing seventy odd PILLARS and COLUMNS, with the appearance of NEPTUNE and AMPHRITRITE, and music suitable thereto. The whole to conclude with a magnificent set of FIREWORKS, such as caterine wheels, *Italian* candles, sea fountains, and sun flowers with the appearance of the sun and moon in their full lustre.

Mr. Gardiner will extend himself between two chairs, and suffer any of the company to break a stone of two hundred weight on his bare breast.

TICKETS to be had at the THEATRE, which are 3/9. for the BOX, PIT 2/6, and GALLERY 1/3. The performance to begin at 6 o'clock.

Vivant Rex & Regina.

⁎⁎⁎ No person can be admitted behind the scenes.

N. B. Between the acts will be instrumental music, consisting of *French* horns and trumpets.

any of the company to break a stone of two hundred weight on his bare breast." Separating these two rather bizarre shows was "instrumental music, consisting of French horns and trumpets."[97] Gardiner's rather unique production, combining the necessary theatrical requirements of spectacle and music, was a fitting last performance for the third Williamsburg theater as it drew its final curtain.

Opposite: The November 19, 1772, *Virginia Gazette* advertisement for the final performance held at the Williamsburg playhouses, shortly before Americans turned their backs on British entertainment. During this show a Mr. Gardiner exhibited a curious set of figures, performed a show called *Bateman and His Ghost,* had a mechanical waterworks and naval reenactment, and utilized other visual displays like fireworks. At the end he extended himself between two chairs so a spectator could break a stone on his chest. Gardiner also had music from French horns and trumpets between the acts.

Epilogue

Altogether the various theatrical companies that visited the Williamsburg playhouses performed approximately one hundred plays, ballad operas, and comic operas, though it is difficult to say for certain due to a lack of written sources. From these plays, however, historian John Molnar estimates "about two hundred songs ... were performed during the action or between the acts" of these plays.[1] The theatrical scene in Williamsburg never again rose to the level of popularity it had in the twenty years starting in 1752. By 1774 Virginians had a potential conflict with Britain on their minds, and public entertainment was not high on their list of priorities. In fact, not only did Americans lose interest in the theater, but they became actively hostile towards it. Some, including the editors of the *Virginia Gazette*, felt plays were becoming immoral and the theater needed to go back to "what it ought to be ... a school of politeness and virtue." This absence of morality in new theatrical pieces, they argued, left the theater lacking "a variety of exhibitions sufficient to engage the attention of the publick," and audiences would not keep watching the same plays over and over as even the "most desirable entertainments, by too frequent a repetition, become insipid."[2] Other colonists were less concerned with the content of the plays than with their origins. As historian Ann Withington argues, "Americans expelled the theater, which was run by English actors and produced English plays."[3] Perhaps due to this hostility, or maybe the prospect of declining income, some of the major players in the theatrical world began to abandon the colonies. A notice in the January 28, 1775, *Virginia Gazette* noted, "The Company of Comedians, with Mr. Douglass, the manager, are preparing to embark for the island of Jamaica, and they will not return to the continent, until its tranquility is restored."[4] The exodus of these theatrical troupes, combined with the increasing likelihood of a war with Britain and a subsequent distrust and hatred of all things British, hastened the decline of the theater in Williamsburg.

This decision to abandon the theater did not come lightly, however, as Virginians, and Americans in general, loved seeing performances despite their British associations, and the outlawing of the theater only came about after a series of less severe measures failed to have the desired effect. In response to Britain's passage of the Stamp Act, Virginia's delegates met in 1769 in the Raleigh Tavern in Williamsburg to draft the first Virginia Nonimportation Resolutions banning the importation of certain British goods, though the theater was not included in the list of banned items.[5] Following the repeal of the Stamp Act the British parliament once again imposed a series of taxes on the colonists, this time in the form of the Townshend Acts, forcing people to pay a fee on paper, lead, tea and other various goods. Once again Virginia's politicians condemned these taxes, and on June 22, 1770, they drafted a bill including fourteen resolutions banning the importation of such various items as wine, slaves, paintings, horses, and more. Once again, however, the theater was not included in the list of banned articles.[6] In fact, following this particular vote many of the bill's signers, including Thomas Jefferson and George Washington, adjourned to attend the theater, as these two individuals alone had purchased more than twenty tickets to that week's performances.[7] Even after the Williamsburg playhouses closed individuals attempted to keep the theatrical arts alive, though they were forced to do so in the comfort of their own homes. As late as 1774 Nicholas Cresswell dined at a Mrs. Leftwiches house "with some young ladies from Virginia. After supper the company amused themselves with several diverting plays. This seems very strange to me, but I believe it is common in this country."[8] This desire to preserve the theater in America could only last so long, however, as a war with Britain soon appeared inevitable.

In the Articles of Association passed in October 1774, the First Continental Congress proposed a series of measures aimed at separating the colonies commercially from Great Britain due to what they considered harsh and destructive taxes levied on the Americans to pay for British debts accrued in the French and Indian War. In one of the final attempts made by the colonists and their congressional leaders to show the seriousness of their grievances with Britain, the Articles declared all imports, exports, and consumption of British goods would henceforth cease. Not only would this ban on trade hurt the importation of music-related items like instruments and music books, but the congress specifically mentioned discouraging plays and other shows: "We will, in our several stations, encourage frugality, economy, and industry, and promote agriculture, arts and the manufactures of this country, especially that of wool; and will discountenance and discourage every species of extravagance and dissipation, especially all horse-racing, and all kinds of games, cock fighting, exhibitions of shews [sic], plays, and other expensive diversions and entertainments."[9] Along with the impending war and growing distrust and hatred of anything British, Americans rapidly lost interest in the stage, closing the Williamsburg playhouses for good.

Theatrical performances in Williamsburg represented the peak of musical commerce in the eighteenth century. As disposable income grew in the 1700s, a wave of social necessity swept over Virginia's wealthier citizens such that becoming more British—in one's personal appearance, belongings, and cultural activities—became the ultimate sign of respectability in the colony. The genteel of the city wanted to experience the same kinds of music and theater enjoyed by the social elites of Britain. Purchasing tickets to shows in Williamsburg that had only recently appeared in London allowed them to feel less rustic and closer to those they admired overseas. Performances put on at the playhouses in town also provided a venue for those citizens of the lower social ranks to experience music in a way they had never been able to in the past. Though folk songs, dances, and music were popular at local events, before the construction of the Williamsburg theaters most large-scale musical performances were held at plantation manors or taverns frequented by the elite, with no potential access for the less well-off. As the century progressed, increasing numbers of individuals from all social levels had disposable income to spend on these performances, and theatrical troupes formed specifically to sell tickets to those willing to part with their money in exchange for a night of entertainment at the theater. These groups integrated music, instruments, and singing, all of which came almost exclusively from Europe and all pastimes of the upper class, into their theatrical shows. Until political conflicts with Britain abruptly brought its expansion to an end, the theater allowed citizens of Williamsburg, both poor and genteel, to immerse themselves in the musical culture of Europe, bringing them closer to the British lifestyles they desired.

Appendix I
Music Master Cuthbert Ogle's Musical Estate

Inventory list of musical items from the estate of Music Master Cuthbert Ogle of Williamsburg, as listed in the *William and Mary Quarterly*, April 1895. All capitalizations are included.

- Some fiddle strings
- A fiddle & case, Harpsichord and 2 Hammers &c
- Musick: 2 sets Pasquatis Overtures
- 10 Books Handels Songs
- 4 large sets Italian songs
- 6 Sonatas by Schickard
- 4 books of Symp. To Handels oratorios
- The Musical entertainment
- Lamps Songs
- Apollos Feast by Handel
- Nares Lessons, Avisons Concertos
- 6 Concertos by Burgess & 6 by Hasse in one book
- 4 small books of Stanley
- 6 Sonatas Degeardino
- Lamps through Bass, Albertis 8 Sonatas
- 5 Concertos by Ramesa, 2 concertos by avison
- 6 Concertos by Hebden
- 1 Concerto in 7 parts by Avison
- 12 English songs by Pasquati
- 1 large Book of songs Palma
- Songs in Acis and Galatea, Handel
- Alcocks Lessons. Grannoms Songs
- 1 Vol Feltons Concertos
- 8 Concertos Avisons
- Feltons Lessons
- Correlli's Sonatas in Score manu

- No. 13
- Leveridges Songs in small
- Songs by Hasse
- Cathces by Purchet & Blow
- Ballards by Grannom
- An unbound book of Italian Songs
- 5 large Books of Concertos manu
- Harlequin Rangers
- Loose Music

Appendix II
Concerts and Dances of Williamsburg

Known organized concerts and public and private dances held in Williamsburg and the surrounding area, as advertised in the *Virginia Gazette*. All advertisements retain their original punctuation and spelling. As the *Gazette* had multiple publishers, often simultaneously, they are identified as follows: Pa=Parks, Hu=Hunter, Ro=Royle, PD=Purdie and Dixon, Ri=Rind, Pi=Pinkney, DH=Dixon and Hunter.

November 5, 1736 (Pa)
Last Saturday being His Majesty's birth-day, the same was observ'd here, with firing of guns, illuminations, and other demonstrations of loyalty: And at night there was a handsome appearance of gentlemen and ladies, at His Honour the Governor's, where was a ball, and an elegant entertainment for them.

November 26, 1736 (Pa)
We hear, from Hanover County, that on Tuesday next, (being St. Andrews Day,) some merry-dispos'd gentlemen of the said county, design to celebrate that festival, by setting up divers prizes to be contended for in the following manner, (to wit,) A neat hunting-saddle, with a fine broad-cloth housing, fring'd and flower'd, &c. to be run for (the quarter,) by any number of horses and mares: a fine Cremona fiddle to be plaid for, by any number of country fiddlers, (Mr. Langford's scholars excepted:) With divers other considerable prizes, for dancing, singing, foot-ball- play, jumping, wrestling, &c. particularly a fine pair of silk stockings to be given to the handsomest maid upon the green, to be judg'd of by the company, At Page's warehouse, commonly call'd Crutchfield in the said County of Hanover, where all persons will find good entertainment.

February 25, 1737 (Pa)
This is to give notice, to all gentlemen and ladies, that Mrs. Barbara Degraffenriedt, intends to have a ball on Tuesday the 26th of next April, and an

assembly, on the 27th, in Williamsburg: For which, tickets will be deliver'd out at her house.

April 22, 1737 (Pa)

To the Gentlemen and Ladies, that Mrs. Stagg proposes to have an Assembly, on Thursday the 28th, and another on Friday the 29th of this instant, at the Capitol; for which tickets are to be delivered out, at half a pistole each, at the Capitol, before the Assemblies begin: And those gentlemen and ladies who will favour her with their company, are requested not to pay any money at the door.

Note, there will be several valuable things set up to be raffled for.

October 14, 1737 (Pa)

This is to inform the Gentlemen and Ladies, that on Tuesday, the first of November next, there will be an assembly, at the capitol, for the benefit of Mrs. Cobb. Tickets to be had of Mrs. Cobb, at Mrs. Staff's, the same day, from ten in the morning til four in the afternoon. Price half a pistole.

October 21, 1737 (Pa)

This is to inform the gentlemen and ladies, that Mrs. Degraffendriedt designs to have a ball at her house, on Tuesday the first of November next, and a collation, for the entertainment of those who are pleased to favour her with their company; for which tickets will be delivered at her house, at five shillings each.

And the next day she designs to have an assembly; for which tickets will be delivered at her house, at half a pistole each.

March 24, 1738 (Pa)

This is to give notice to the gentlemen and ladies, that there will be a publick and assembly, at the Capitol, on Thursday evening the 27th of April next:

Also several grotesque dances, never yet perform'd in Virginia. Tickets to be had of Mrs. Stagg.

Several valuable goods will be put up to be raffled for; also a likely young Negro fellow.

March 31, 1738 (Pa)

This is to give notice to all gentlemen and ladies, that there will be a ball on Wednesday evening, the 26th of April next, and an Assembly on Friday the 28th, at the house of Mrs. Degraffenreidt, in Williamsburg. Tickets to be had of her.

April 21, 1738 (Pa)

Next Thursday evening, there is to be a publick and assembly, at the Capitol; for which, tickets may be had of Mrs. Stagg, at the usual price.

April 21, 1738 (Pa)

On Wednesday next there is to be a ball, and on Friday an assembly, at Mrs. Degraffenriedt's, of whom tickets may be had, for the ball 5s. and for the assembly half a pistole.

October 13, 1738 (Pa)

This is to give notice, that for the entertainment of the gentlemen and ladies, Mrs. Stagg intends to have two assemblies, at the Capitol; the first on Tuesday evening, the 31st of this instant October, and the second on Wednesday evening, the first of November; for which tickets may be had of Mrs. Stagg, at her house in Williamsburg, or at the Capitol, the evenings before the assemblies begin.

Price half a pistole. Several things will be set up to be raffled for.

November 3, 1738 (Pa)

Williamsburg, Nov 3. Last Monday being the anniversary of His Majesty's birth-day, was observ'd in this city with all the distinguishing marks of loyalty we are capable of shewing. In the morning the publick flag was hoisted on the Capitol; at noon the cannon at the governor's house were trebly discharg'd; and at night, most of the gentlemens and other houses of note were illuminated. His Honour the Governor, was pleas'd to give a handsome entertainment for the gentlemen and ladies, together with a ball; and the evening concluded with agreeable mirth, in every respect, suitable to the occasion. The King's ships, and the forts, in this colony, also proclaimed their loyalty from the mouths of their cannon.

April 20, 1739 (Pa)

This is to give notice to all gentlemen and ladies, that Mrs. Degraffenreidt's long indisposition hath render'd her incapable of keeping an assembly, as usual; but if they please to except of a dance at her house in Williamsburg, on Wednesday the second of May, she will find them a room, musick, candles, and liquors, for five shillings a ticket.

November 2, 1739 (Pa)

Williamsburg, Nov 2. Tuesday last, being the anniversary of His Majesty's birth day, it was observ'd here, with great decency and respect. In the morning, the flag was display'd at the Capitol. At noon the great guns at the Governor's, were thrice discharg'd. And in the evening the Governor's House, the college, several gentlemens, and other houses, were beautifully illuminated. His Honour the Governor entertained a great number of gentlemen and ladies at his house, with a ball, and an elegant supper. And the night was concluded with great demonstrations of joy, suitable to the happy occasion, and agreeable to the distinguish'd loyalty of this colony in general, to His Majesty, and His illustrious family.

August 28, 1746 (Pa)

The gentlemen of Hanover county, being desirous of following the example of Williamsburg, Norfolk, Suffolk, and other places, in expressing their joy and loyalty, on occasion of the defeat of the Rebels in Scotland, voluntarily raised a sum of money, for making a publick entertainment; which was appointed to be at Newcastle, yesterday was se'nnight:

Accordingly, that day, a great number of gentlemen and ladies, inhabitants of that and the adjacent counties, met at the house of Mr. Waters; where a handsome dinner was provided; a long arbour was set up, in which 50 gentlemen and ladies din'd, and several other tables were full, in the house. After dinner, the healths of the king, prince and princess of Wales, the Duke of Cumberland, and the rest of the royal family, success to his majesty's arms, the governor and prosperity to Virginia, &c. were chearfully drank in the best of liquors. A large quantity of punch was given to the populace; and at each health there was a volley of small arms discharged, and three chearfull huzza's at each volley. A large bonfire was made in the evening, and the windows of the loyalists in town were illuminated. The ladies were entertained with dancing; and the evening concluded with the utmost demonstrations of loyalty, and all was conducted with decency and good order. There never was seen such a concourse of people at that place, on any occasion; and the hearty zeal and unaffected joy which appear'd in general, was sufficient to put the few (suppos'd to be) disaffected quite out of countenance.

September 11, 1746 (Pa)

This is to give notice, that for the entertainment of gentlemen and ladies, there will be balls and assemblies at the Capitol, every other night, during the court, by their humble servant, [signed] William Dering.

January 17, 1751 (Hu)

This is to give notice to all gentlemen and ladies, that on the 27th and the 29th instant, I intend to have an assembly at my dwelling-house, in Norfolk Town. Where all gentlemen and ladies, who will favour me with their good company, may depend on kind entertainment. Tickets to be had as usual, from their most humble servant, [signed] Edward Dial.

February 7, 1751 (Hu)

This is to give notice to all gentlemen and ladies, that on the 20th and the 22th instant, I intend to have an assembly at my dwelling-house, in Norfolk Town. Where all gentlemen and ladies, who will favour me with their good company, may depend on kind entertainment. Tickets to be had as usual, from their most humble servant, [signed] Edward Dial.

March 7, 1751 (Hu)

This is to give notice to all gentlemen and ladies, that on the 20th and the 22th instant, I intend to have an assembly at my dwelling-house, in Norfolk Town. Where all gentlemen and ladies, who will favour me with their good company, may depend on kind entertainment. Tickets to be had as usual, from their most humble servant, [signed] Edward Dial.

April 4, 1751 (Hu)

This is to give notice to all gentlemen and ladies, that on the 17th and the 20th instant, I intend to have an assembly at my dwelling-house, in Norfolk Town, where all gentlemen and ladies, who will favour me with their good company, may depend on kind entertainment. Tickets to be had as usual, from their most humble servant, [signed] Edward Dial.

April 11, 1751 (Hu)

On Tuesday the 23d instant, at the court house in Williamsburg, will be a ball for the entertainment of gentlemen and ladies. Tickets to be had of Mrs. Anne Shields, at her house in Williamsburg, at half a pistole each.

May 2, 1751 (Hu)

This is to give notice to all gentlemen and ladies, that on Thursday the 16th instant, I intend to have an assembly at my dwelling-house, in Norfolk Town, where all gentlemen and ladies, who will favour me with their good company, may depend on kind entertainment. Tickets to be had as usual, from their most humble servant, [signed] Edward Dial.

June 6, 1751 (Hu)

This is to give notice to all gentlemen and ladies, that on Thursday the 20th instant, I intend to have an assembly at my dwelling-house, in Norfolk Town, where all gentlemen and ladies, who will favour me with their good company, may depend on kind entertainment. Tickets to be had as usual, from their most humble servant, [signed] Edward Dial.

October 24, 1751 (Hu)

At the court-house in Williamsburg, on Thursday the 31st of October, I purpose to have a ball for my scholars: Such gentlemen and ladies who are pleased to favour me with their company, may have tickets at half a pistole each, at Mr. Finnie's, or from their most obedient humble servant, Richard Coventon.

N.B. The doors will be open at 6 o'clock.

February 27, 1752 (Hu)

Notice is hereby given to the ladies and gentlemen, that the subscriber purposes to have a ball, at the Apollo, in Williamsburg, once every week, during the sitting of the general assembly and court. [signed] Alexander Finnie.

March 5, 1752 (Hu)

For the ladies and gentlemen, there will be a ball, at Henry Wetherburn's, on Tuesday evening next, the 10th instant and on every Tuesday during the sitting of the general assembly.

Tickets half a pistole.

November 17, 1752 (Hu)

Friday last, being the anniversary of his majesty's birth-day, in the evening, the whole city was illuminated. There was a ball, and a very elegant entertainment, at the palace, where were present, the emperor and empress of the Cherokee nation, with their son the young Prince, and a brilliant appearance of ladies and gentlemen; several beautiful fireworks were exhibited in Palace

Street, by Mr. Hallam, manager of the theatre in this city, and the evening concluded with every demonstration of our zeal and loyalty.

June 13, 1755 (Hu)

Wednesday the 4th instant being the birth-day of his Royal Highness George Prince of Wales, his Honor the Governor gave a ball and entertainment at the palace, where was a splendid appearance of gentlemen and ladies, and the evening was concluded with the greatest demonstrations of mirth and loyalty.

June 6, 1766 (PD)

Norfolk, May 24. On the 13th instant the ship Peggy, Capt. Andrew, arrived from Glasgow, by whom we received the interesting and agreeable news that his majesty had been graciously pleased to give his royal assent to the bill for repealing the Stamp Act; upon which it was immediately and unanimously determined, by the gentlemen of this corporation, that Thursday the 22d should be devoted to decent rejoicings on that ever memorable event, that has so happily reconciled the differences subsisting between Great Britain and her colonies....

At sunset there was another discharge of the artillery, when the colours were struck; and general illuminations, bonfires, and various exhibitions of fireworks, took place, and great quantities of liquor were given to the populace: The evening concluded with a very elegant ball and entertainment, given at the house of Mr. Stephen Tanchard, at which was present a very numerous company of ladies and gentlemen, who made a brilliant appearance, and seemed to vie with each other in demonstrations of loyalty and joy on the happy occasion. The whole was conducted with the utmost regularity, dignity, and decorum.

June 20, 1766 (PD)

On Friday last, a good deal of company being in town at the Oyer and Terminer court, our gratitude and thankfulness upon the joyful occasion of the repeal of the Stamp Act, and the universal pleasure and satisfaction it gives that all differences between the Mother Country and her colonies are so happily terminated, was manifested here by general illuminations, and a ball and elegant entertainment at the Capitol, at which was present his honour the governour, many of the members of his majesty's council, and a large and genteel company of ladies and gentlemen, who spent the evening with much mirth and decorum, and drank all the loyal and patriotick toasts.

December 11, 1766 (Ri)

On the thirtieth of December 1766, will be a concert of musick in Fredericksburg, for the entertainment of all gentlemen and ladies, who will favour the subscriber with their company. Several of the best hands in Virginia will assist in the concert, which will be composed as follows, viz.

3 violins, 1 tenor, 1 bass, 2 fluits, 1 hautboy, 1 horn, 1 harpsichord.

The concert to begin precisely at six o'clock in the evening. A genteel supper, and liquor suitable for such an occasion, will be prepared. After supper, a ball, which will be free to all encouragers of the above scheme, as long as the ladies stay.

Tickets at 7s. 6d. which may be had at Port-Royal, Fredericksburg, Falmouth, and of the subscriber, [signed] John Schnieder.

December 24, 1767 (Ri)

On Tuesday the 29th of December will be performed, in the Town-house of Fredericksburg, a concert for the entertainment of all ladies and gentlemen who will favour the subscriber with their company. After the concert a ball, the expence of which will be defrayed by the subscriber, till the ladies depart.

Tickets at 7s6. [signed] John Schneyder.

March 17, 1768 (PD)

On Monday the 4th of April will be fought, at Sussex Court-house, a match of cocks, between the Brunswick and Sussex gentlemen; to show 30 cocks a side, for 5 l. a battle, and 50 l. the odd.

At night there will be a ball, for the reception of the ladies and gentlemen.

October 27, 1768 (Ri)

At the particular request of several ladies and gentlemen, on Wednesday the 16th of November next, will be performed in King-William court-house, a concert of instrumental musick, by gentlemen of note, for their own amusement. After the concert will be a ball, if agreeable to the company.

Tickets to be had, at five shillings each, of Mr. Holt Richeson, at King-William court-house; of Mr. Claiborne, at the ferry; at Mr. Pearson's store, in Newcastle; at Fleet's and Fraser's ferries; and at the new printing-office, in Williamsburg.

May 11, 1769 (Ri)

At the request of several ladies and gentlemen, on Friday the 19th instant, will be performed, at Mr. Thomas Tinsley's, in Hanover town, a concert of instrumental music; to consist of various instruments, by gentlemen of note, for their own amusement. It is requested by the ladies, that the company may be governed by a becoming silence and decorum, during the performance.

After the concert there will be a ball, if agreeable to the company. The music will begin precisely at 7 o'clock, before which time it is requested that all persons will be provided with tickets, as it will be inconvenient to receive money at the door.

Tickets to be had, at a dollar each, of Mr. Thomas Tinsley in Hanover-town, Mr. Lewis Jordan at Hanover court-house, and of Francis Albertie.

May 25, 1769 (PD)

Last Friday, being the Queen's birthday, the flag was displayed on the Capitol; and in the evening his Excellency the Governour gave a splendid ball and entertainment at the palace, to a very numerous and polite company of ladies and gentlemen.

October 26, 1769 (Ri)

Yesterday being the day appointed for celebrating the anniversary of his Majesty's birth day, his Excellency the Governor gave an elegant ball at the palace, where there was a numerous and very brilliant assembly of ladies and gentlemen.

December 28, 1769 (PD)

Last Tuesday his Excellency the Governour gave a ball and elegant entertainment at the palace to the gentlemen and ladies of this city.

April 19, 1770 (PD)

On Friday the Lady Mayoress will give a grand rout and a ball; afterwards there will be an elegant supper, at which many of the nobility are expected to be present.

June 7, 1770 (PD)

Monday last, the birthday of our most gracious sovereign, there was a grand ball and entertainment at the capitol, given by his Majesty's Council to his Excellency the Governour, the Hon, the Speaker and Gentlemen of the House of Burgesses, and the magistrates and other principal inhabitants of this city. The capitol was finely illuminated upon the occasion.

October 17, 1771 (Ri)

On Friday evening his Excellency the Governor gave a ball at the palace, in honour of our gracious sovereign, it being the anniversary of his accession to the throne. The company was numerous and brilliant, and the entertainment elegant.

The Raleigh tavern was likewise opened for the reception of those who did not chuse to attend at the palace. The city was handsomely illuminated, and plenty of liquor was given to the populace.

October 31, 1771 (PD)

Last Friday being the anniversary of our most gracious Sovereign's [missing] accession to the Throne, his Excellency the governour gave a ball and elegant entertainment at the palace, to a numerous and splendid company of ladies and gentlemen. The Raleigh Tavern likewise, by direction of his Excellency, was opened for the entertainment of such as might incline to spend the evening there; plenty of liquor was given to the populace; and the city handsomely illuminated.

November 7, 1771 (Ri)

At the Raleigh, on Wednesday next, being the 13th instant, will be performed, A Concert of Vocal and Instrumental Music:

The vocal parts by Miss Hallam, Miss Storer, and Mr. Woolls. With select pieces on the Musical Glasses, and Piano-Forte. To begin exactly at eight o'clock.

Tickets to be had at the bar of the Raleigh, and at the post office, at five shilings each. There will be music provided for such of the ladies and gentlemen as chuse to dance after the concert.

March 19, 1772 (PD)

Last night there was a ball and elegant entertainment at the Capitol, given by the gentlemen of the Honourable the House of Burgesses to his Excellency the Governour and the people of rank in this city.

May 19, 1774 (PD)

Norfolk, [Virginia] May 3. Yesterday was celebrated in this place the anniversary of St. Tamminy, the tutelar Saint of the American Colonies. At one o'clock a Royal salute of 21 guns, from a battery erected for the purpose, ushered in the rejoicings of the day; and in the evening a grand entertainment was given, at the Masons Hall, by the Sons of the Saint, to which there was a general invitation, and the company exceedingly numerous and brilliant, consisting of near 400 persons. At six the Ball was opened, by one of our worthy Burgesses, in the character of King Tamminy, properly accoutred in the ancient habit of this country, at which time another royal salute was given. The ladies, whose fair bosoms on this occasion seemed more particularly animated with a generous love of their country, indulged the company with their presence till four in the morning, and after their retirement, the Sons of St. Tamminy, according to the immemorial custom of these countries, encircled their King, and practised the ancient mysterious War Dance, so highly descriptive of the warmest attachment and freedom of spirit.

May 26, 1774 (PD)

This evening there is to be a Ball and entertainment at the Capitol, given by the Honourable the House of Burgesses to welcome Lady Dunmore and the rest of our Governour's family to Virginia.

May 26, 1774 (Ri)

A grand ball and entertainment is this evening to be given at the Capitol by the Burgesses, on account of the arrival of the Right Honourable the Countess of Dunmore and family.

Appendix III
Slaves and Servants Valued for Their Music or Dancing Skills

Listing of for sale, runaway, or missing slaves and servants valued for their music or dancing skills from Williamsburg and the surrounding area, as advertised in the *Virginia Gazette*. Some of the listed runaways only pretended to have musical skills in the hope of increasing their chances of escaping from their overseers.

January 11, 1737 (Pa)
On Sunday last, ran away from Col. Benjamin Harrison, in Charles City, a servant man, named Thomas Cellars, who was a servant of Mrs. Stagg's: He is a small man, of about five feet two inches high; his left eye quite out, by a blow from a horse; very much battle ham'd, and a long, flat foot, an Englishman by birth, plays very well on the violin, or fiddle, and is a great lover of strong drink: He has a wigg, a lightish Kersey. coat and waistcoat, blew cotten breeches, with silk puffs; a pair of gray worsted stockings, and Virginia common shoes. He went off in company with a little shoemaker, who ran away for debt, named Richard Hooper. Whoever will bring the said runaway to me, shall be handsomely rewarded, besides what the law directs.

May 19, 1738 (Pa)
Ran away from the subscriber, in Charles City County, on Wednesday the 9th of this instant, a servant man, named Thomas Sellers, who formerly belong'd to Mrs. Stagg: He is a small man, very battle-ham'd, a flat foot, and has but one eye; plays well on the fiddle, and is a great lover of strong drink: Had on when he went away, a light colour'd coat and waistcoat, and a pair of blue shagg breeches; he has also with him a small trotting bay horse, with a blaze in his face, branded thus, B H. He was seen the day after, going over Chickahominy long bridge, in New-Kent County. Whoever will take up the said runaway and carry him before some justice, that he may be dealt with

according to law, and conveyed to me, shall be handsomely rewarded, besides what the law allows. [signed] Benjamin Harrison.

September 26, 1745 (Pa)

Ran away from the subscriber, in Prince George county, on the 18th of this instant, an Irish servant man, named Thomas Hoy, aged about 31 years, of a middle stature, with a scar under one of his eyes, and some scars on his head; his little finger of his left hand has been broke, and is very crooked; he is very much given to strong drink, and lisps when he is in liquor; plays very well on the violin, and pretends to teach dancing: He took with him when he went away, a large gray gelding, branded on the near buttock CDG in a piece but not very plain, also a saddle and bridle, a light colour'd broad-cloth coat, two check shirts, a pair of books, one brown and one small black wig, and a pair of leather breeches patch'd between the thighs. Whoever secures the said servant, so that I may have him again, if above 10 miles from home, shall have ten pounds reward, if under, four pounds, paid by [signed] Tsh. Degraffenried.

July 4, 1751 (Hu)

Ran away from the subscriber, living in Hanover County, on the 10th day of June last, a convict servant man, named Hugh Dean, about 35 years of age, of a middle stature, very much pitted with the small-pox, has a roguish look, pretends to be a German, but is thought to be an Irishman; he plays well on the violin, is a great drunkard, says he was brought up a refiner of metals, a chymist, and a doctor; he pretends to understand all sorts of metals, and talks of several countries; he was seen on Rappahanock River the 18th of June, near Port-Royal. Therefore all masters of wealth are hereby forewarn'd from taking him on board. Had on when he went away, [illegible] jacket with brass buttons, a blue and white ditto, a brown linen shirt, leather breeches, shoes, and [illegible], a large felt hat, and his own long brown hair. Whoever will take up the said run-away, and deal with him according to law, so that I may have him again, shall have a pistole reward, besides what the law allows. [signed] Morgan Graven.

March 27, 1752 (Hu)

By the Honourable Robert Dinwiddie, Esq; ... Whereas Guy, a Negroe man slave, belonging to George Purcell, about two years ago being covicted of felony, in the county of Northumberland, broke the goal of the said county, and is fled from justice: The said Guy is of a yellow complexion, much like a Mulatto, about 5 feet 6 inches high, and is thought to be in the county of Frederick, and to pass for a Free-man by the name of Nicken, he plays on the violin. And whereas Dick, a Negroe man slave, belonging to William Hutchings, in the county of Lancaster, about five months ago ran away from his said master, and refuses to surrender himself although the process of outlawry hath issued against him, according as the law directs: and there is good reason to suspect, that the said Dick intends to escape out of this colony; he is about 5 feet 10 inches high, a strong active fellow, and can play on the fiddle.

There are therefore in his Majesty's name, to command and require all sheriffs, constables, and other his Majesty's liege people, within this colony, to make diligent search and pursuit, by way of hue and cry, within their several counties and precincts, after the said Guy and Dick; and them, or either of them having found, to apprehend and carry before the next justice of the peace, to be dealt with according to law: And I do desire the governors of the neighbouring colonies and provinces to be aiding and assisting in apprehending and bringing the said offenders to justice, hereby promising a reward of ten pounds, for apprehending the said Guy.

Given under my hand, and the seal of the colony, at Williamsburg, this thirteenth day of March, one thousand seven hundred and fifty two, in the twenty fifth year of the reign of our sovereign lord King George the second. [signed] Robert Dinwiddie.

July 3, 1752 (Hu)

Ran away from the subscriber in Lancaster County, a convict servant woman, named Sarah Knox, alias Howard, of middle size, a swarthy complexion and has a short nose, talks broad, and says she was born in Yorkshire, had been in the Army for several years with the camp in Flanders, and at the Battle of Culoden, where she lost her husband; she had on when she went away, a woman's black hat, an old red silk handkerchief round her neck, an old dirty blue stuff gown, with check linen cuffs, old stays, a black and white strip'd country cloth petticoat, an old blue quilted ditto, a check linen apron, and a brown linen shift. She may go by the name of Sarah Howard, Wilson, or something else, pretend to be a dancing mistress, will make a great many courtesies, is a very deceitful insinuating woman, and a great lyar. Whoever apprehends and conveys her to me shall have a pistole reward besides what the law allows, or if any person find her qualified to teach dancing, or to serve in any other way he may purchase between 5 and 6 years service of her at fifteen pounds currency, from [signed] David Currie.

August 21, 1752 (Hu)

Ran away from the subscriber, living in King & Queen County, on the 10th day of July last, a servant man, named Christopher Lewelin, about 21 or 22 years of age, of a middle stature, and somewhat pitted with the small-pox; has a sly look, pretends to be a fine singer, has a large scar on the out-side of his right legg, a great many letters and flowers mark'd on his arms in blue, with the letters C L on one of his hands, very dull: He is a blacksmith by trade, and was imported in the ship Rachael, Capt. Armstrong, in the year 1750. Whoever secures the said run-away, so that I may have him again, shall have two pistole reward if taken up in Virginia, and five pistols taken in any other province, paid by William Taliaferro.

October 20, 1752 (Hu)

Ran away from the subscriber, living in Fredericksburg, on the 27th day of July last, a servant man, named Thomas Gray; he is about 36 years of age, of a brown complexion, about 5 feet 10 inches high, a cabinet-maker and joiner by trade; had on when he went away an old hat, a grizled wig, a check'd shirt, a pair of light coloured fustian breeches, with flat metal buttons, black stockings, and old shoes without buckles; but 'tis suppos'd may have changed his dress; he is very talkative, much addicted to drinking, and plays well on the violin; was imported by indenture from London in the ship Rachel, Capt. Armstrong, this summer, and is supposed to have gone towards North-Caroline, having been seen lately at Richmond town on James River. Whoever apprehends and conveys him to me, shall have thirteen pistole reward, paid by James Ailan.

October 27, 1752 (Hu)

Ran away from the subscriber, on the 9th of this instant, a small short dark-skin'd Mulatto slave, about 43 years of age, endeavours to pass for a freeman, his cloathing was a cinnamon colour'd coat, much worn, an old cotton wastecoat, white linen long breeches, yarn stocking, English shoes, a half-worn wide-brimm'd hat, and a Virginia linen shirt: He can play on the violin, and pretends to understand making of tobacco very well. Whoever will apprehend and secure him, so that I may have him again, shall have a pistole reward, besides what the law allows, paid by [signed] James Cocke.

June 6, 1755 (Hu)

Ran away from the subscriber, living at Norfolk Glebe, on Tuesday the 14th of May last, a Negroe man, named Dick; he is a very likely fellow, about 24 years of age, speaks good English, plays on the violin, will endeavour to pass for a seaman, and freeman, being very cunning and artful; had on when he went away, an half-worn grey suit, a brown wig, a pair of large trousers, with shoes and stockings, and is supposed to have crossed the bay to the eastern shore. Whoever apprehends then secures him, so that I may have him again, shall have two pistoles reward, besides what the law allows. [signed] Charles Smith.

August 1, 1755 (Hu)

To be sold, at public sale, at the Royal-Exchange, in Norfolk, on Thursday, the 21st day of August next, the estate of Edward Dial, deceased, consisting of sundry pictures, household furniture, and wearing apparel: Also a valuable Negroe slave, about 28 years of age, belonging to the said estate; he is well qualified for a waiting man, and taking care of horses, &c. and plays well on the violin. All persons indebted to the said estate, to prevent costs, are desired to pay their respective debts to the subscriber, some time before the first day of September next. [signed] William young, administrator, with the will annexed.

March 28, 1766 (PD)

To be sold, a young healthy Negro fellow, who has been used to wait on a gentleman, and plays extremely well on the French horn. For further particulars apply to the printer.

April 4, 1766 (PD)

Run away from the subscriber in Hanover, about the middle of December last, a likely Negro man named Damon, about 5 feet 9 or 10 inches high, has a scar on his forehead and cheek, is a brisk lively fellow, speaks good English, was born in the West Indies, beats the drum tolerable well, which he is very fond of, and loves liquor; had on when he went away Negro cotton clothes, and an old hat bound round with linen. I expect he will get on board some vessel, as I understand he was seen in Yorktown. Whoever takes up the said Negro, and contrives him to me, shall have 3 £. reward. [signed] Sarah Gist.

N.B. The said Negro was formerly a sailor, has a smattering of the French language, and is outlawed.

May 7, 1767 (PD)

King William, April 29, 1767. Run away from the subscriber, on Monday the 20th of this instant, a mulatto slave, named David Gratenread; he is an arch fellow, very well known by most people, plays the fiddle extremely well, has a wide mouth, a little piece bit out of one of his ears, has a large bump upon on of his shins, about 37 years of age, 5 feet 6 or 7 inches high, and may perhaps change his name, and pretend to pass as a free man; he carried with him a new brown cloth waistcoat, lappelled, lined with white timiny, and yellow gilt buttons, a new pair of buckskin breeches, gold laced hat, a fine Holland shirt, brown cut wig, and several old clothes that I cannot remember, except an old lappelled kersey waistcoat. I believe he has carried his fiddle with him. He may endeavour to get onboard some vessel, and make his escape out of the colony; I therefore forewarn all masters of vessels, or others, from harbouring him. Whoever apprehends the said runaway, and brings him to me, or commits him to any gaol, so that I get him again, shall have five pounds reward if taken in this colony, if out therefore ten pounds. [signed] Richard King.

July 23, 1767 (PD)

To be sold, a valuable young handsome Negro fellow, about 18 or 20 years of age, has every qualification of a genteel and sensible servant, and has been in many different parts of the world. He shaves, dresses hair, and plays on the French horn. He lately came from London, and has with him two suits of new cloths, and his French horn, which the purchaser may have with him. Inquire at the Printing office of Mess. Purdie and Dixon.

August 4, 1768 (PD)

Ten pounds reward. Run away from the Occoquan furnace, in Prince William county, on the 14th instant, a country born Negro man named Billy, the property of the Hon. John Tayloe, Esq; he is a very well set fellow, about 5 feet 8 or 9 inches high, chews tobacco, can play on a violin, which he carried away with him, and is by trade a ship carpenter; had on and with him when he went away a black cotton velvet jacket, two white shirts, one pair of brown and a pair of check linen trousers, an old fine hat bound round the brim with black tape, two pair of shoes, and plated buckles. He was lately brought from Carolina, where, by virtue of a forged pass that some good natured person had wrote for him, he had travelled without much interruption, and very possibly may prevail on some other of his acquaintance to forge another, to assist him in prosecuting his intended scheme of getting to South Carolina, where he expects to be free. Whoever takes up the said slave, and brings him to the said furnace, shall receive a reward of 5 £. if taken in Virginia, and 10 £. if taken any where out of it. [signed] Thomas Lawson.

August 18, 1768 (PD)

Run away from the subscriber in Amelia, in the year 1766, a black Virginia born Negro fellow, named Sambo, about 6 feet high, about 32 years old, and bends in one of his knees, but which I cannot tell. He makes fiddles, and can play upon the fiddle, and work at the carpenters trade. I have heard that he passes for a free fellow. Whoever brings the said Negro to me shall have 10 £. reward. [signed] Mark Jackson.

November 3, 1768 (PD)

Run away from the subscriber in Halifax county, North Carolina, last April, a Virginia born Negro many named Ned, about 5 feet 9 or 10 inches high, has a high forehead, a bold look, has very good sense, talks good English, one of his under fore teeth out, and as for his clothing I cannot describe them. He is branded on the inside of his right thigh B, and has been branded on the left do. and left breast IL in a piece, though I am not sure they are plain, but the first is plain. He is a good sawer and hewer, and part of a carpenter, can play on the violin, and will endeavour to impose upon the public and pass for a freeman. As I understand he intends to leave the colony, I must therefore entreat all commanders of vessels, and others, that if such a person should offer his service they will have him secured and delivered to the subscriber, who will give 5 £. reward [signed] James Barnes.

December 22, 1768 (PD)

Just arrived, the Justitia, Captain Colin Somervell, with about 120 healthy servants, consisting of men, women, and boys, among which are many tradesmen, vix. Shoemakers, tailors, weavers, hatters, diers, carpenters, joiners, house painters, a tanner, a bookbinder, a stone mason, a good wheelwright, a tallow handler, farmers, and other country labourers. There are, I doubt not, other tradesmen; but not having yet examined the servants, I cannot now mention them. The sale will commence on Thursday the 19th of this instant (Dec.) at Leed's town, on Rappahannock. A reasonable credit will be allowed, on giving bond with approved security to [signed] Thomas Hodge.

N.B. There is one of the servants who plays well on the French horn, flute, and other instruments.

March 9, 1769 (PD)

Ten pounds reward. Run away from the subscriber's plantation, in Loudoun county, from James Whaley, overseer, on last Easter Monday, Tom, a Negro man slave, by some called Tom Salter, of a middle size, well made for strength, about 38 years old, has bad teeth, and many small pimples about his beard; he can read, and play on the fiddle, and had a variety of clothes, but his common working dress was died brown cotton. He managed several years as an overseer for me, under Capt. Robert Downman, at a plantation of mine on Morattico creek, in Richmond county, where he always lived until lately. He is a dissembling artful fellow, and generally smiles when he speaks. I suspect he is lurking about a plantation belonging to Charles Carter, Esq; in Hanover county, at or near South Wales, where he has a wife named Sebra, and perhaps at times about his old haunts at Morattico. Whoever will deliver him to me, in Prince William county, shall have the [illegible] reward; or if they will [illegible] him to any of his majesty's [illegible], so that I may get him [illegible] 5 £. and if he is taken out of the colony, and brought back to me, 10 £. paid by [signed] Henry Lee.

May 4, 1769 (PD)

Run away from the subscriber in Charles City county, the 14th of April last, a Virginia born Negro fellow named Peter, about 44 years of age, of a black complexion, a slim fellow, his teeth out before as if broke off, and is a sly artful rogue if not watched; he carried with him sundry clothes, such as crop Negroes usually wear, also a white Virginia cloth waistcoat and petticoat, a tarlton plaid gown, and sundry other of his wife's clothes. He also carried away a gun of an uncommon large size, and a fiddle, which he is much delighted in when he gets any strong drink, which he is remarkably fond of, and then very talkative and impudent. I suspect he is gone to Amelia county, to Mr. Tanner's, as Mrs. Tanner, alias Mrs. Johnson, sold him to Mr. Richard Hayles, and by him sold him to the subscriber, as he often told the other Negroes that if ever I used him ill he would go to his old mistress, as she never sold him to Mr. Hayles, but only lent him during pleasure, and that he would go to her and be protected. The said Negro is outlawed; and I will give 10 £. to any person or persons that will kill him and bring me his head, separate from his body, or 40 s. if delivered to the subscriber near the Long Bridge. [signed] William Gregory.

September 14, 1769 (Ri)

Wanted, to buy or to hire, an orderly Negro or Mulatto man, who can play well on the violin. Whoever has such a one may have good wages, or a good price, and ready money, if to be sold. Enquire of the printer, or apply to [signed] William Fearson.

October 19, 1769 (Ri)

To be sold, for ready money, a very valuable young Negro man, who understands cleaning of a house, and is well qualified to wait on a single gentleman, or a family, a very good gardener, and a tolerable good cook, butcher, and plaisterer, and in short very handy at any thing. He is also sober, very honest, and can play on the violin. Enquire of the printer hereof.

December 28, 1769 (PD)

Run away from the subscriber in Lancaster, a Virginia born Negro man named George, about 25 years old, about 5 feet 8 or 9 inches high, a middling black well made fellow, of a clear speech, plays on the fiddle, reads, can write a little, and is a very smart fellow. I imagine he has by some means got a pass. He was seen about the middle of November in Norfolk, and I suppose will make for Carolina. Whoever contrives him to me shall have 10 £. reward, if [missing], if out therefore 15 £. [signed] Richard Chilton.

May 14, 1772 (PD)

Prince George, May 6, 1772. Run away from the subscriber, a Negro man named Derby, about twenty five years of age, near six feet high, a slim black fellow, and plays on the fiddle with his left hand, which he took with him; he had on, when he went away, a Virginia cloth jacket, an osnabrug shirt, and a pair of blue broadcloth breeches. I have some reason to think he will make for Piersylvania, as his wife has been lately sent there to one of Mr. John Baird's quarters. Whoever brings him to me, or secures him so that I may get him again, shall have three pounds reward if he is taken within fifty miles, and eight pounds if above that distance. [signed] Robert Hunnicutt, Junior.

April 1, 1773 (PD)

Run away from Burwell's Ferry, about the 1st of February last, a Negro boy named Pompey, about eighteen years old, five feet three inches high, remarkably black, and proportionately made; he is a native of Africa, speaks English tolerably, stoops when he walks, and plays on the French horn. He had on a dark coloured duffil short coat, waistcoat, and breeches, and I have been informed he went on board a country craft up James River; he has been bred to the sea, and may probably endeavor to get on board a ship, and make his escape out of the colony. All masters of vessels are forewarned from harbouring or carrying him out of the colony, at their peril. I will give fifty shillings reward, with reasonable expenses, to any person who will deliver him to me at Portsmouth, or thirty shillings to secure him in any jail, and give me notice therefore. [signed] John Goodrich, Junior.

November 4, 1773 (PD)

Run away from the subscriber, the Negro boy so well known in this city by the name of Fiddler Billy, who is of a yellowish cast, smart and likely. He belongs to the estate of Edward Nicholson, deceased; and I hired him of Mr. Benjamin Weldon, the executor. Whoever delivers him to me shall have 20 s. reward, besides what the law allows; and I hereby forwarn all persons from harbouring him. [signed] William Fearson.

June 16, 1774 (PD)

Run away from the subscriber, about the 20th of April, a mulatto man named Peter Brown, by trade a painter, about 35 or 40 years of age, five feet eight or nine inches high, of a dark complexion, slim made, thin visage, has lost several of his upper fore teeth, is fond of singing and sings well, has several suit of clothes, therefore I cannot describe his dress. He was some years past tried for a robbery, and found guilty, but obtained the governour's pardon on suffering one year's imprisonment. After that time he was sold to Mr. John Fox of Gloucester, with whom he lived one or two years; he then ran away and passed for a freeman in the counties of King William, Caroline, and Hanover, where he was taken up and brought home. As he has a wife at Mr. Benjamin Hubbard's, it is likely he may be lurking in that neighbourhood, or near Petersburg, where he was raised. Whoever takes up the said runaway, and delivers him to me at Osborne's, shall have 40 s. reward. All persons are forbid from harbouring or carrying him out of the colony. [signed] Peterfield Trent.

August 18, 1774 (Ri)

Fredericksburg, August 9, 1774. A person of the name of William Foster Crosby having procured a recommendation to me, I lent him, the 19th of last month, my single chair and a mare to visit Captain John Lee, on Rappahannock, to whom he said he was recommended, to return in four days at the most; but not hearing of him since, except that he had mistaken his way, and got to Richmond, on James River, and colonel William Fleming from Cumberland county, I am obliged to take this method of recommending him to all honest men, as a profound knave. Such a flagrant act of injustice, accompanied with such ingratitude to me, will no doubt engage every gentleman to endeavor to strip him of the price of his villainy. But I will gladly pay forty shillings to have my mare and chair detained till I can send for them, or five pounds to be delivered here. As the knave is young, I had rather he should turn from his wickedness and live!

He is about twenty, of slim and genteel make, and fair complexion, rather pale and foul skin, black hair, very long and clubbed like a macaroni! He is exceeding vain, boasts much of his learning, particularly of geography, and professes teaching the classics, music, dancing, and fencing. He grins much when he laughs, which he often does at his own wit. His dress was shabby; I believe one only coat, formerly a pale blue, or [illegible] green, the cuffs of which have been lately let down, and the original colour makes a remarkable ring round his arm. He passed on my friend [illegible] from New England, and said he intended to visit Virginia, on his way to Charlestown, South Carolina, from New England, in order to see the country; expecting here some supplies he had ordered.

I cannot recollect whether the mare had any brand or flesh marks; she is about 14 hand and a half high, half blooded, well made, rather round, a chestnut bay, with a full long bob tail, and hog mane, very small feet, and shod before, trots very nimbly, and remarkably low. The carriage of the chair is new, the axletree hangs on iron springs, the body is painted green, with the [illegible] of my name on the back, in a double cypher, in blue letters, in a gilt ground; it has been new lined, and has now a carpet bottom, but suspect he will quit the chair for a saddle.

He borrowed a silver watch here, which, I presume, the owner will pay something to recover. [signed] James Mercer.

December 1, 1774 (PD)

Run away from the subscriber's plantation in Manakin Town, the last of July or first of August last, a black Negro man named Tom, formerly the property of Major Henry Gaines of King William, but since the said Gaine's death has been sold several times, and is now my property. He was bred by Major Gaines to keeping horses and riding races, but is now a good Sawyer. He is not tall, knock-kneed, full eyes, and I believe a speck in one of them, caused by a chip as he was cutting with an axe. He values himself for his fine dancing, is subject to liquor, and fond of talking about religion. If he is taken in the colony, and brought to me, near the old courthouse, in Albemarle County, or my overseer, James Scott, at Manakin Town, I will give 3 £. and if out of the colony 10 £. [signed] John Scott.

Appendix IV
Plays and Performances at the Williamsburg Theatres

Known plays, performances, and musical acts performed at the Williamsburg Theatres and the surrounding areas, as advertised in the *Virginia Gazette*.

September 10, 1736 (Pa)
This evening will be performed at the theatre, by the young gentlemen of the college, The Tragedy of Cato: And, on Monday, Wednesday, Friday next, will be acted the following comedies, by the gentlemen and ladies of this country, viz. The Busy-Body, The Recruiting-Officer, and The Beaux-Stratagem.

September 17, 1736 (Pa)
Williamsburg, Sept 17. Next Monday night will be perform'd, the Drummer; or the Haunted House, by the young gentlemen of the college.

April 21, 1738 (Pa)
Williamsburg, Apr 21. There lately arriv'd here, a man and his wife, and with them two children, who perform the agility of body, by various sorts of postures, tumbling, and sword dancing, to greater perfection than has been known in these parts for many years, if ever.

July 14, 1738 (Pa)
Williamsburg, Jul 14. We hear from Hampton, that on Thursday next, there is to be a tryal of skill, with back-swords, perform'd on a publick stage, by two gladiators, one an Englishman, the other a Barbadian. They both desire sharp swords, a clear stage, and no favour; and it's expected there will be abundance of company to see them perform.

September 26, 1751 (Hu)
By permission of his honour, the President, on Monday the 21st of October next, will be perform'd, at the new theatre, in Williamsburg; the tragical history

Plays and Performances at the Williamsburg Theatres   155

of King Richard the Third; to which will be added, a grand tragic dance; compos'd by Monsieur Denoier, call'd The Royal Captive, after the Turkish manner, as perform'd at his majesty's opera house, in the Hay-Market.

October 17, 1751 (Hu)

By permission of his honour the President, at the new theatre in Williamsburg, on Monday the 21st instant, will be presented a tragedy, called King Richard the Third: To which will be added, a grand tragic dance, compos'd by Monsieur Denoier, called The Royal Captive. After the Turkish manner, as perform'd at his majesty's opera house, in the Hay Market.
Boxes 7s. 6d. Pit 5s. 9d. Gallery 3s. 9d.
No person to be admitted behind the scenes.

November 14, 1751 (Hu)

By permission of his Honour the President, on Monday the 18th of November inst. will be perform'd, at Capt. Newton's great room in Norfolk, a comedy call'd, The Recruiting Officers. With entertainments as express'd in the bills.

April 17, 1752 (Hu)

By permission of his honour the governor, at the new theatre, in Williamsburg, for the benefit of Mrs. Beccely, on Friday, being the 24th of this instant will be performed, a comedy, called The Constant Couple: or A Trip to the Jubilee.
The part of Sir Harry Wildair to be perform'd by Mr. Kean. Colonel Standard, by Mr. Murray. And the part of Angelica to be perform'd by Mrs. Beccely. With entertainment of singing between the acts: Likewise a dance, called The Drunken Peasant. To which will be added, a farce, called The Lying Valet. Tickets to be had at Mrs. Vobe's, and at Mr. Mitchel's, in York.

April 30, 1752 (Hu)

The Company of Comedians, from the New Theatre at Williamsburg, propose playing at Hobbs's-Hole, from the 10th of May to the 24th; from thence they intend to proceed to Fredericksburg, to play during the continuance of June Fair. We therefore hope, that all gentlemen and ladies, who are lovers of theatrical entertainments, will favour us with their company.

August 21, 1752 (Hu)

We are desired to inform the publick, that as the Company of Comedians, lately from London, have obtain'd his honour the Governor's permission, and have, with great expence, entirely altered the play-house at Williamsburg to a regular theatre, fit for the reception of ladies and gentlemen, and the execution of their own performances, they intend to open on the first Friday in September next, with a play, call'd The Merchant of Venice, (written by Shakespear) and a farce, call'd The Anatomist, or, Sham Doctor.
The ladies are desired to give timely notice to Mr. Hallam, at Mr. Fisher's, for their places in the boxes, and on the day of performance to send their servants early to keep them, in order to prevent trouble and disappointment.

August 28, 1752 (Hu)

By permission of the Honble Robert Dinwiddie,, Esq; his Majesty's Lieutenant-Governor, and Commander in Chief of the colony and dominion of Virginia. By a Company of Comedians, from London, at the theatre in Williamsburg, on Friday next, being the 15th of September, will be presented, a play, call'd, The Merchant of Venice. (Written by Shakespear.)

The part of Antonio (The Merchant) to be perform'd by Mr. Clarkson. Gratiano, by Mr. Singleton, Lorenzo, (with songs in character) by Mr. Adcock. The part of Bassanio to be perform'd by Mr. Rigby. Duke, by Mr. Wynell. Salanio, by Mr. Herbert. The part of Launcelot, by Mr. Hallam. And the part of Shylock (the Jew) to be perform'd by Mr. Malone. The part of Nerissa, by Mrs. Adcock, Jessica, by Mrs. Rigby. And the part of Portia, to be perform'd by Mrs. Hallam. With a new occasional prologue, To which will be added, a farce, call'd The Anatomist: or, Sham Doctor. The part of Monsieur le Medicin, by Mr. Rigby. And the part of Beatrice, by Mrs. Adcock.

No person, whatsoever, to be admitted behind the scenes.

Boxes, 7s. 6d. Pit and balconies, 5s. 9d. Gallery, 3s. 9d.

To begin at six o'clock.

Vivat rex.

September 22, 1752 (Hu)

On Friday last the Company of Comedians from England, open'd the theatre in this city, when The Merchant of Venice, and the Anatomist, were perform'd, before a numerous and polite audience, with great applause; the following prologue, suitable to the occasion, was spoken by Mr. Rigby.

> PROLOGUE.
> O! for the tuneful voice of eloquence.
> Whose numbers flow with harmony and sense,
> That I may soar above the common wing,
> In lively strains the grateful subject sing;
> To celebrate the laurel'd poet's fame,
> And thro' the world the stage's use proclaim.
> To charm the fancy, and delight the soul,
> To deal instruction, without harsh controul,
> To cultivate (by pleasing arts) the mind,
> To win to reason, and with wit refin'd
> To check each error, and reform mankind.
> For this the bard, on Athen's infant stage,
> At first produc'd the drama's artful page;
> At once to please and satyrize he knew,
> And all his characters from nature drew;
> Without restriction then, as nature taught
> The player acted, and the poet wrote;
> The tragic muse did honour to the state,
> And in a mirrour taught them to be great;
> The comick too, by gentle means reprov'd,
> Lash'd every vice, and every vice remov'd.

For tho' the foible, or the crime she blam'd,
Smil'd on the man, and with a smile reclaim'd.
Thus was the Grecian stage, the Romans too,
When e'er they wrote, had virtue in their view;
In this politer age, on British ground,
The sprightly scenes, with wit and sense abound,
The brilliant stage with vast applause is crown'd,
And shouts of joy thro' the whole house resound;
Yet not content to bear so great a name,
The muse still labour'd to encrease her fame;
Summon'd her agents quickly to appear,
Haste, to Virginia's plains, my sons, repair,
The goddess said, go, confident to find
An audience sensible, polite and kind.
We heard and strait obey'd; from Britain's shore
These unknown chimes advent'ring to explore;
For us then, and our muse, thus low I bend,
Nor fear to find in each the warmest friend;
Each smiling aspect dissipates our fear,
We ne'er can fail of kind protection here;
The stage is ever wisdom's fav'rite care;
Accept our labours then, approve our pains,
Your smiles will please us equal to our gains;
And as you all esteem the darling muse,
The gen'rous plaudit you will not refuse.

November 17, 1752 (Hu)

The Emperor of the Cherokee nation with his Empress and their son, the young Prince, attended by several of his warriors and great men and their ladies, were received at the palace by his honour the governor, attended by such of the council as were in town and several other gentlemen, on Thursday the 9th instant, with all the marks of civility and friendship, and were that evening entertained, at the theatre, with the play, (the tragedy of Othello) and a pantomime performance, which gave them great surprize, as did the fighting with naked swords on the stage, which occasioned the Empress to order some about her to go and prevent their killing one another. The business of their coming is not yet made publick; but it is said to relate to the opening and establishing a trade with this colony, which they are very desirous of. They were dismissed with a handsome present of fine cloaths, arms, and amunition; and expressed great satisfaction in the governor's kind reception, and from several others; and left this place this morning.

September 5, 1755 (Hu)

To be seen and heard, at the Exchange Tavern, Norfolk, that elaborate and celebrated piece of mechanism, called The Microcosm: or, The World in Miniature.

Built in the form of a Roman temple, after 22 years close study and application, by the late ingenious Mr. Henry Bridges, of London; who, having received the approbation and applause of the Royal Society, &c, afterwards made considerable additions and improvements; so that the whole, being now completely finished; is humbly offered to the curious in this colony, as a performance which has been the admiration of every spectator, and proved itself by its singular perfections the most instructive as well as entertaining piece o' work in Europe, &c.

A piece of such complicated workmanship, that affords such a variety of representations, (tho' all upon the most simple principles) can but very imperfectly be described in words the best chosen; therefore it is desire, what little is said in the advertisement may not pass for an account of the Microcosm, but only what is thought merely necessary in the title of such an account, &c.

Its outward structure is a most beautiful composition of architecture, sculpture and painting. The inward contents are as judiciously adapted to gratify the ear, the eye, and the understanding; for it plays with great exactness several fine pieces of musick, and exhibits, by an amazing variety of moving figures, scenes diversified with natural beauties, operations of art, of human employments and diversions, all passing as in real life, &c.

The first shews all the celestial phaenomena, with just regard to the proportionable magnitudes of their bodies, the figures of their orbits, and the periods of their revolutions, with the doctrine of Jupiter's satellites, of eclipses, and of the Earth's annual and diurnal motions, which are all rendered familiarly intelligible. In particular will be seen the trajectory and type of a comet, predicted by Sir Isaac Newton, to appear the beginning of 1758; likewise a transit of Venus over the sun's disk, the 6th of June 1761, also a large and visible eclipse of the sun, the 1st of April 1764, &c.

Secondly, are the nine muses playing in concert on divers musical instruments, as the harp, hautboy, bass viol, &c.

Thirdly, is Orpheus in the forest, playing on his lyre, and beating exact time to each tune; who, by his exquisite harmony, charms even the wild beasts.

Fourthly, is a carpenter's yard wherein the various branches of that trade are most naturally represented, &c.

Fifthly, is a delightful grove, wherein are birds flying, and in many other motions warbling forth their melodious notes, &c.

Sixthly, is a fine landslip, with a propect of the sea, where ships are failing with a proportionable motion according to their distance. On the land are coaches, carts, and chaises passing along, with their wheels turning round as if actually on the road, and altering their positions as they ascend and descend a steep hill; and nearer, on a river, is a gunpowder mill at work. On the same river are swans swimming, fishing and bending their necks backwards, to feather themselves; as also the sporting of the dog and duck, &c.

Seventhly and lastly, is shewn, the whole machine in motion at one view, when upwards of twelve hundred wheels and pinnions are in motion at once; and during the whole performance it plays several fine pieces of music, on the organ and other instruments, both single and in concert, in a very elegant manner, &c.

As this machine cannot be moved without a considerable expense and loss of time, 'tis hoped gentlemen and ladies will be as expeditious as convenient, for it will be shewn in this town positively no longer than the 13th of September, being obliged to be in Philadelphia, at a determined time, (if possible) and the price not lowered, as is generally expected in common shews, which was sufficiently experienced in the West-Indies, to the great disappointment of many.

To begin exactly at seven o'clock every Monday, Wednesday, and Saturday. Tickets to be had at the above place at a crown each; and tickets for children, under ten years of age, at half a crown, tho' a price quite inferior to the great expence and merits of this machine.

N.B. Any select company (not less than five) that may be desirous of seeing this piece, by day light, shall be obliged by sending half an hour's notice, and 7s. 6d. each, which entitles them to see the internal parts of this machine in motion, so worthy the notice of the curious, and upon what principle the whole is performed, &c.

January 8, 1767 (PD)

The celebrated Lecture upon Heads, so much admired and applauded by all who have heard it performed, will be delivered, on Monday and Tuesday next, at 6 o'clock in the evening, in the Great Room of the Rawleigh tavern, by Mr. William Verling, who is just arrived in this city. He does not intend to exhibit but these two nights.

March 31, 1768 (PD)

By permission of the worshipful the mayor of Williamsburg, at the old theatre, near the capital, by the Virginia Company of Comedians, on Monday the 4th of April will be presented a tragedy, called Douglas.

Lord Randolph, by Mr. Bromadge. Glenalvon, Mr. Goodwin. Norval, Douglas, Mr. Verling. Old Norval, Mr. Parker. Officer, Mr. Walker. Lady Randolph, by Mrs. Osborne. Anna, Mrs. Parker. An occasional prologue by Mr. Verling, and after the play a dance by Mr. Godwin. To which will be added a farce, called The Honest Yorkshireman. Sir Penurious Muckworm, by Mr. Bromadge. Gaylove, Mr. Verling. Sapscull, Mr. Parker. Slango, Mr. Godwin. Blunder, Mr. Walker. Arabella, by Mrs. Osborne. Combrush, Mrs. Parker.

Tickets to be had of Mr. William Russell, at his store next door to the post office, and at the door of the theatre.

Boxes 7s. 6d. Pit 5s. Gallery 3s 9d.

Vivant rex & regina.

N.B. No person whatever can be admitted behind the scenes.

(On Wednesday The Drummer, with Miss in Her Teens.)

April 7, 1768 (PD)

By permission of the worshipful the mayor of Williamsburg, at the old theatre, near the capital, by the Virginia Company of Comedians, on Friday the 8th of April will be presented a tragedy, called Venice Preserved, or A Plot Discovered.

Duke, by Mr. Charlton. Priuli, Mr. Bromadge. Jaffeir, Mr. Godwin. Pierre, Mr. Verling. Redamar, Mr. Bromadge. Renault, Mr. Parker. Eliot, Mr. Walker.

Belvidera, by Mrs. Osborne. To which will be added a ballad opera, called Damon and Phillida. Arcas, by Mr. Bromadge. Corydon, Mr. Godwin. Damon, Mr. Osborne. Cymon, Mr. Parker. Mopsus, Mr. Verling. Phillida, by Mrs. Parker.

Tickets to be had of Mr. William Russell, at his store next door to the post office, and at the door of the theatre. The doors to be opened at six, and the play to begin at seven o'clock precisely.

Boxes 7s. 6d. Pit 5s. Gallery 3s 9d.

Vivant rex & regina.

N.B. No person whatever can be admitted behind the scenes.

April 14, 1768 (PD)

By permission of the worshipful the mayor of Williamsburg, at the old theatre, near the capitol, by the Virginia Company of Comedians, on Friday, being the 15th instant, will be performed a tragedy, called The Orphan, or the Unhappy Marriage.

Acasto, Mr. Bromadge. Castalio, Mr. Verling. Polydore, Mr. Parker. Chamont, Mr. Godwin. Chaplain, Mr. Charlton. Ernesto, Mr. Walker. Page, Miss Dowthaitt. Monimia, Mrs. Osborne. Serina, Mrs. Parker. Maid, Mrs. Dowthaitt. After the play, a new comic dance, call'd The Bedlamites. Bedlamite, Mr. Godwin. Mad Doctor, Mr. Charlton. Simon, Mr. Walker. To which will be added, (the second night) a pantomime entertainment, in which will be introduced a new scene not before presented, called, Harlequin Skeleton, or The Burgomaster Trick'd. Harlequin, by Mr. Godwin. Pantaloon, Mr. Verling. Conjurer, Mr. Bromadge. Merchant, Mr. Walker. Frenchman, Mr. Charlton. Clown, Mr. Parker. Scaramouch, Mr. Walker. Columbine, by Mrs. Parker.

Tickets to be had of Mr. William Russell, at his store, next door to the post-office, and at the door of the theatre.

Boxes 7s6. pit 5s. gallery 3s9.

N.B. No person whatever can be admitted behind the scenes.

May 12, 1768 (PD)

By permission of the worshipful the mayor of Williamsburg (for the benefit of Mrs. Osborne) at the old theatre near the capitol, on Wednesday next, being the 18th instant, will be presented a comedy, called The Constant Couple or A Trip to the Jubilee.

Sir Harry Wildair by Mrs. Osborne, Colonel Standard by Mr. Charlton, Vizzard by Mr. Bromadge, Alderman Smuggler by Mr. Parker, Beau Clincher by Mr. Vering, Clincher, Junior by Mr. Godwin, Dicky by Mr. Farrell, Tom Errand by Mr. Walker. Lady Darling by Mrs. Dowthaitt. Angelica by Miss Dowthaitt. Parley by Miss Yapp, Lady Lurewell, by Mrs. Parker. Between the 1st and 2d acts a prologue, in the character of a country boy, spoken by Mr. Parker. After the second act a dance, called The Coopers, by Mr. Godwin, Mess. Bromadge, Walker, &c. After the 3d act a cantata, sung by Mr. Parker. And in the 5th act a minuet, by Miss Yapp and Mrs. Osborne, in the character of Sir Harry Wildair. After the play a hornpipe, by Mr. Godwin. To which will be added a farce, called The Miller of Mansfield. King by Mr. Verling, Miller by Mr. Parker,

Lord Lurewell by Mr. Godwin, Dick by Mr. Bromadge, First Courtier by Mrs. Osborne, Second Courtier by Mr. Charlton. Joe by Mr. Farrell. Madge by Mrs. Dowthaitt, Kate by Miss Dowthaitt, Peggy, Mrs. Parker. Keepers, Mess. Walker, Farrell, &c.

Tickets to be had of Mrs. Osborne, at Mrs. Rathell's store, and at the door of the theatre. To being at 7 o'clock.

Boxes 7s 6d. pit 5s. gallery 3s 9d.

May 19, 1768 (PD)

By permission of the worshipful the mayor of Williamsburg (for the benefit of Mr. Bromadge) at the old theatre near the capitol, tomorrow evening, being the 20th instant, will be presented a tragedy, called The Gamester. After the play a new dance called The Cowkeepers, by Mess. Godwin, Walker, and Farrell. To which will be added a farce, called Polly Honeycomb.

Tickets to be had of Mr. Bromadge, at Mrs. Ratbell's store, and at the door of the theatre. To begin at 7 o'clock.

Boxes 7s.6d. Pit 5s. Gallery 3s. 9d.

Vivant rex & regina.

For the benefit of Mr. Parker. On Wednesday the 25th instant will be presented the historical tragedy of Henry the Fourth. With a new farce, never performed here, called The Old Maid.

Tickets to be had at the post office, and of Mr. Parker, at his lodgings near Mrs. Vobe's tavern. For the benefit of Miss Yapp, Friday the 27th instant will be presented a comedy, written by Shakespeare, called The Merchant of Venice.

Shylock the Jew, by Mr. Verling. Portia, by Mrs. Osborne.

To which will be added a comedy of two acts, never performed here, called High Life Below Stairs. With entertainments of dancing and singing, which will be expressed in the bills of the day.

Tickets to be had at the post office, and of Miss Yapp, at her lodgings near Mrs. Vobe's tavern.

May 26, 1768 (PD)

For the benefit of Mrs. Parker. On Friday the 3d of June next will be presented The Beggar's Opera.

The part of Captain Macheath by Mr. Verling, being his first appearance in that character; and the part of Miss Polly Peachum by Mrs. Parker.

After the opera a dance, called The Drunken Peasant, by Mr. Godwin. To which will be added a farce, called The Anatomist, or Sham Doctor. The musick of the opera to be conducted by Mr. Pelham, and others.

Tickets to be had at the post office, Mr. Rind's, Mrs. Ratbell's, Mr. Hay's, Mr. Charlton's, and of Mrs. Parker.

April 20, 1769 (PD)

By permission of his Excellency the Governour. For the entertainment of the curious, on Thursday the 27th of this instant (April) will be exhibited, at the theatre in Williamsburg, by Peter Gardiner, a curious set of figures, richly dressed, four feet high, which shall appear upon the stage as if alive; to which will be added a curious View of Water Works, representing the Sea, with all manner of Sea Monsters sporting upon the waves. Likewise will be presented a set of fireworks, together with the taking of the Havannah, with ships, forts, and batteries, continually firing, until victory crowns the conquest; To which will be added, a curious Field of Battle, containing the Dutch, French, Prussian, and English forces, which shall regularly march and perform the different exercises to great perfection. Likewise will he presented a comedy called Whittington and his Cat, the surprising art of legerdemain, &c. &c. &c. as will be expressed in the bills on that day.

May 4, 1769 (PD)

We hear a noted clergyman and poet is preparing an entertainment for the theatre, entitled Liberty's Last Stake, but whether it be tragedy or comedy is yet uncertain.

June 14, 1770 (PD)

Yesterday Mr. Douglass, with his Company of Comedians, arrived in town from Philadelphia; and; we hear, intend opening the theatre in this city, on Saturday, with the Beggar's Opera, and other entertainments.

April 25, 1771 (PD)

At the theatre to-morrow evening, The Tender Husband, with The Honest Yorkshireman.

May 16, 1771 (PD)

The American Company of Comedians will open the theatre in Fredericksburg the latter end of this month, and perform every Tuesday, Wednesday, and Thursday, during their residence there.

October 17, 1771 (PD)

On Wednesday next the theatre in this city will be opened with the comedy of The West Indian, and The Musical Lady. A prologue and epilogue will be likewise spoken.

November 7, 1771 (PD)

At the theatre, on Tuesday next being the 12 instant, a tragedy (never performed in Virginia) called King Lear; with a farce, that will be expressed in the bill.

December 19, 1771 (PD)

On Saturday evening, at the Theatre, The Jealous Wife, and The Padlock.

January 2, 1772 (PD)

Next week the theatre in Norfolk will be opened by the American Company of Comedians, where they are to remain but a short while, as they intend for this place again by the meeting of the General Assembly, and to perform till the end of the April court. They then proceed to the northward, by engagement, where it is probable they will continue some years.

March 12, 1772 (PD)

We hear that a new comedy, called The Brothers, written by Mr. Cumberland, author of the much approved West Indian, is now in rehearsal, and will soon make its appearance on our theatre; also that False Delicacy, and A Word to the Wise, the productions of the ingenious Mr. Hugh Kelly, whose spirited letter to the Lord Mayor (Beckford) has been read by most people, are in great forewardness.

April 2, 1772 (PD)

Mr. Kelly's new comedy of A Word to the Wise was performed at our theatre last Thursday, for the first time, and repeated on Tuesday to a very crowded and splendid audience. It was received both nights with the warmest marks of approbation; the sentiments with which this excellent piece is replete were greatly, and deservedly applauded; and the audience, while they did justice to the merit of the author, did no less honour to their own refined taste. If the comick writers would pursue Mr. Kelly's plan, and present us only with moral plays, the stage would become (what it ought to be) a school of politeness and virtue. Truth, indeed, obliges us to confess, that, for several years past, most of the new plays that have come under our observation have had a moral tendency, but there is not enough of them to supply the theatre with a variety of exhibitions sufficient to engage the attention of the publick; and the most desirable entertainments, by too frequent a repetition, become insipid.

April 9, 1772 (PD)

On Tuesday next, being the 14th instant, a new comedy, called False Delicacy, by the author of A Word to the Wise.

It may not be improper to give notice that the theatre in Williamsburg will be closed at the end of the April Court, the American Company's engagements calling them to the northward, from whence, it is probable, they will not return for several years.

April 23, 1772 (PD)

On Tuesday next, being the 28th instant, a comedy, (never performed there) written by Arthur Murphey, Esquire, called The Way to Keep Him. To which will be added, The Oracle.

Singing by Mrs. Stamper.

It may not be improper to give notice that the theatre in Williamsburg will be closed at the end of the April Court, the American Company's engagements calling them to the northward, from whence, it is probable, they will not return for several years.

May 7, 1772 (PD)

We are authorised to inform the publick that the new comedy of The Fashionable Lover, now acting at the Theatres Royal in Drury Lane and Edinburgh, with the utmost applause, will shortly appear on our theatre. Such is the industry of the American Company, that, though the piece has not been above ten days in the country, it has been rehearsed more than once, and is already, we hear, fit for representation.

November 19, 1772 (RI)

By authority. At the theatre in Williamsburg, on Monday the 23d of this instant (November) will be exhibited, by Mr. Gardiner, a curious set of figures, richly dressed, four feet high; they are to appear on the stage as if alive, and will perform a tragic performance, called Bateman and his Ghost.

Likewise a set of waterworks, representing the sea, and all manner of sea monsters sporting on the waves. With the taking of the Havannah, with ships, forts, and batteries, continually firing, until victory crowns the British forces; with the appearance of the two armies. To which will be added, a magnificent piece of machinery, called Cupid's Paradise, representing seventy odd pillars and columns, with the appearance of Neptune and Amphritrite, and music suitable thereto.

The whole to conclude with a magnificent set of fireworks, such as caterine wheels, Italian candles, sea fountains, and sun flowers with the appearance of the sun and moon in their full lustre.

Mr. Gardiner will extend himself between two chairs, and suffer any of the company to break a stone of two hundred weight on his bare breast.

Ticket to be had at the theatre, which are 3s9. for the box, pit 2s6, and gallery 1s3. The performance to begin at 6 o'clock.

Vivant Rex & Regina.

No person can be admitted behind the scene.

N.B. Between the acts will be instrumental music, consisting of French horns and trumpets.

Appendix V
Articles of Association,
October 20, 1774

The Articles of Association were passed by the First Continental Congress on October 20, 1774 (courtesy National Archives).

We, his majesty's most loyal subjects, the delegates of the several colonies of New-Hampshire, Massachusetts-Bay, Rhode-Island, Connecticut, New-York, New-Jersey, Pennsylvania, the three lower counties of Newcastle, Kent and Sussex on Delaware, Maryland, Virginia, North-Carolina, and South-Carolina, deputed to represent them in a continental Congress, held in the city of Philadelphia, on the 5th day of September, 1774, avowing our allegiance to his majesty, our affection and regard for our fellow-subjects in Great-Britain and elsewhere, affected with the deepest anxiety, and most alarming apprehensions, at those grievances and distresses, with which his Majesty's American subjects are oppressed; and having taken under our most serious deliberation, the state of the whole continent, find, that the present unhappy situation of our affairs is occasioned by a ruinous system of colony administration, adopted by the British ministry about the year 1763, evidently calculated for enslaving these colonies, and, with them, the British Empire. In prosecution of which system, various acts of parliament have been passed, for raising a revenue in America, for depriving the American subjects, in many instances, of the constitutional trial by jury, exposing their lives to danger, by directing a new and illegal trial beyond the seas, for crimes alleged to have been committed in America: And in prosecution of the same system, several late, cruel, and oppressive acts have been passed, respecting the town of Boston and the Massachusetts-Bay, and also an act for extending the province of Quebec, so as to border on the western frontiers of these colonies, establishing an arbitrary government therein, and discouraging the settlement of British subjects in that wide extended country; thus, by the influence of civil principles and ancient prejudices, to dispose the inhabitants to act with hostility against the free Protestant colonies, whenever a wicked ministry shall chuse so to direct them.

Appendix V

To obtain redress of these grievances, which threaten destruction to the lives liberty, and property of his majesty's subjects, in North-America, we are of opinion, that a non-importation, non-consumption, and non-exportation agreement, faithfully adhered to, will prove the most speedy, effectual, and peaceable measure: And, therefore, we do, for ourselves, and the inhabitants of the several colonies, whom we represent, firmly agree and associate, under the sacred ties of virtue, honour and love of our country, as follows:

1. That from and after the first day of December next, we will not import, into British America, from Great-Britain or Ireland, any goods, wares, or merchandise whatsoever, or from any other place, any such goods, wares, or merchandise, as shall have been exported from Great-Britain or Ireland; nor will we, after that day, import any East-India tea from any part of the world; nor any molasses, syrups, paneles, coffee, or pimento, from the British plantations or from Dominica; nor wines from Madeira, or the Western Islands; nor foreign indigo.

2. We will neither import nor purchase, any slave imported after the first day of December next; after which time, we will wholly discontinue the slave trade, and will neither be concerned in it ourselves, nor will we hire our vessels, nor sell our commodities or manufactures to those who are concerned in it.

3. As a non-consumption agreement, strictly adhered to, will be an effectual security for the observation of the non-importation, we, as above, solemnly agree and associate, that from this day, we will not purchase or use any tea, imported on account of the East-India company, or any on which a duty bath been or shall be paid; and from and after the first day of March next, we will not purchase or use any East-India tea whatever; nor will we, nor shall any person for or under us, purchase or use any of those goods, wares, or merchandise, we have agreed not to import, which we shall know, or have cause to suspect, were imported after the first day of December, except such as come under the rules and directions of the tenth article hereafter mentioned.

4. The earnest desire we have not to injure our fellow-subjects in Great-Britain, Ireland, or the West-Indies, induces us to suspend a non-exportation, until the tenth day of September, 1775; at which time, if the said acts and parts of acts of the British parliament herein after mentioned, ate not repealed, we will not directly or indirectly, export any merchandise or commodity whatsoever to Great-Britain, Ireland, or the West-Indies, except rice to Europe.

5. Such as are merchants, and use the British and Irish trade, will give orders, as soon as possible, to their factors, agents and correspondents, in Great-Britain and Ireland, not to ship any goods to them, on any pretence whatsoever, as they cannot be received in America; and if any merchant, residing in Great-Britain or Ireland, shall directly or indirectly ship any goods, wares or merchandize, for America, in order to break the said non-importation agreement, or in any manner contravene the same, on such unworthy conduct being well attested, it ought to be made public; and, on the same being so done, we will not, from thenceforth, have any commercial connexion with such merchant.

The Articles of Association, October 20, 1774

6. That such as are owners of vessels will give positive orders to their captains, or masters, not to receive on board their vessels any goods prohibited by the said non-importation agreement, on pain of immediate dismission from their service.

7. We will use our utmost endeavours to improve the breed of sheep, and increase their number to the greatest extent; and to that end, we will kill them as seldom as may be, especially those of the most profitable kind; nor will we export any to the West-Indies or elsewhere; and those of us, who are or may become overstocked with, or can conveniently spare any sheep, will dispose of them to our neighbours, especially to the poorer sort, on moderate terms.

8. We will, in our several stations, encourage frugality, economy, and industry, and promote agriculture, arts and the manufactures of this country, especially that of wool; and will discountenance and discourage every species of extravagance and dissipation, especially all horse-racing, and all kinds of games, cock fighting, exhibitions of shews, plays, and other expensive diversions and entertainments; and on the death of any relation or friend, none of us, or any of our families will go into any further mourning-dress, than a black crepe or ribbon on the arm or hat, for gentlemen, and a black ribbon and necklace for ladies, and we will discontinue the giving of gloves and scarves at funerals.

9. Such as are venders of goods or merchandize will not take advantage of the scarcity of goods, that may be occasioned by this association, but will sell the same at the rates we have been respectively accustomed to do, for twelve months last past. -And if any vender of goods or merchandise shall sell such goods on higher terms, or shall, in any manner, or by any device whatsoever, violate or depart from this agreement, no person ought, nor will any of us deal with any such person, or his or her factor or agent, at any time thereafter, for any commodity whatever.

10. In case any merchant, trader, or other person, shall import any goods or merchandize, after the first day of December, and before the first day of February next, the same ought forthwith, at the election of the owner, to be either re-shipped or delivered up to the committee of the country or town, wherein they shall be imported, to be stored at the risque of the importer, until the non-importation agreement shall cease, or be sold under the direction of the committee aforesaid; and in the last-mentioned case, the owner or owners of such goods shall be reimbursed out of the sales, the first cost and charges, the profit, if any, to be applied towards relieving and employing such poor inhabitants of the town of Boston, as are immediate sufferers by the Boston port-bill; and a particular account of all goods so returned, stored, or sold, to be inserted in the public papers; and if any goods or merchandizes shall be imported after the said first day of February, the same ought forthwith to be sent back again, without breaking any of the packages thereof.

11. That a committee be chosen in every county, city, and town, by those who are qualified to vote for representatives in the legislature, whose business it shall be attentively to observe the conduct of all persons touching this association; and when it shall be made to appear, to the satisfaction of a majority of any such committee, that any person within the limits of their appointment

has violated this association, that such majority do forthwith cause the truth of the case to be published in the gazette; to the end, that all such foes to the rights of British-America may be publicly known, and universally contemned as the enemies of American liberty; and thenceforth we respectively will break off all dealings with him or her.

12. That the committee of correspondence, in the respective colonies, do frequently inspect the entries of their customhouses, and inform each other, from time to time, of the true state thereof, and of every other material circumstance that may occur relative to this association.

13. That all manufactures of this country be sold at reasonable prices, so-that no undue advantage be taken of a future scarcity of goods.

14. And we do further agree and resolve that we will have no trade, commerce, dealings or intercourse whatsoever, with any colony or province, in North-America, which shall not accede to, or which shall hereafter violate this association, but will hold them as unworthy of the rights of freemen, and as inimical to the liberties of their country.

And we do solemnly bind ourselves and our constituents, under the ties aforesaid, to adhere to this association, until such parts of the several acts of parliament passed since the close of the last war, as impose or continue duties on tea, wine, molasses, syrups paneles, coffee, sugar, pimento, indigo, foreign paper, glass, and painters' colours, imported into America, and extend the powers of the admiralty courts beyond their ancient limits, deprive the American subject of trial by jury, authorize the judge's certificate to indemnify the prosecutor from damages, that he might otherwise be liable to from a trial by his peers, require oppressive security from a claimant of ships or goods seized, before he shall be allowed to defend his property, are repealed.-And until that part of the act of the 12 G. 3. ch. 24, entitled "An act for the better securing his majesty's dock-yards magazines, ships, ammunition, and stores," by which any persons charged with committing any of the offenses therein described, in America, may be tried in any shire or county within the realm, is repealed- and until the four acts, passed the last session of parliament, viz. that for stopping the port and blocking up the harbour of Boston-that for altering the charter and government of the Massachusetts-Bay-and that which is entitled "An act for the better administration of justice, &c."-and that "for extending the limits of Quebec, &c." are repealed. And we recommend it to the provincial conventions, and to the committees in the respective colonies, to establish such farther regulations as they may think proper, for carrying into execution this association.

The foregoing association being determined upon by the Congress, was ordered to be subscribed by the several members thereof; and thereupon, we have hereunto set our respective names accordingly.

IN CONGRESS, PHILADELPHIA, October 20, 1774.

Signed, PEYTON RANDOLPH, President.

Chapter Notes

Chapter 1

1. *Virginia Gazette*, 22 October 1767 (PD). As the *Gazette* had multiple publishers, often simultaneously, they are identified as follows: Pa=Parks, Hu=Hunter, Ro=Royle, PD=Purdie and Dixon, Ri=Rind, Pi=Pinkney, DH=Dixon and Hunter.
2. "Diary of Col. Landon Carter," *William and Mary Quarterly* vol. 13, no. 3 (Jan. 1905): 159.
3. *Virginia Gazette*, 24 January 1752 (Hu).
4. Richard L. Bushman, *The Refinement of America: Persons, Houses, Cities* (New York: Alfred A. Knopf, 1992), 153.
5. Carl Bridenbaugh, *Seat of Empire: The Political Role of Eighteenth-Century Williamsburg* (Williamsburg: Colonial Williamsburg, 1958), 30.
6. Hugh F. Rankin, *The Theater in Colonial America* (Chapel Hill: University of North Carolina Press, 1965), 143.
7. *Travels Through the Middle Settlements in North America in the Years 1759 and 1760; With Observations Upon the State of the Colonies by the Rev. Andrew Burnaby, Archdeacon of Leicester and Vicar of Greenwich* (London: Printed for T. Payne, at the Mews-Gate, 1798), 5–6.
8. Ibid.
9. Hugh Jones, *The Present State of Virginia* (New York: Reprinted for Joseph Sabin, 1865. Originally published 1724), 31.
10. *Virginia Gazette*, 11 September 1746 (Pa).
11. Mary Newton Stanard, *Colonial Virginia: Its People and Customs* (Philadelphia: J.B. Lippincott Company, 1917), 241.
12. *Virginia Gazette*, 5 September 1755 (Hu).
13. *Ibid.*, 17 November 1752 (Hu). See also Rankin, *Theater*, 57.
14. Helen Cripe, *Thomas Jefferson and Music* (Chapel Hill: University of North Carolina Press, 2009), 14, 44.
15. Ronald L. Davis, *A History of Music in American Life, vol. 1: The Formative Years, 1620–1865* (Malabar, FL: Robert Krieger Publishing Company, 1982), 47.
16. Daniel Mendoza de Arce, *Music in North America and the West Indies from the Discovery to 1850* (Lanham, MD: Scarecrow Press, 2006), 134–35.
17. "Order in Council restoring William Byrd Esq. to the Council of Virginia," *Calendar of Virginia State Papers* vol. 1: 194–95.
18. Louis B. Wright and Marion Tinling, eds., *William Byrd of Virginia, The London Diary (1717–1721) and Other Writings* (New York: Oxford University Press, 1958), 400.
19. Louis B. Wright, *The Cultural Life of the American Colonies 1607–1763* (New York: Harper & Row, 1957), 188.
20. William C. Ewing, *The Sports of Colonial Williamsburg* (Richmond: The Dietz Press, 1937), 11–13.
21. *Virginia Gazette*, 5 November 1736 (Pa).
22. *Ibid.*, 13 June 1755 (Hu).
23. *Ibid.*, 14 November 1755 (Hu).
24. *Ibid.*, 6 June 1766 (PD).
25. *Ibid.*, 25 October 1765 (Ro).
26. *Ibid.*, 26 September 1766 (PD).
27. *Ibid.*, 20 June 1766 (PD).
28. *Ibid.*, 23 May 1766 (PD).

29. *Ibid.*, 6 June 1766 (PD).
30. "Proceedings of the Visitors of the William and Mary College, 1716," *The Virginia Magazine of History and Biography* vol. 4, no. 2 (Oct. 1896): 169.
31. Hugh Jones, *Virginia*, 87.
32. Rhys Isaac, *The Transformation of Virginia, 1740–1790* (Chapel Hill: University of North Carolina Press, 1982), 81.
33. Thomas Story, *A Journal of the Life of Thomas Story* (Newcastle Upon Tyne: Isaac Thompson and Company, 1747), 388.
34. "Report of the Journey of Francis Louis Michel from Berne, Switzerland, to Virginia, October 2, 1701-December 1, 1702. Part II," *The Virginia Magazine of History and Biography* vol. 24, no. 2 (April 1916): 126–27.
35. Bushman, *Refinement*, 61.
36. *Ibid.*, 27.
37. *Virginia Gazette*, 29 January 1767 (PD).
38. Bushman, *Refinement*, 31.
39. *George Washington's Rules of Civility & Decent Behaviour in Company and Conversation* (Massachusetts: Applewood Books, 1988). See rules 5 and 12.
40. Gilbert Chase, *America's Music: From the Pilgrims to the Present*, 3rd edition (Chicago: University of Illinois Press, 1987), 73.
41. Hunter Dickinson Farish, ed., *Journal & Letters of Philip Vickers Fithian, 1773–1774: A Plantation Tutor of the Old Dominion* (Charlottesville: Dominion Books, 1968), 212.
42. Davis, *History of Music*, 44.
43. Farish, *Fithian*, 43.
44. Davis, *History of Music*, 44.
45. Isaac, *Transformation*, 86.
46. Carter, quoted in *ibid.*, 49. Carter was concerned Judy would become ill from dancing in the heat as it was her "Lunar period."
47. Louis B. Wright and Marion Tinling, eds., *The Secret Diary of William Byrd of Westover, 1709–1712* (Richmond: The Dietz Press, 1941), 296–97.
48. Farish, *Fithian*, 220.
49. *Ibid.*, 48.
50. *Virginia Gazette*, 27 March 1752 (Hu).
51. Bushman, *Refinement*, 47.
52. *Ibid.*, 166.
53. *Ibid.*, 185.
54. Mendoza, *North America*, 26.
55. Bushman, *Refinement*, 164.
56. *Ibid.*, 5.
57. *Ibid.*, 15.
58. *Ibid.*, 16.
59. *Virginia Gazette*, 4 October 1770 (Ri).
60. Farish, *Fithian*, XXI.
61. Hugh Jones, *Virginia*, 81, 102.
62. *Virginia Gazette*, 28 September 1769 (PD). The queen referenced in this quote was the wife of King George III, Charlotte of Mecklenburg-Strelitz.
63. *Ibid.*, 14 March 1751 (Hu). 60,000 French livres was valued at approximately 4,500 pounds, or 383,000 pounds in today's currency.
64. *Ibid.*, 8 August 1751 (Hu).
65. *Ibid.*, 15 May 1752 (Hu).
66. *Ibid.*, 21 August 1752; 15 September 1752 (both Hu).
67. *Ibid.*, 2 May 1766 (PD).
68. *Ibid.*, 30 June 1768 (PD).
69. T.H. Breen, *The Marketplace of Revolution: How Consumer Politics Shaped American Independence*. (New York: Oxford University Press, 2004), 38.
70. *Ibid.*, 61.
71. *Ibid.*, 60.
72. *Ibid.*, 52.
73. *Ibid.*, 61.
74. Mendoza, *North America*, 44.
75. Davis, *History of Music*, 43–44.
76. *Washington's Rules of Civility*. See rule 16.
77. Davis, *History of Music*, 51.
78. Lyon G. Tyler, "Diary of John Blair," *William and Mary Quarterly* vol. 7, no. 3 (Jan. 1899): 135.
79. Farish, *Fithian*, 88–90.
80. Davis, *History of Music*, 43.
81. "Minutes of the Council and General Court, 1622–1624" *The Virginia Magazine of History and Biography* vol. 19, no. 4 (Oct. 1911): 374–76.
82. *Virginia Gazette*, 7 October 1737 (Pa).
83. Davis, *History of Music*, 43.
84. Henry S. Randall, *The Life of Thomas Jefferson* (New York: Derby & Jackson, 1858), 1:132.
85. Julian P. Boyd et al., eds, *The Papers of Thomas Jefferson* (Princeton: Princeton University Press, 1950), 1:8.
86. Cripe, *Jefferson*, 15.
87. *Virginia Gazette*, 20 January 1774 (Ri).

88. Farish, *Fithian*, 57, 68.
89. Cripe, *Jefferson*, 42.
90. Farish, *Fithian*, 58.
91. Cripe, *Jefferson*, 73–76.
92. Benjamin Franklin, *Experiments and Observation Made on Electricity, Made at Philadelphia in America* (London: Printed for David Henry; and sold by Francis Newbery, at the corner of St. Paul's Church Yard, 1769), 428–433.
93. Chase, 79. According to Chase, the reason the colonists preferred "harmonica" to "armonica" is that in the English language an aspirate, or the pronunciation of a sound with an exhalation of breath, is more comfortable to the speaker.
94. Cripe, *Jefferson*, 42.
95. Farish, *Fithian*, 49.
96. Cripe, *Jefferson*, 65. Cripe notes Jefferson was never satisfied with these instruments as they were, instead desiring to have them personally modified to fit his meticulous musical tastes.
97. Chase, *America's Music*, 94.
98. Mendoza, *North America*, 152.
99. John W. Molnar, *Songs from the Williamsburg Theatre* (Charlottesville: University Press of Virginia, 1972), xviii.
100. Ron Byrnside, *Music in Eighteenth-Century Georgia* (Athens: The University of Georgia Press, 1997), 11.
101. Thomas Jefferson, *Notes on the State of Virginia*, ed. William Peden (Chapel Hill: University of North Carolina Press, 1955), 288.
102. *Virginia Gazette*, 8 January 1767 (PD).
103. Albert Stoutamire, *A History of Music in Richmond, Virginia from 1742 to 1865* (PhD diss, Florida State University, 1960), 20.
104. Davis, *History of Music*, 44. See also *Virginia Gazette*, 6 August 1767 (PD).
105. Cripe, *Jefferson*, 10.
106. *Ibid.*, 11.
107. *Virginia Gazette*, 16 May 1771 (PD).
108. Frances Norton Mason, ed, *John Norton & Sons, Merchants of London and Virginia: Being the Papers from their Counting House for the Years 1750 to 1795* (New York: Augustus M. Kelley, 1968), 15–16.
109. Hugh Jones, 32.
110. *Virginia Gazette*, 6 August 1767 (PD).
111. *Ibid.*, 3 November 1768 (Ri).
112. *Ibid.*, 17 September 1767 (PD).
113. *Ibid.*, 18 January 1770 (PD).
114. *Ibid.*, 27 May 1773 (Ri). This item was listed at 22 pounds, or approximately 1,400 pounds in today's money.
115. For an example of this see James A. Bear, Jr., and Lucia C. Stanton, eds., *Jefferson's Memorandum Books: Accounts, with Legal Records and Miscellany, 1767–1826* (Princeton: Princeton University Press, 1997), 1:82.
116. *Virginia Gazette*, 11 April 1771 (PD).
117. Maurer Maurer, "The Library of a Colonial Musician, 1755," *The William and Mary Quarterly* vol. 7, no. 1 (Jan. 1950): 50.
118. *Virginia Gazette*, 29 August 1771 (PD).
119. *Ibid.*, 29 November 1770 (PD).
120. Farish, *Fithian*, 167.
121. *Virginia Gazette*, 3 December 1772 (Ri).
122. Molnar, *Theater*, 143.
123. H. Wiley Hitchcock, *Music in the United States: A Historical Introduction*, 3rd edition (Englewood Cliffs, NJ: Prentice Hall, 1988), 33.
124. *Virginia Gazette*, 18 August 1774 (Ri).
125. Lawrence C. Wroth, *The Colonial Printer* (Charlottesville: Dominion Books, 1964), 234–35.
126. *Virginia Gazette*, 8 October 1736 (Pa).
127. The first listing of an instrument for sale was from John Mitchelson selling "a spinett" in the *Virginia Gazette*, 5 September 1751 (Hu).
128. *Virginia Gazette*, 23 February 1739 (Pa); See also *ibid.*, 24 May 1751 (Hu).
129. Breen, *Marketplace*, 55. See *Virginia Gazette*, 12 February 1762 (PD) for an example of this.
130. Breen, *Marketplace*, 55.

Chapter 2

1. *Virginia Gazette*, 7 October 1737. See also 9 December 1737 (both Pa).
2. *Ibid.*
3. Mendoza, 43.
4. Hitchcock, *Music*, 8.
5. Irving Lowens, *Music and Musi-*

cians in *Early America* (New York: W.W. Norton, 1964), 281–82.

6. *Virginia Gazette*, 3 November 1752 (Hu).

7. Farish, *Fithian*, 256. Fithian wrote that he attended service in Ucomico-Church, which is most likely the unincorporated community of Wicomico Church in Northumberland County, VA.

8. Lowens, 283.

9. See *Virginia Gazette*, 25 February 1768 (PD) for an example of this.

10. *Ibid.*, 10 June 1773 (PD).

11. York County Probate Inventories (hereafter referred to as YCPI), "An Inventory of the Estate of Cuthbert Ogle taken April 23, 1755," Colonial Williamsburg Digital Library, http://research.history.org/DigitalLibrary/View/index.cfm?doc=Probates\PB00349.xml (accessed Oct. 16, 2013).

12. Davis, *History of Music*, 44.

13. Boyd, *Jefferson*, 1:12–13.

14. Farish, *Fithian*, 163.

15. *Virginia Gazette*, 29 December 1774 (PD).

16. Farish, *Fithian*, 163.

17. Davis, *History of Music*, 45–46.

18. *Ibid.*

19. *Virginia Gazette*, 24 June 1773 (PD).

20. Farish, *Fithian*, 105.

21. *Virginia Gazette*, 12 June 1752 (Hu).

22. *Ibid.*, 28 March 1755 (Hu).

23. Maurer, "Library," 40. Ogle died on April 23, 1755.

24. *Virginia Gazette*, 16 May 1771 (PD).

25. *Ibid.*, 27 February 1772 (PD).

26. Molnar, *Theater*, xviii.

27. Cripe, *Jefferson*, 6.

28. Molnar, *Theater*, 20.

29. James S. Darling, *Let the Anthems Swell: Musical Traditions at Bruton Parish Church, Williamsburg, Virginia* (Williamsburg: Burton Parish Church, 2003), 13–19.

30. Mendoza, *North America*, 47.

31. Cripe, *Jefferson*, 6.

32. Arthur C. Edwards and W. Thomas Marrocco, *Music in the United States* (Dubuque, IA: WM C. Brown Company, 1968), 13. See also Darling, *Anthems*, 16.

33. Mendoza, *North America*, 47.

34. *Virginia Gazette*, 11 March 1773 (PD).

35. Molnar, *Theater*, 20.

36. Charles Hamm, *Music in the New World* (New York: W.W. Norton, 1983), 82–83.

37. Mendoza, *North America*, 150.

38. Hamm, *New World*, 85.

39. *Virginia Gazette*, 27 October 1768 (Ri).

40. Farish, *Fithian*, 28, 34, 37, 57, 110, 160.

41. Cripe, *Jefferson*, 7.

42. *Virginia Gazette*, 11 December 1766 (Ri).

43. Cripe, *Jefferson*, 7.

44. Hugh Jones, 48.

45. Hamm, *New World*, 67–71.

46. Kate Van Winkle Keller, *Dance and Its Music in America, 1528–1789* (New York: Pendragon Press, 2007), 184, 186.

47. Joy Van Cleef and Kate Van Winkle Keller, "Selected American Country Dances and Their English Sources," in *Music in Colonial Massachusetts, 1630–1820, I: Music in Public Places, A Conference Held by the Colonial Society of Massachusetts, May 17 and 18, 1973* (Boston: The Colonial Society of Massachusetts, 1980), 11.

48. Stanard, *Virginia*, 140.

49. 1755 letter of John Kello, as found in Charles M. Andrews, *Guide to the Materials for American History, to 1783, in the Public Record Office of Great Britain*, vol. II (Washington, D.C.: Carnegie Institution of Washington, 1914), 322.

50. Farish, *Fithian*, 232.

51. Burnaby, *Travels*, 28.

52. Farish, *Fithian*, 163.

53. Davis, *History of Music*, 46.

54. Bushman, *Refinement*, 68.

55. Byrnside, *Georgia*, 32.

56. *Virginia Gazette*, 25 November 1737 (Pa).

57. *Ibid.*, 20 March 1752 (Hu).

58. *Ibid.*, 16 May 1771 (PD).

59. Keller, *Dance*, 203.

60. *Virginia Gazette*, 26 September 1745 (Pa).

61. *Ibid.*, 6 April 1739 (Pa).

62. Keller, *Dance*, 199.

63. *Ibid.*, 214.

64. Stanard, *Virginia*, 144.

65. Farish, *Fithian*, 42, for reference to dancing lessons at Nomini Hall; *Ibid.*, 68, for reference to the children attending dancing class in Stratford.

66. *Ibid.*, 205.

67. Wright, *London Diary*, 456.

68. Farish, *Fithian*, 44.

69. "Letters of William Byrd, 2d, of Westover, Va. (Continued)," *The Virginia Magazine of History and Biography* vol. 9, no. 3 (Jan. 1902), 240. Lucretia was a Roman woman who, according to legend, was raped by the son of the last Roman king and killed herself afterwards, leading to the revolution which overthrew the monarchy and established the Roman Republic.
70. *Virginia Gazette*, August 17, 1775 (Pi).
71. Bushman, *Refinement*, 64–65.
72. *Washington's Rules of Civility*. See rules 10 and 53.
73. Davis, *History of Music*, 46.
74. Stanard, *Virginia*, 182.
75. Rankin, *Theater*, 17.
76. Wright, *London Diary*, 470–71.
77. *Virginia Gazette*, 25 February 1737; 21 October 1737; 31 March 1738; 21 April 1738; 20 April 1739 (all Pa).
78. *Ibid.*, 22 April 1737 (Pa).
79. *Ibid.*, 24 March 1738. See also 13 October 1738 (both Pa).
80. Keller, *Dance*, 201.
81. *Virginia Gazette*, 21 April 1738 (Pa).
82. *Ibid.*, 11 April 1751 (Hu).
83. *Ibid.*, 24 October 1751 (Hu).
84. *Ibid.*, 27 February 1752 (Hu).
85. Stanard, *Virginia*, 182.
86. Farish, *Fithian*, 44–45.
87. *Ibid.*, 75.
88. *Ibid.*, 63.
89. *Ibid.*, 117.
90. Wright, *London Diary*, 391–92.
91. *Ibid.*, 404. Byrd is referring to the Council of Virginia, to which he had just been reinstated by the King over the objections of the governor, though they eventually reconciled.
92. Wright, *Secret Diary*, 297.
93. Mendoza, *North America*, 102, 146. See also Davis, *History of Music*, 48.
94. Farish, *Fithian*, 165.
95. *Ibid.*, 69.
96. Wright, *Secret Diary*, 297.
97. *Ibid.*, 75–76.
98. *Ibid.*, 203–04.
99. *The Journal of Nicholas Cresswell, 1774–1777* (New York: Kennikat Press, 1968), 52–53.
100. Hamm, *New World*, 71.
101. Cresswell, *Journal*, 52–53.
102. Wright, *Secret Diary*, 296.
103. Bushman, *Refinement*, 52–57.
104. Isaac, *Transformation*, 81, 84.
105. Bushman, 51.
106. Jared Sparks, ed., *The Writings of George Washington; Being his Correspondence, Addresses, Messages, and other Papers, Official and Private, Selected and Published from the Original Manuscripts; with A Life of the Author, Notes, and Illustrations*, vol. II (New York: Harper & Brothers, 1847), 512–13.

Chapter 3

1. "Letter of Anne Blair to Martha Braxton," *William and Mary Quarterly* vol. 16, no. 3 (Jan. 1908), 178.
2. Hitchcock, *Music*, 29.
3. Hamm, *New World*, 48.
4. Davis, *History of Music*, 51.
5. See Cripe, *Jefferson*, 88–130, for an index of the music collection of Monticello.
6. Anne Dhu McLucas, *The Musical Ear: Oral Tradition in the USA* (Burlington, VT: Ashgate, 2010), 82–83.
7. Wroth, *Printer*, 234.
8. *Virginia Gazette*, 20 January 1774 (PD).
9. "William Logan's Journal of a Journey to Georgia, 1745," *The Pennsylvania Magazine of History and Biography* vol. 36, no. 1 (1912), 5–6.
10. Sharon V. Salinger, *Taverns and Drinking in Early America* (Baltimore: Johns Hopkins University Press, 2002), 2.
11. Ewing, *Sports*, 18.
12. *Virginia Gazette*, 29 January 1767 (PD).
13. McLucas, *Musical Ear*, 89–91.
14. Leonard W. Labaree, ed. *The Papers of Benjamin Franklin*, vol. 12 (New Haven: Yale University Press, 1968), 158–165.
15. Hamm, *New World*, 65.
16. Bushman, *Refinement*, 49.
17. Devereux Jarratt, *The Life of the Reverend Devereux Jarratt* (Baltimore: Warner & Hanna, 1806), 42–43.
18. *Ibid.*, 43–44.
19. Bushman, *Refinement*, 49.
20. *Ibid.*, 57.
21. Cresswell, *Journal*, 30.
22. *Ibid.*, 26.
23. Hitchcock, *Music*, 43.
24. Burnaby, *Travels*, 28.
25. *Ibid.*

26. Keller, *Dance*, 180.
27. Don Jordan and Michael Walsh, *White Cargo: The Forgotten History of Britain's White Slaves in America* (New York: New York University Press, 2008), 86–87.
28. Richard Jobson, *The Golden Trade; Or, a Discovery of the River Gambra, and the Golden Trade of the Aethiopians* (New York: Speight and Walpole, 1623), 133.
29. Eileen Southern, *The Music of Black Americans: A History, 2nd Edition* (New York: W.W. Norton, 1983), 7. See also Byrnside, *Georgia*, 19.
30. Olaudah Equiano, *The Interesting Narrative of the Life of Olaudah Equiano* (London, 1793), 7.
31. Byrnside, *Georgia*, 19.
32. Hamm, *New World*, 122.
33. Quote in *Ibid.*, 123.
34. Chase, 59.
35. Shane White and Graham White, "'Us Likes a Mixtery': Listening to African-American Slave Music," in *The Slavery Reader*, Gad Heuman and James Walvin, eds. (London: Routledge, 2003), 414–16.
36. Equiano, *Narrative*, 8.
37. Jobson, *Golden Trade*, 135–36.
38. Southern, *Black Americans*, 10–13.
39. Richard Cullen Rath, *How Early America Sounded* (New York: Cornell University Press, 2003), 90.
40. Southern, *Black Americans*, 51–52.
41. Chase, *America's Music*, 68. See also: Hamm, *New World*, 123.
42. Jefferson, *Notes*, 140.
43. Cripe, *Jefferson*, 7.
44. Byrnside, *Georgia*, 11.
45. Chase, *America's Music*, 66.
46. Mendoza, *North America*, 131.
47. Wright, *Secret Diary*, 298.
48. Philip Alexander Bruce, *Social Life of Virginia in the Seventeenth Century* (Richmond: Whittet & Shepperson, 1907), 181–82.
49. Richard Crawford, *America's Musical Life: A History* (New York: W.W. Norton, 2001), 107.
50. *Virginia Gazette*, 1 August 1755 (Hu).
51. *Ibid.*, 23 July 1767 (PD).
52. *Ibid.*, 14 September 1769 (Ri).
53. *Ibid.*, 27 March 1752 (Hu).
54. *Ibid.*, 4 November 1773 (PD).
55. *Ibid.*, 1 April 1773; 1 December 1774 (both PD).
56. *Ibid.*, 4 August 1768; 18 August 1768 (both PD).
57. J.F.D. Smyth, *A Tour in the United States of America* (London: G. Robinson, 1784), 46.
58. Southern, *Black Americans*, 48.
59. Cresswell, *Journal*, 18.
60. Farish, *Fithian*, 137.
61. Cresswell, *Journal*, 18–19.
62. Farish, *Fithian*, 82–83.
63. Cresswell, *Journal*, 30.

Chapter 4

1. "Letter from Hudson Muse, of Virginia, to His Brother, Thomas Muse, of Dorchester Co., Maryland," *William and Mary Quarterly* vol. 2, no. 4 (April 1894), 240–41.
2. Accomac County Records, vol. 1663–66, folio 102.
3. Rankin, *Theater*, 7.
4. Hunter D. Farish, "The Playhouse (First Theater) Historical Report Block 29 Building 17B Lots 163, 164, 169," 1940, *eWilliamsburg*, http://research.history.org/ewilliamsburg/document.cfm?source=ResearchReports/XML/RR1583.xml&rm_id=RM00091.
5. *Ibid.*
6. Molnar, *Theater*, xiii.
7. Farish, "Playhouse."
8. R.A. Brock, ed., *The Official Letters of Alexander Spotswood, Lieutenant-Governor of the Colony of Virginia, 1710–172, vol. 1* (Richmond, VA: Virginia Historical Society, 1882), 284.
9. Ann Morgan Smart, "The Playhouse Archeological Report Block 29 Building 17A," 1986, *eWilliamsburg*, http://research.history.org/ewilliamsburg/document.cfm?source=ResearchReports/XML/RR1589.xml&rm_id=RM00091.
10. Rankin, *Theater*, 14–15.
11. Cripe, *Jefferson*, 15.
12. Molnar, *Theater*, 117.
13. Smart, "Archeological Report."
14. Gregory A. Stiverson and Patrick H. Butler, III, eds., "Virginia in 1732: The Travel Journal of William Hugh Grove," *The Virginia Magazine of History and Biography* vol. 85, no. 1 (January 1977), 26. Bowes's identity is unknown, though Rankin speculates he may have been an employee of Archibald Blair, the owner of the play-

house when Grove visited. See Rankin, *Theater*, 16.
  15. Carl Lounsbury, "'To Emulate the British Stage': The Research and Design of the Douglass Theatre, Block 8," 2015, *eWilliamsburg*, http://research.history.org/DigitalLibrary/view/index.cfm?doc=ResearchReports\RR1763.xml&highlight=theater.
  16. *Virginia Gazette*, 10 September 1736; *Ibid.*, 17 September 1736 (both Pa).
  17. *Ibid.*, 19 December 1745 (Pa).
  18. Molnar, *Theater*, xiii.
  19. *Virginia Gazette*, 29 August 1751 (Hu).
  20. Rankin, *Theater*, 143
  21. *Ibid.*, 37.
  22. *Virginia Gazette*, 26 September 1751 (Hu).
  23. Tyler, "Diary of John Blair," 147.
  24. Rankin, *Theater*, 37.
  25. *Virginia Gazette*, 17 October 1751 (Hu).
  26. Rankin, *Theater*, 37.
  27. *Virginia Gazette*, 24 October 1751 (Hu).
  28. Wright, *Cultural Life*, 182.
  29. *Virginia Gazette*, 12 June 1752 (Hu).
  30. Molnar, *Theater*, xiii-xiv.
  31. *Virginia Gazette*, 12 June 1752 (Hu).
  32. *Ibid.*
  33. Rankin, *Theater*, 50–51.
  34. Dr. George Gilmer to Dr. Thomas Walker, 30 June 1752, as quoted in Odai Johnson and William J. Burling, *The Colonial American Stage, 1665–1774: A Documentary Calendar* (London: Associated University Presses, 2001), 157.
  35. Rankin, *Theater*, 51.
  36. *Ibid.*, 52.
  37. *Ibid.*
  38. *Virginia Gazette*, 21 August 1752 (Hu).
  39. Rankin, *Theater*, 52–54.
  40. Odai Johnson, *Absence and Memory in Colonial American Theatre* (New York: Palgrave Macmillan, 2006), 69.
  41. Rankin, *Theater*, 52–54.
  42. Johnson, *Absence*, 68.
  43. *Virginia Gazette*, 21 August 1752 (Hu).
  44. *Ibid.*; See also 28 August 1752 (Hu).
  45. Rankin, *Theater*, 54.
  46. *Virginia Gazette*, 28 August 1752 (Hu).
  47. Molnar, *Theater*, 73.

  48. *Ibid.*, xvii.
  49. *Ibid.*, 93.
  50. Rankin, *Theater*, 56.
  51. *Virginia Gazette*, 22 September 1752 (Hu).
  52. Rankin, *Theater*, 56.
  53. Hamm, *New World*, 89.
  54. *Virginia Gazette*, 17 November 1752 (Hu).
  55. Rankin, *Theater*, 89.
  56. Hamm, *New World*, 90–91; see also Mendoza, *North America*, 121. It makes one wonder how the genteel sitting in the box seats reconciled their view of the theater as a genteel activity with the raucousness of the crowds below them.
  57. *Virginia Gazette*, 8 October 1772 (PD).
  58. *New York Mercury*, 3 May 1773.
  59. *Virginia Gazette*, 29 October 1736 (Pa).
  60. *Ibid.*, 5 December 1751 (Hu).
  61. *Ibid.*, 8 December 1752 (Hu).
  62. *Ibid.*, 28 November 1771 (PD).
  63. Mendoza, *North America*, 113.
  64. Molnar, *Theater*, xiv-xv.
  65. *Virginia Gazette*, 12 May 1768 (PD).
  66. Hamm, *New World*, 88.
  67. Byrnside, *Georgia*, 48–49.
  68. Hamm, *New World*, 48.
  69. Mendoza, *North America*, 141.
  70. Hamm, *New World*, 52–53.
  71. Molnar, *Theater*, 20, 23.
  72. Wright, *London Diary*, 626–27.
  73. Rankin, *Theater*, 58–59.
  74. *Virginia Gazette*, 5 September 1755 (Hu).
  75. Lounsbury, "Stage."
  76. Mary A. Stephenson, "Second Theatre Historical Report Block 7," 1946, *eWilliamsburg*, http://research.history.org/ewilliamsburg/document.cfm?source=ResearchReports/XML/RR1107.xml&rm_id=RM00049.
  77. Rankin, *Theater*, 74.
  78. *Ibid.*, 89.
  79. Lounsbury, "Stage."
  80. *Ibid.*
  81. *Ibid.*
  82. *Ibid.*
  83. Burling and Johnson, *American Stage*, 212. See also Rankin, *Theater*, 90–91.
  84. W.W. Abbot, ed., *The Papers of George Washington, Colonial Series, vol. 6, 4 September 1758–26 December 1760*

(Charlottesville: University Press of Virginia, 1988), 465–66.

85. W.W. Abbot and Dorothy Twohig, eds., *The Papers of George Washington, Colonial Series, vol. 7, 1 January 1761–15 June 1767* (Charlottesville: University Press of Virginia, 1990), 1–11. The group stayed in the Williamsburg area until at least May 14 of that year because leatherworker Alexander Craig sold Lewis Hallam, Jr. a pair of shoes on that date. See Harold B. Gill, Jr., "Leather Workers in Colonial Virginia," August 1966, *eWilliamsburg*, http://research.history.org/DigitalLibrary/View/index.cfm?doc=ResearchReports%5CRR0107.xml.

86. Burling and Johnson, *American Stage*, 231.

87. *Virginia Gazette*, 8 January 1767 (PD).

88. Ibid., 24 March 1768 (Ri).

89. Ibid., 31 March 1768 (PD).

90. Mary Stephenson, "Second Theatre Historical Report Block 7."

91. Bear and Stanton, *Jefferson's Memorandum Books*, 1:74–75.

92. *Virginia Gazette*, 30 June 1768 (PD).

93. As quoted in Johnson, *Absence*, 29.

94. Ibid.

95. Burling and Johnson, *American Stage*, 354.

96. *Virginia Gazette*, 7 May 1772 (PD). According to Burling and Johnson in *The Colonial American Stage*, this play had premiered in London January 20, 1772, making it four months old at its premiere in Williamsburg. See p. 403.

97. *Virginia Gazette*, 19 November 1772 (Ri).

Epilogue

1. Molnar, *Theater*, ix.
2. *Virginia Gazette*, 2 April 1772 (PD).
3. Ann Fairfax Withington, *Toward a More Perfect Union: Virtue and the Formation of American Republics* (New York: Oxford University Press, 1991), 21–22.
4. *Virginia Gazette*, 28 January 1775 (DH).
5. Johnson, *Absence*, 90.
6. Boyd, *Jefferson*, 1: 43–48.
7. Johnson, *Absence*, 91.
8. Cresswell, *Journal*, 23.
9. "The Articles of Association." *Journals of the Continental Congress 1774–1779*. Edited from the original records in the Library of Congress by Worthington Chauncey Ford; Chief, Division of Manuscripts. Washington, D.C.: Government Printing Office, 1905.

Bibliography

Primary Sources

Abbot, W.W., ed. *The Papers of George Washington, Colonial Series, vol. 6, 4 September 1758–26 December 1760.* Charlottesville: University Press of Virginia, 1988.

Abbot, W.W., and Dorothy Twohig, eds. *The Papers of George Washington, Colonial Series, vol. 7, 1 January 1761–15 June 1767.* Charlottesville: University Press of Virginia, 1990.

Accomac County Records, vol. 1663–66, folio 102.

"Appraisement of the estate of Mr Cuthbert Ogle dec'd April 23, 1755." *William and Mary Quarterly* vol. 3, no. 4 (April 1895): 246–253.

"The Articles of Association." *Journals of the Continental Congress 1774–1779.* Edited from the original records in the Library of Congress by Worthington Chauncey Ford; Chief, Division of Manuscripts. Washington, D.C.: Government Printing Office, 1905.

Bear, James A., Jr., and Lucia C. Stanton, eds. *Jefferson's Memorandum Books: Accounts, with Legal Records and Miscellany, 1767–1826.* Princeton: Princeton University Press, 1997.

Boyd, Julian P., et al., eds. *The Papers of Thomas Jefferson.* Princeton: Princeton University Press, 1950.

Brock, R.A., ed. *The Official Letters of Alexander Spotswood, Lieutenant-Governor of the Colony of Virginia, 1710–1722, vol. 1.* Richmond, VA: Virginia Historical Society, 1882.

"Diary of Col. Landon Carter." *William and Mary Quarterly* vol. 13, no. 3 (Jan. 1905): 157–164.

Dr. George Gilmer to Dr. Thomas Walker, as quoted in Odai Johnson and William J. Burling, *The Colonial American Stage, 1665–1774: A Documentary Calendar.* London: Associated University Presses, 2001.

Equiano, Olaudah. *The Interesting Narrative of the Life of Olaudah Equiano.* London, 1793.

Farish, Hunter Dickinson, ed. *Journal & Letters of Philip Vickers Fithian, 1773–1774: A Plantation Tutor of the Old Dominion.* Charlottesville: Dominion Books, 1968.

Franklin, Benjamin. *Experiments and Observation Made on Electricity, Made at Philadelphia in America.* London: Printed for David Henry; and sold by Francis Newbery, at the corner of St. Paul's Church Yard, 1769.

George Washington's Rules of Civility & Decent Behaviour in Company and Conversation. Massachusetts: Applewood Books, 1988.

Bibliography

Jarratt, Devereux. *The Life of the Reverend Devereux Jarratt.* Baltimore: Warner & Hanna, 1806.

Jefferson, Thomas. *Notes on the State of Virginia.* Edited by William Peden. Chapel Hill: University of North Carolina Press, 1955.

Jobson, Richard. *The Golden Trade; Or, A Discovery of the River Gambra, and the Golden Trade of the Aethiopians.* London: Speight and Walpole, 1623.

Jones, Hugh. *The Present State of Virginia.* New York: Reprinted for Joseph Sabin, 1865. Originally published 1724.

The Journal of Nicholas Cresswell, 1774–1777. New York: Kennikat Press, 1968.

Labaree, Leonard W. *The Papers of Benjamin Franklin, vol. 12.* New Haven: Yale University Press, 1968.

"Letter from Hudson Muse, of Virginia, to His Brother, Thomas Muse, of Dorchester Co., Maryland." *William and Mary Quarterly* vol. 2, no. 4 (April 1894): 239–241.

"Letter of Anne Blair to Martha Braxton." *William and Mary Quarterly* vol. 16, no. 3 (Jan. 1908): 174–180.

Letter of John Kello, 1755, as found in Charles M. Andrews, *Guide to the Materials for American History, to 1783, in the Public Record Office of Great Britain, vol. II.* Washington, D.C.: Carnegie Institution of Washington, 1914.

"Letters of William Byrd, 2d, of Westover, Va. (Continued)." *The Virginia Magazine of History and Biography* vol. 9, no. 3 (Jan. 1902): 225–251.

Mason, Frances Norton, ed. *John Norton & Sons, Merchants of London and Virginia: Being the Papers from their Counting House for the Years 1750 to 1795.* New York: Augustus M. Kelley, 1968.

"Minutes of the Council and General Court, 1622–1624." *The Virginia Magazine of History and Biography* vol. 19, no. 4 (Oct. 1911): 374–389.

New York Mercury, 1768–1783.

"Order in Council restoring Wm Byrd Esq. to the Council of Virginia." *Calendar of Virginia State Papers* vol. 1 (194–95).

Pemberton, E. "An Essay For the further Improvement of Dancing; Being a Collection of Figure Dances, of Several Numbers, Compos'd by the most Eminent Masters; Describ'd in Characters after The newest Manner of Monsieur Feuillet." London, 1711.

"Proceedings of the Visitors of William and Mary College, 1716." *The Virginia Magazine of History and Biography* vol. 4, no. 2 (Oct. 1896): 161–175.

"Report of the Journey of Francis Louis Michel from Berne, Switzerland, to Virginia, October 2, 1701–December 1, 1702. Part II." *The Virginia Magazine of History and Biography* vol. 24, no. 2 (April 1916): 113–141.

Smyth, J.F.D. *A Tour in the United States of America.* London: G. Robinson, 1784.

Sparks, Jared, ed. *The Writings of George Washington; Being his Correspondence, Addresses, Messages, and other Papers, Official and Private, Selected and Published from the Original Manuscripts; with A Life of the Author, Notes, and Illustrations,* vol. II. New York: Harper & Brothers, 1847.

Stiverson, Gregory A., and Patrick H. Butler, III, eds. "Virginia in 1732: The Travel Journal of William Hugh Grove." *The Virginia Magazine of History and Biography* vol. 85, no. 1 (Jan. 1977): 18–44.

Story, Thomas. *A Journal of the Life of Thomas Story.* Newcastle Upon Tyne: Isaac Thompson and Company, 1747.

Travels Through the Middle Settlements in North America in the Years 1759 and 1760; With Observations Upon the State of the Colonies by the Rev. Andrew Burnaby, Archdeacon of Leicester and Vicar of Greenwich. London: Printed for T. Payne, at the Mews-Gate, 1798.

Tyler, Lyon G. "Diary of John Blair." *William and Mary Quarterly* vol. 7, no. 3 (Jan. 1899): 133–153.
Virginia Gazette, 1736–1780.
"William Logan's Journal of a Journey to Georgia, 1745." *The Pennsylvania Magazine of History and Biography* vol. 36, no. 1 (1912): 1–16.
Wright, Louis B., and Marion Tinling, eds. *The Secret Life of William Byrd of Westover, 1709–1712* Richmond: The Dietz Press, 1941.
Wright, Louis B., and Marion Tinling, eds. *William Byrd of Virginia, The London Diary (1717–1721) and Other Writings.* New York: Oxford University Press, 1958.
York County Probate Inventories.

Secondary Sources

Breen, T.H. *The Marketplace of Revolution: How Consumer Politics Shaped American Independence.* New York: Oxford University Press, 2004.
Bridenbaugh, Carl. *Seat of Empire: The Political Role of Eighteenth-Century Williamsburg.* Williamsburg: Colonial Williamsburg, 1958.
Bruce, Philip Alexander. *Social Life of Virginia in the Seventeenth Century.* Richmond: Whittet & Shepperson, 1907.
Burling, William J., and Odai Johnson. *The Colonial American Stage, 1665–1774: A Documentary Calendar.* London: Associated University Presses, 2001.
Bushman, Richard L. *The Refinement of America: Persons, Houses, Cities.* New York: Alfred A. Knopf, 1992.
Byrnside, Ron. *Music in Eighteenth-Century Georgia.* Athens: The University of Georgia Press, 1997.
Carson, Cary, Ronald Hoffman, and Peter J. Albert, eds. *Of Consuming Interests: The Style of Life in the Eighteenth Century.* Charlottesville: University Press of Virginia, 1994.
Chase, Gilbert. *America's Music: From the Pilgrims to the Present, 3rd edition.* Chicago: University of Illinois Press, 1987.
Cleef, Joy Van, and Kate Van Winkle Keller. "Selected American Country Dances and Their English Sources." In *Music in Colonial Massachusetts, 1630–1820, I: Music in Public Places, A Conference Held by the Colonial Society of Massachusetts, May 17 and 18, 1973.* Boston: The Colonial Society of Massachusetts, 1980.
Coffin, Charles Carleton. *Building the Nation: Events in the History of the United States from the Revolution to the Beginning of the War Between the States.* New York: Harper & Brothers, 1883.
Crawford, Richard. *America's Musical Life: A History.* New York: W.W. Norton, 2001.
Cripe, Helen. *Thomas Jefferson and Music.* Chapel Hill: University of North Carolina Press, 2009.
Darling, James S. *Let the Anthems Swell: Musical Traditions at Bruton Parish Church, Williamsburg, Virginia.* Williamsburg: Bruton Parish Church, 2003.
Davis, Ronald L. *A History of Music in American Life, vol. 1: The Formative Years, 1620–1865.* Malabar, FL: Robert Krieger Publishing Company, 1982.
DelDonna, Anthony R., ed. *Genre in Eighteenth-Century Music.* Ann Arbor: Steglein Publishing, 2008.
Edwards, Arthur C., and W. Thomas Marrocco. *Music in the United States.* Dubuque, IA: WM C. Brown Company, 1968.
Ellinwood, Leonard. *The History of American Church Music.* New York: Da Capo Press, 1970.

Ewing, William C. *The Sports of Colonial Williamsburg.* Richmond, VA: The Dietz Press, 1937.

Farish, Hunter D. "The Playhouse (First Theater) Historical Report Block 29 Building 17B Lots 163, 164, 169," 1940. *eWilliamsburg,* http://research.history.org/ewilliamsburg/document.cfm?source=ResearchReports/XML/RR1583.xml&rm_id=RM00091.

Gill, Harold B., Jr. "Leather Workers in Colonial Virginia," August 1966. *eWilliamsburg,* http://research.history.org/DigitalLibrary/View/index.cfm?doc=ResearchReports%5CRR0107.xml.

Grashel, John W. "John Playford's 'An Introduction to the Skill of Musick' and Its Influence on the Musical Textbooks of Colonial America." *The Bulletin of Historical Research in Music Education* vol. 5, no. 2 (July 1984): 39–54.

Hamm, Charles. *Music in the New World.* New York: W.W. Norton, 1983.

Heuman, Gad, and James Walvin. *The Slavery Reader.* London: Routledge, 2003.

Hitchcock, H. Wiley. *Music in the United States: A Historical Introduction,* 3rd edition. Englewood Cliffs, NJ: Prentice Hall, 1988.

Howard, John Tasker. *Our American Music: A Comprehensive History from 1620 to the Present.* New York: Thomas Y. Crowell Company, 1965.

Isaac, Rhys. *The Transformation of Virginia, 1740–1790.* Chapel Hill: University of North Carolina Press, 1982.

Johnson, Odai. *Absence and Memory in Colonial American Theatre.* New York: Palgrave Macmillan, 2006.

Johnson, Odai, and William J. Burling. *The Colonial American Stage, 1665–1774: A Documentary Calendar.* London: Associated University Presses, 2001.

Jordan, Don, and Michael Walsh. *White Cargo: The Forgotten History of Britain's White Slaves in America.* New York: New York University Press, 2008.

Keller, Kate Van Winkle. *Dance and Its Music in America, 1528–1789.* New York: Pendragon Press, 2007.

Keller, Kate Van Winkle. *Popular Secular Music in America through 1800.* Metuchen, NJ: Scarecrow Press, 1981.

Lounsbury, Carl. "'To Emulate the British Stage': The Research and Design of the Douglass Theatre, Block 8," 2015. *eWilliamsburg,* http://research.history.org/DigitalLibrary/view/index.cfm?doc=ResearchReports\RR1763.xml&highlight=theater.

Lowens, Irving. *Music and Musicians in Early America.* New York: W.W. Norton, 1964.

Maurer, Maurer. "The Library of a Colonial Musician, 1755." *The William and Mary Quarterly* vol. 7, no. 1 (Jan. 1950): 39–52.

Maurer, Maurer. "A Musical Family in Colonial Virginia." *The Musical Quarterly* vol. 34, no. 3 (July 1948): 358–364.

Maurer, Maurer. "The 'Professor of Musick' in Colonial Virginia." *The Musical Quarterly* vol. 36, no. 4 (Oct. 1950): 511–524.

McLucas, Anne Dhu. *The Musical Ear: Oral Tradition in the USA.* Burlington, VT: Ashgate, 2010.

Mendoza de Arce, Daniel. *Music in North America and the West Indies from the Discovery to 1850.* Lanham, MD: Scarecrow Press, 2006.

Millar, John Fitzhugh. *Country Dances of Colonial America.* Williamsburg: Thirteen Colonies Press, 1990.

Molnar, John W. *Songs from the Williamsburg Theatre.* Charlottesville: University Press of Virginia, 1972.

Moody, Jane, and Daniel O'Quinn, eds. *The Cambridge Companion to British Theatre, 1730–1830.* New York: Cambridge University Press, 2007.

Pencak, William. *Riot and Revelry in Early America*. University Park: Pennsylvania State University Press, 2002.
Radocy, Rudolf, and J. David Boyle. *Psychological Foundations of Musical Behavior, 3rd edition*. Springfield, IL: Charles C. Thomas, 1997.
Randall, Henry S. *The Life of Thomas Jefferson*. New York: Derby & Jackson, 1858.
Rankin, Hugh F. *The Theater in Colonial America*. Chapel Hill: University of North Carolina Press, 1965.
Rath, Richard Cullen. *How Early America Sounded*. New York: Cornell University Press, 2003.
Salinger, Sharon V. *Taverns and Drinking in Early America*. Baltimore: The Johns Hopkins University Press, 2002.
Smart, Ann Morgan. "The Playhouse Archeological Report Block 29 Building 17A," 1986. *eWilliamsburg*, http://research.history.org/ewilliamsburg/document.cfm?source=ResearchReports/XML/RR1589.xml&rm_id=RM00091.
Sonneck, Oscar G. *A Bibliography of Early Secular American Music (18th Century)*. New York: Da Capo Press, 1964.
Sonneck, Oscar G. *Early Concert Life in America (1731–1880)*. New York: Musurgia, 1949.
Southern, Eileen. *The Music of Black Americans: A History, 2nd Edition*. New York: W.W. Norton, 1983.
Stanard, Mary Newton. *Colonial Virginia: Its People and Customs*. Philadelphia: J.B. Lippincott Company, 1917.
Stephenson, Mary A. "Second Theatre Historical Report Block 7," 1946. *eWilliamsburg*, http://research.history.org/ewilliamsburg/document.cfm?source=ResearchReports/XML/RR1107.xml&rm_id=RM00049.
Stiverson, Cynthia Zignego. *Colonial Williamsburg Music: A Descriptive Catalogue of Printed Eighteenth and Nineteenth-Century Music in the Collections of the Colonial Williamsburg Foundation*. West Cornwall, CT: Locust Hill Press, 1988.
Stoutamire, Albert. *A History of Music in Richmond, Virginia from 1742 to 1865*. PhD diss., Florida State University, 1960.
Talley, John B. *Secular Music in Colonial Annapolis: The Tuesday Club, 1745–56*. Chicago: University of Illinois Press, 1988.
Virga, Patricia H. *The American Opera to 1790*. Ann Arbor: UMI Research Press, 1982.
Withington, Ann Fairfax. *Toward a More Perfect Union: Virtue and the Formation of American Republics*. New York: Oxford University Press, 1991.
Wright, Louis B. *The Cultural Life of the American Colonies 1607–1763*. New York: Harper & Row, 1957.
Wroth, Lawrence C. *The Colonial Printer*. Charlottesville: Dominion Books, 1964.

Index

Numbers in **_bold italics_** refer to pages with photographs.

advertisements 8, 37; *see also* broadsides; *Virginia Gazette*
Africans *see* slaves
alcohol *12*, 16, 40, 61, 71, 74, 76, 78–83, 93, 97
Alexandria 66, 69, 83
American Company 35, 125–127, 130, 162–164
American Revolution 1–3, 13, 59, *79*, 127, 130–131
American Syren 35, 43
armonica *see* glass harmonica
Articles of Association 131, 165–168

Bach, Johann Sebastian 34
ballad operas 74, 119–121
balls *see* dances
banjo 31, 83, 89–90, 95–*96*; *see also* instruments
The Bear and the Cub 100–*101*
The Beggar's Opera 35, 43, 47, 105, 113, 119–121, 161–162
Blair, John, Sr. 26, 106
Bodleian Plate *10*
books 17, *36*, 38, 40, 42–43, 74; acquisition 8, 25, 34–35, 39, 47, 121; printing 35, 37, 73–74
Boston 3, 9, 47
Boston Tea Party 75–76
Botetourt, Gov. Norborne 47, 71–72, 93
Briggs, Landon 93
Britain *see* Europe
broadsides 42, 74–75, 119
Bruton Parish Church 2, 8, 42, 47, *101*, 113, 120
Bucktrout, Benjamin 31
Burnaby, Andrew 9, 54, 84

Byrd, William, II 11–*12*, 18–19, 28, 40, 56, 58–60, 63–64, 67, 93, 120–121

capitol 8–10, 13, 20, *101*, 106, 123; construction of 8; dances in 14, 61
Carter, Landon 8, 18, 127
Carter, Robert, I 58
Carter, Robert, III 18, 26, 28–31, 35, 45, 56, 58, 63–64, 90
Charles Town 3, 9, 55, 120
Cherokee *see* Native Americans
Christian, Francis 56–58, 64
College of William and Mary 6, 8–*10*, *12*, 15–16, 42, 47, 55, 92, 104, 115, 154
Colonial Williamsburg 3, 9–*10*, 106, 124
concerts 5, 26, 31, 46, 48, 50, 69; music selection 81; ticket sales 5, 49; *see also* governor's palace
The Constant Couple, or A Trip to the Jubilee 113, 118, 126, 155, 160
cotillions 24, 52, 64
country dances 6, 15, 24, 52–54, 58, 64–66, 74, 81–85, 97; *see also* dancing
Cresswell, Nicholas 66, 83, 95–97, 131
Cumins, Edward 35

dances (formal) 5, 13–15, 38, 60–62, 69–70, 92; ticket sales 5, 48, 60–62; *see also* dancing; dancing masters; governor's palace
dancing 18–19, 21, 40, 52–55, 58, 61–67, 69, 76, *79*, 83, 85, 93, 95–96, 118; school 15, 55; on slave ships 87; social importance of 18–19, 54, 63–67, 69, 81–82; use in courtship 18, 42, 63, 66; *see also* country dances; dances (formal); dancing masters; governor's palace; slaves

183

dancing masters 5, 27, 34, *52*–60, 69, 84–85, 102
Degraffenreidt, Barbara 58–61, 135–137
Dinwiddie, Robert 11, 13, 94, 109–110, 112, 156
Douglass, David *see* American Company; Douglass Company
Douglass Company 115, 122–125, 162
Duke of Gloucester Street 9, *12*–13, 15, 20, 71, 123
dulcimer 31, 34; *see also* instruments
Dunmore, Governor 21

Equiano, Olaudah 86, 89
Europe: celebration of events 13, 15–16, 67, 75; cultural emulation 9, 11, 22, 24–26, 34, 39, 43, 45, 49, 54–55, 66, 69, 81, 100, 109, 114, 117; performers from 44–45, 107

Fauquier, Francis 11, 13, 47, 123, 125
fiddle *see* violin
Finnie, Alexander 55, 62, 105, 110, 123–124
Fithian, Philip 7, 18–19, 26, 31, 35, 40, 42–45, 50, 54, *57*–58, 63, 65–66, *79*–80, 95, 97
flute 26, 31, 33, 35, 46, 50, 93; *see also* German flute; instruments
folk songs 6, 73–74, 76, 78, 80–81, 84; *see also* songs
fortepiano *see* piano forte
France *see* Europe
Franklin, Benjamin 30–32, 81
Fredericksburg 50, 56, 125
French horn 14, 55, 65, 93–94, 129; *see also* instruments

General Assembly 14, 62, 125, 162
gentility 8–9, 14, 34, 49–52, 63–67, 69, 92; behavior of 16–25, 54–56, 59–60, 83–84, 94; desire to be British 22, 100, 109, 114; financial costs 32–33, 106, 114–115; necessity of music 24, 41, 43–44, 103, 106; social separation 20–21, 80–81, 110–111, 115
George I, king of England 11, 102
George II, king of England 13, 24
George III, king of England 13, 24, 43, 140
German flute 28, 31, 35, 46; *see also* flute; instruments
Gilliat, Simeon 92–93
Gilmer, George 110
glass harmonica 30–32; *see also* instruments
Gooch, William 13

governor: use of music 9–11, 13–14, 67, 103
governor's palace 8–9, 11, 13, 20, 27, *101*–103; concerts in 11–*12*, 27, 92; construction of 8, 15; dances in 13, 18–19
Great Awakening 41; *see also* religion
guitar 26, 28, 31, 34, 43, 45; *see also* instruments

Hallam, Lewis 107, 110, 112, 114, 117, 119, 121–123, 140, 155–156
Hallam, Sarah 59, 99, 107, 112, 122–123, 142, 156
hand organ 33; *see also* instruments
Handel, George 4, 34, 43, 47, 49, 73
harpsichord 22, 26, 28, 31–35, 43, 45–47, 50, 113; *see also* instruments
Haydn, Franz 34, *51*, 84
Henry, Patrick 11
Hosier's Ghost 75–77
House of Burgesses 27, 73, 110
Hunter, William 19

illuminations *12*–14
instruments: acquisition 8, 25–26, 28, 31–34, 39, 73; maintenance *29*–30, 34, 47; social status 32–33; *see also* slaves

James River 8, 56
Jamestown 2, 8, 27, 85–86
Jarratt, Devereux 81–82
Jefferson, Thomas 6, 11, 27–31, 34, 43, *51*, 60, 62–63, 74, 92, 126, 131
jig 18, 52, 65–66, 84–85
Jobson, Richard 86, 89
Jones, Hugh 9, 15, 22, 33, 50

Kean, Thomas 105, 107, 109–110, 121
Kirkman, Jacob 32–33

Levingston, William 2, 15, 102, 104
London 11, 22–25, 32–33, 35, 43, *53*–54, 94, 100, 109, 112, 114–115, 127; *see also* Europe
London Company of Comedians 107, 110, 114, 117, 119, 121, 155–156
Love, Charles 31
Love in a Village 35

Mercer, George 13–14
The Merchant of Venice 112–113, 155–156, 161
metronome *29*–30; *see also* instruments
minuet 5, 15, 24, 52, 54, 58, 64–65, *79*, 118
Monticello 31

Index

Mozart, Wolfgang Amadeus 34, 73, 84
Murray, Walter 105, 107, 109–110, 121
Muse, Hudson 99, *101*, 127
music books *see* books
music masters 5, 44–50, 56, 60, 69, 90, 92

Native Americans 11, 114, 156
New York Company of Comedians 105–107, 109–110, 121
Nomini Hall 18, 26, 28–*29*, 56, 58, 63, 65–66, *79*
Norfolk 14, 46, 125

oboe 16, 31; *see also* instruments
Ogle, Cuthbert 2, 4, 34, 43, 46–47, 113, 133–134
organ 22, 28, 31, 43, 46–48; *see also* instruments
Othello 11, 23, 114
Oxford University *10*

Pachelbel, Charles Theodore 47
Pachelbel, Johann 47
The Padlock 35, 162
Palace Green 15, 20, *101*–103
Parks, William 37–38, 104
Pelham, Peter, Jr. 47–48, 113, 120
Philadelphia 9, 123
piano 43; *see also* instruments
piano forte 22, 26, 28, 45; *see also* instruments
plantations 20–21, 28, 45, 56, 58, 62–64, 66, 78, 81
playhouse *see* theater
Plenius, Roger 32
Portsmouth 14, 151
Prentis, John 34
The Present State of Virginia 9, 15
psalmody 42; *see also* religion; singing; singing schools
Purdie & Dixon 35

Raleigh Tavern 21, 60, 62, 105, 110, 126, 131, 142–143
Rameau, Jean-Philippe 34
Rappahannock River 56, 58
reel 52–*53*, 64–65, *79*
religion 41–43, 47, 82
Revolutionary War *see* American Revolution
Richmond 47, 56
Rolfe, John 85
Russworm, Francis 45–46, 55

Shakespeare, William 23, 120, 161
singing 21, 35, 40, 42–44, 47, 71–73, 76, 78–80, 113, 118; *see also* ballad operas; singing schools; songs
singing schools 42
slaves 2, 5–6, 31, 37, *51*, 61, 66, 72, 83, 85–86, 92–93; advertisements for 93–94, 144–153; dancing 95–97; first arrival 85; instruments 31, 89–92; singing 88; transportation of 87–88; use of music in Africa 86, 88–89
songs 73–76, 78–81, 84; *see also* ballad operas; folk songs; singing
spinet 31–34, 43, 46; *see also* instruments
Spotswood, Alexander *10–12*, 102–103
Stagg, Charles 56, 58–59, 61, 102
Stagg, Mary 61–62, 102, 136–137
Stainer, Jacob 32
Stamp Act 13, 131, 140
Stradivari, Antonio 32
Stratford Hall 31, *79*

taverns 20–21, 73, 75–76, 78–*79*, 83
The Tempest 120
The Tender Husband 103–104
theater 6, 22–23, 46, 80; acquiring performers 102, 105, 115–117; audience 114–117; building descriptions 103, 110–112, 123–125; closures 104–105, 121–122, 132; first in America 2, 100, 102; funding 105, 123; laws *101*; music masters in 48, 113; plays performed 100, 103, 106, 109, 112–114, 126–127, 130, 154–164; rejection of 130–132; selection of music 114; tickets 80, 106, 118, 122, 124–125; types of performances 117–118, 127–129; use of music 103, 113
Townshend Act 131
trumpet 14, 40–41, 129; *see also* instruments
Tyler, John 11
Tyler, William 27

Utie, John 2, 27

Verling, William 126–127, 159–160
violin 15–16, 18, 26–28, 31–32, 34–35, 40, 45–46, 50, *53*, 65–67, *79*, 83–84, 87, 90, 92–95, 97; *see also* instruments
Virginia: economy 25; first play 100–*101*; flora and fauna *10*; housing 21; love of dancing 54
Virginia Company of Comedians 118, 126–127, 159–160
Virginia Gazette: advertising in 4, 31, 34–35, 37, 43, 45–46, 49–50, 55, 60–62, 74, 93–94, 104–106, 112; content 75; stories about Europe 5, 19, 22–24, 115–117

Virginia Reel *see* reel
Vivaldi, Antonio 34–35, 47, 49

Washington, George 6, 17, 26, 28, **57**, 59, 69, 125–126, 131
Westover Plantation 11, 56
William and Mary *see* College of William and Mary

Williamsburg: alcohol 78, 82; becoming capital 8; map ***101***; mercantilism 33, 76; musical education in 15, 42, 45–46, 55, 59; population 9; public spaces in 20
Wythe, George 11, 126

York River 8, 56

www.ingramcontent.com/pod-product-compliance
Ingram Content Group UK Ltd.
Pitfield, Milton Keynes, MK11 3LW, UK
UKHW042013140426
5217IPUK00015B/1146